CONVERSATIONS ACROSS OUR AMERICA

JOE R. AND TERESA LOZANO LONG SERIES
IN LATIN AMERICAN AND LATINO ART AND CULTURE

LOUIS G.
MENDOZA

CONVERSATIONS
ACROSS OUR AMERICA

TALKING ABOUT IMMIGRATION
AND THE LATINOIZATION
OF THE UNITED STATES

University of Texas Press ⌇ *Austin*

Requests for permission to reproduce material from this work should be sent to:
Permissions
University of Texas Press
P.O. Box 7819
Austin, TX 78713-7819
www.utexas.edu/utpress/about/bpermission.html

∞ The paper used in this book meets the minimum requirements of
ANSI/NISO Z39.48-1992 (R1997) (Permanence of Paper).

LIBRARY OF CONGRESS CATALOGING-IN-PUBLICATION DATA

Mendoza, Louis Gerard, 1960–
    Conversations across our America : talking about immigration and the Latinoization of the United States / by Louis G. Mendoza.
        p.   cm. — (Joe R. and Teresa Lozano Long series in Latin American and Latino art and culture)
    Includes bibliographical references and index.
    ISBN 978-0-292-73738-9 (cloth : alk. paper) — ISBN 978-0-292-73883-6 (pbk. : alk. paper) — ISBN 978-0-292-73739-6 (e-book)
    1. Hispanic Americans—Interviews. 2. Hispanic Americans—Social conditions. 3. Immigrants—United States—Interviews. 4. Immigrants—United States—Social conditions. 5. United States—Emigration and immigration—Social aspects. 6. United States—Civilization—Hispanic influences. I. Title.
    E184.S75M453 2012
    973'.0468—dc23   2011048138

This book is dedicated to my loving parents, Joe and Mary Mendoza, for their lifetime of faith in me and to the spirit of my friend and teacher, raúlrsalinas, for his inspiration and modeling of what it means to undertake a transformative journey and the value of sharing that story with others.

LISTENING IS A MAGNETIC AND STRANGE THING, A CREATIVE
FORCE. THE FRIENDS WHO LISTEN TO US ARE THE ONES WE MOVE
TOWARD. WHEN WE ARE LISTENED TO, IT CREATES US, MAKES US
UNFOLD AND EXPAND.

Karl Menninger

CONTENTS

ACKNOWLEDGMENTS

This project would not have been possible without the benefit and the luxury of the University of Minnesota's faculty sabbatical program. Additional assistance was received from the College of Liberal Arts under the leadership of Dean Steven Rosenstone; the Office for Equity and Diversity under the leadership of Vice President and Vice Provost Rusty Barceló; Edén Torres, Chair of the Department of Chicano Studies; and a McKnight Foundation Summer Research Grant.

Edna Day, Lisa Sass-Zaragoza, Miguel Vargas, and Jennifer Nevitt, staff members in the Department of Chicano Studies, provided much-needed logistical support along the way. My beloved parents, Joe and Mary Mendoza, and siblings, Rosemary, Mary Ann, Robert, Beatrice, Margie, Cynthia, and Gilda, as well as their spouses and my nieces and nephews, provided support, encouragement, and faith in me. Many of my dear friends provided me with lodging and/or emotional nourishment along the way. Among these are Marianne Bueno; Ben Olguín; Sandy Soto; Miranda Joseph; Sherry Edwards; Jennifer Caron; Emiliano Compean; Omar Valerio and Cathy Komisaruk; Yolanda Chávez Leyva; Verónica Carbajal; Ralph Rodriguez; Luis Marentes and Negar Taradji and their children, Kasra and Katayoun; Sheila Contereas and Salah Hassan and their daughters, Paz and Noor; Rita Alcalá and Raúl Villa and their son, Joseph; Tamara Belknap; Kisa Takesue; Ralph Rodriguez; Brent Beltran; Consuelo Manriquez; Antonio Díaz and Beth Ching and their son, Antonito; Cristal Casares; Kelly O'Brien; and George O'Brien.

With more than eighty-five hours of audio to transcribe, resulting in nine hundred pages of text, this work would not have been possible without the assistance of many people, including Sarah Beck-Esmay, Rachel Jennings, Kamala Platt, Terrell Webb, Dora Chalmers, Rene Valdez, Irene Lara Silva, and especially Steven Renderos, who tackled and beautifully captured the nuances of some of the most difficult interviews containing Tex-Mex code switching. I also received invaluable assistance from a number of friends who took the time to help me evaluate which interviews were richest and most insightful. For their time and insights, I would like to thank Angélica Afanador Pujol, Marianne Bueno, Rachel Jennings, Ben V. Olguín, Kamala Platt, Omar Valerio Jimenez, and Sandy Soto.

This project has continued to live in numerous ways, including the opportunity to share my experiences and the words of those I met along the way. A special thanks to the many people and places that hosted me upon my return and have provided me numerous opportunities to speak about this project at academic conferences, universities, K-12 schools, and community settings.

At the University of Texas Press, Theresa May, editor in chief, and her staff deserve a special thanks for their skillful guidance in preparing the manuscript for publication. A special thanks to Professor Roberto Calderon for his extraordinarily helpful suggestions for improving the manuscript.

Finally, it must be said that above all other types of support, this project absolutely depended on the willingness of strangers to meet with me and trust me with their stories. I am deeply indebted to those whose voices are included here, as well as those whose interviews I could not include due to space limitations. They ensured that my experience conducting research in this manner was not only successful but also life altering. Likewise, there were many, many people who reached out to provide friendship and words of support along the way via the Internet, at rest stops, in stores, or on the road. Among these were strangers who helped me when I needed a ride or assistance or simply provided acts of kindness to remind me of my connection to others through our common humanity.

To all those listed here by name and the many out there who believe in a vision of the United States that is enriched by our multicultural, multilingual, and multinational heritage, I offer my gratitude for working to make this vision a reality.

CONVERSATIONS ACROSS OUR AMERICA

THE LATINOIZATION OF THE U.S. AND "OUR" NATIONAL CULTURE

In the spring of 2006, the U.S. experienced a series of unprecedented immigrant rights marches involving hundreds of thousands of people across the country as they sought to shift the rising tide of anti-immigrant discourse in the media and among the public at large. In recent years, anti-immigrant sentiments, particularly those aimed at undocumented workers and families, have given rise to hundreds of local ordinances prohibiting access to housing, education, and jobs. Amid this climate, efforts to reform outdated immigration policies stalled at the federal level as the country became polarized by competing perspectives on the benefits and liabilities of immigrant workers to the U.S. economy and culture.

That fall, I began developing plans for a year-long research sabbatical. Like many Chicana/o scholars, I want my research to be relevant to events affecting our community. Having moved to Minnesota in the summer of 2004, as one of only a handful of Chicana/o scholars on campus, I found myself constantly having to speak about migration and immigration to my students and the greater Minnesota community, which was experiencing a rapid influx of Latino immigrants. Though I came of age politically as an undergraduate student in Houston during the 1986 immigration reform era, living in Minnesota, one of the nation's exemplars of the new geography of Latino immigration, was eye-opening. My position at the university provided me with a unique opportunity to be a resource of information and facilitator of people's understanding of this "emerging" population. As I forged alliances and friendships with new immigrants and engaged with a broader public concerned about the impact of immigration on the state's well-being, I gained new insight and appreciation for the complexities and harsh realities that influenced immigrants' decisions to leave home and risk life in *el norte*. I also witnessed firsthand what it is like to be considered a problem, an unwelcome presence, even though workers and industries that depend on immigrant labor thrive in a mutually beneficial relationship. Further, despite the pervasive media portrayal of a strong anti-immigrant movement and the intensification of rhetoric by politicians, I have seen how immigrant families often forge strong intercultural community relationships at work and in their personal lives. As an educator I have been stunned to learn how little many Minnesotans know about Latin American and Latinos' long history in their own backyard, despite the fact that a Chicano/Latino presence in the urban and rural communities of Minnesota is a century-long phenomenon, not something new at all. In fact, this dynamic environment, the coexistence of older and newer Mexican and Latino communities, had been one of the intriguing factors that led to my move from San Antonio to the Twin Cities.

Determined to conceptualize a project on immigration and the short- and long-term impact of the emergence of Latinos as the nation's largest ethnic minority, I was obliged to reckon with the role the media and its pundits play in shaping public perception of Latinos in the national imaginary. As an avid consumer of media, I often feel inundated by the negative coverage of Latinos and crime, our portrayal as "illegals," as interlopers, as a cultural and economic threat to be regulated and micromanaged by laws writ large and small. All of these concerns strike many Latinos as absurd given that our existence in the Americas, either as indigenous people or settlers, predates the existence of the U.S., even as we also share status with most Americans as multigenerational immigrants. For better or worse, we embody the history of the Americas, including the U.S., which arrogantly proclaims itself America in a bold act of effacement of its intercontinental neighbors. The conflicts, conquests, commingling, and contradictions that comprise this identity form the core of our historical experience as transnational migrants. Moreover, what is lost on so many people is that the upsurge in immigration across the southern border since the 1960s, in fact throughout the twentieth century, is a direct result of U.S. policies that have actively recruited immigrant workers into the labor force and intervened repeatedly in the economic and political self-determination of Latin American countries—policies and practices that continue to this day.

Wanting to get beyond the mostly superficial accounts of media coverage on conflict between newcomers and "citizens," I reached the conclusion that the best way to really explore this problem was to travel across the country and *see* firsthand the impact of new (im)migrations, to *speak* firsthand with folks within and outside the Latino community about what the Latino presence here means, and to *listen and learn* from their experiences as a means of broadening and deepening my perspective. My intention was to let the experience of others inform my own experience as a Chicano in the U.S.

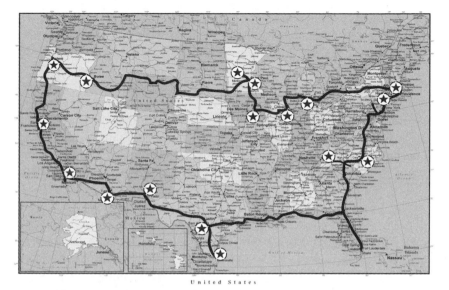

A map of the route I traveled in the United States and Ontario, Canada. Drawn by Louis Mendoza.

With a few important exceptions, the vast majority of the interviews and oral histories that constitute this book were collected as I traveled approximately 8,500 miles through thirty states around the perimeter of the country on a bicycle from July 1 to December 19, 2007. I departed from Santa Cruz, California, following a route that took me clockwise around the country and back to my final destination in Oakland, California. While my means of travel was nontraditional for scholarly research, it ensured that I would go off the beaten path to meet people in small towns whom I would not have met if I had traveled by other means. It had this and many other benefits, including the acquisition of new insights on the complexity of the social landscape and a renewed respect for the natural environment that immigrants traverse and toil within. My trip was characterized by hundreds of chance meetings and introductions by friends via phone or e-mail to immigrant rights advocates in various regions of the country. I conducted more than seventy-five formal interviews and held countless less formal conversations with people about Latino demographic changes, the new geography of Latino immigration, and the social, cultural, and political challenges associated with both.

Immigration and its consequences, the ensuing friction, fears, and fights, are not to be escaped. This is particularly true in a state like Minnesota whose former governor eagerly embraced the Republican National Party's directive to exploit this as a wedge issue, to make political gain by being distinctive in promoting policies and practices that made easy targets of economically, socially, and politically vulnerable newcomers, despite the fact that across the country they buttress state economies and have renewed devastated rural and urban communities through their labor, entrepreneurship, civic participation, and community-building efforts. How cheap and easy and sad that political power can be used to fracture communities and individual lives in the name of patriotism, homeland security, or political ambition.

But this is not the first time this has happened. The U.S. is a country beset by historical amnesia, the systematic inability to learn painful lessons from our past that might help us unlearn destructive behaviors.

ORGANIZATION OF THIS BOOK

In *A Journey Around Our America*, a companion book to *Conversations Across Our America*, I documented the five and a half months I spent on the road and share my experiences and perspective alongside those whom I encountered along the way, in stores, in cafés, and as they extended a helping hand to me when my very survival depended on it. The book represented a journey across the land in a particular time and place—the interactive and mutually informing dynamics of the social, political, and natural climate that made up the summer and fall of 2007. In contrast, *Conversations* is intended to foreground the words and experiences of those people I met who took time to have an extended conversation with me. Due to space limitations, included here are portions of thirty-three conversations involving forty-two people of various Latino nationalities, in diverse regions of the country and both urban and rural locales, in diverse professional and nonprofessional occupations, as well as activists, artists, students, and retirees.

I should note that even as I considered the criteria above to determine which interviews I would be able to include and which it would be necessary to exclude, I realized that among the final slate of interviewees were many activists working to effect positive social change around immigration reform and community empowerment. As activists, this is a group of people who may or may not have access to having their voice heard in public discourse but who are nevertheless experienced in articulating the values and beliefs that motivate their work. I recognize that this may have placed them at an advantage for being included here, as they are perhaps more cogent and practiced in expressing their thoughts on the issues we discussed. Thus I was obliged to evaluate the limited extent to which I was giving prominence to the voices of "everyday people," that is, people whose lives are directly affected by local and national contingencies but whose lives are not marked

On the Stone Arch Bridge in Minneapolis, Minnesota, before leaving on my trip.
Photo by Kelly MacDonald, College of Liberal Arts, University of Minnesota.

by immersion in political discourse. As I pondered the implications of this, I considered two things. First, excerpts of numerous conversations I had with others who were not selected for inclusion here are given voice in *A Journey Around Our America*. Second, though the majority of folks whose interviews are included here are activists, their involvement is often a consequence of a process of conscientization that has led them to become agents of change. In other words, with perhaps one or two exceptions, these are people who are not intergenerational activists. They were driven by their everyday life circumstances and experiences—as workers, immigrants, children of immigrants, and descendants of Mexican settlers who arrived before the establishment of the U.S., and students—across generations and geography to acquire the needed knowledge base and the organizing and speaking skills to be effective activists and advocates. In this way, they are quintessential practitioners of cultural citizenship who seek to advance community well-being by advocating for social and institutional reforms through formal and informal means. And in this way, their politics situates them within the historical trajectory of the Latino civil rights movement.

The interviews are organized in seven chapters, each of which covers a primary theme that emerged from my conversations. Each chapter is preceded by background information on the issue being addressed, and each interview segment provides background information on the interviewee. It is important to note, however, that I have chosen to preserve the integrity and complexity of my conversations with each speaker by not reducing their contribution only to what they have to say about the prevailing theme. The insights they share are dynamic and enriched by the complexity of the issue as a whole—both diachronically and synchronically—even when, at times, these contradict one another.

What follows next is an overview of my "process" for identifying interviewees, how I structured our conversation, and my method for determining what to include in this collection and how I approached editing the massive amount of raw data I collected during my trip. Preceding each interview is a brief description of how I was introduced to or met the interviewee. Though I began the trip without scheduled interviews, I was able to make numerous initial contacts with potential interviewees through my network of coworkers and friends. What is included in this collection are portions taken from more sustained conversations; there were countless additional informal conversations and interviews that I have not been able to include. Many people I spoke with referred me to other interviewee candidates. In some cases, I made "cold calls," or unannounced visits, to people in their offices who appeared likely to be good sources of information. While not all of them were able to take the time to speak with me, and given my mode of travel I was not able to schedule meetings in advance or even defer meetings because I needed to maintain my travel schedule, many people dropped what they were doing and took time to visit with me.

I returned home with close to ninety hours of video- and audiotape and notes. With lots of assistance, I transcribed these recordings and ended up with almost a thousand pages of material. As I hope is evident from the brief overview above, the voices and personal experiences vary across time and space. Though I was limited in my ability to conduct extended interviews with young people, they are present here and occupy a prominent space in the imagined future of the immigrant population and the very real future of this country as they come of age and participate in or lead the way to finding resolutions to the enduring challenges associated with immigration. As I made selections of whom to include and exclude, I considered geography, the overall quality of the interview, the age of the interviewee, the range of topics addressed, the status of the interview, and how the particular experiences fit the overall historical experience of Latinos in the U.S. In addition, I considered the ethnicity of the interviewee, as I wanted to include a diversity of Latino and non-Latino voices. No attempt was made to achieve a perfectly proportionate representation of the population.

I approached each interview as a conversation rather than a structured interview or survey. While I had some guiding questions, these were designed to be open-ended so as to let the conversation flow according to the interviewees' interests and experience. For some people this worked quite well, but with many I had to actively elicit detailed responses. The concerns below guided me and influenced with whom I sought to converse.

- What is the individual story of someone's arrival to a particular location? How did they or their family get from point A to point B (as an immigrant or as an internal migrant)?
- How is Latino immigration changing the U.S.?
- How is recent immigration similar to and/or different from past waves of immigration?
- Is there a basis for people's fear about new immigrants changing "the" national culture?
- What are the benefits and challenges of Latinoization to local communities?
- Do the benefits of being in the U.S. outweigh sacrifices made by new immigrants? Has it been worth it?

As I edited the conversations, some of them, like those with Humberto Fuentes, Adela Marmion, Magda Iriarte, and Ernesto Portillo, were akin to oral histories. I strove to remove my voice as much as possible to give their stories prominence. In many cases, the dialogue is necessarily dynamic, and this required that my questions and responses remain intact, so I shortened the interviews by removing portions of the conversation that were less interesting or repeated topics addressed more provocatively in other interviews. Since I was meeting many of the interviewees for the first time, I often told them my personal and family story as a second-generation Mexican American and a professor as a way to earn their trust and make clear my intentions and my willingness to reciprocate. I was often asked questions about the experiences I was having on my trip, which I have chosen to delete here.

During my trip, I met people from all walks of life. I also read local and national newspapers on a daily basis to keep apprised of immigration issues as they arose during this time period. I often found strong resonance between the two, but there were many instances in which local coverage of events was dissonant with what was occurring nationally or not in line with the conversations I had with local community members. My perspective on small-town America was changed as I realized that despite the fact that many parochial attitudes persist, in many instances these communities were extraordinarily open-minded.

There are a few interviews and oral histories that were collected prior to and following the trip in Minnesota, which I have inserted alongside others from this state. Finally, I should note that I have striven to retain the integrity

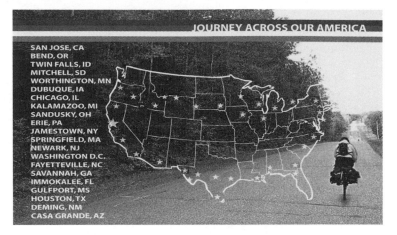

SAN JOSE, CA
BEND, OR
TWIN FALLS, ID
MITCHELL, SD
WORTHINGTON, MN
DUBUQUE, IA
CHICAGO, IL
KALAMAZOO, MI
SANDUSKY, OH
ERIE, PA
JAMESTOWN, NY
SPRINGFIELD, MA
NEWARK, NJ
WASHINGTON D.C.
FAYETTEVILLE, NC
SAVANNAH, GA
IMMOKALEE, FL
GULFPORT, MS
HOUSTON, TX
DEMING, NM
CASA GRANDE, AZ

A postcard created by Kelly MacDonald to advertise my journey. It became my calling card for people I met along the way. Photo by Lisa Sass-Zaragoza. Design by Kelly MacDonald, College of Liberal Arts, University of Minnesota.

of language usage by each interviewee—be it English, Spanish, Spanglish, or code-switching. As a child of the pre-bilingual education era whose parents' educational experience was steeped in a period of American socialization that disallowed speaking anything other than English in school, I am not fully bilingual. As I have written elsewhere, my own linguistic history is part of the Latino experience in the U.S.[1] Consequently, most of the interviews here were held with people who had at least some English facility. My lack of full fluency in Spanish surely prohibited me from fully engaging some potential interviewees and/or establishing the rapport necessary to hold a more meaningful dialogue. I address this issue more fully in *A Journey Around Our America*, where I share my awareness of and frustrations with how my language limitations had a detrimental impact on my experience and this project.

In the book's conclusion I offer some reflections on the historical and contemporary factors that influence immigration policy and practice that should be taken into account for a more comprehensive understanding of how this issue shapes people's lives. It is my hope that readers will gain further insight into the enormous complexity of immigration and the simple yet profound truths about the human will for basic survival. The voices heard in this collection provide an array of perspectives from the ground level of those whose lives are affected most immediately as they struggle to deal with a sustained American ambivalence, if not antipathy, toward Latinos and the increasingly draconian and Janus-faced attitude directed at new immigrants.

ONE

LEAVING
HOME IS NO LONGER HOME

IN ORDER TO CHANGE, WE MUST BE SICK AND TIRED OF BEING

SICK AND TIRED. *Anonymous*

As will become abundantly clear throughout this book, each immigrant's experience is idiosyncratic even as his or her individual story resonates with common themes: motivations for leaving home, the emotional pain resulting from being separated from loved ones and one's homeland, the struggle to adapt to a new society. In addition, for many immigrants there is the recognition that their primary home is now here, and home is no longer home. Obviously this recognition depends on the migrant's expectations about returning home. Until recently, inter-American migrants to the U.S. who had served as seasonal and temporary migrant workers did not necessarily have to make the decision about returning to their homelands at the time of leaving. In fact, many assumed that crossing was temporary and the return home unequivocal. But those who come to work in jobs that require staying in a fixed location often find it tempting to establish a second or more permanent and comfortable home here as they raise families and build social networks. Moreover, with the increased militarization of the border since 2001, undocumented seasonal migration has been severely curtailed, and migrants must now contend with the higher risks and costs of crossing. The decision by seasonal migrants to settle in a community is often the first step toward permanent settlement in the U.S.

The interviewees in this section speak from their unique situations. There are differences in their legal status, in the time they have been in the U.S. (from five to twenty-five years), and in terms of political and emotional perspectives on what it means to be here as an exile, a migrant, a world citizen. They are not the only ones who reflected on this condition of migrancy, but they each resonate in complementary ways with mutable and poignant notions of home that simultaneously entail a sense of loss and an ardent embrace of something new, though in some cases what defines the new is still in formation. In many respects, there is ambivalence, there is gratitude, and there is sometimes a reluctant critique of the homeland even as there is nostalgia for that which has irrevocably changed. It is the attitude of the contemporary pioneer—the economic refugee whom no one wants to claim as a by-product of globalization and free trade. While leaving one's homeland is never easy, often conditions there had made remaining untenable, a fact even more apparent after having arrived in the U.S.

Coming from a socialist country, Gloria Caballero is here to make her family whole, but she has nothing but disdain for the rampant consumerism and waste associated with capitalism and the violence that permeates everyday life in the U.S. Unlike the others in this section, she longs for permanent residency as a truly global citizen. In contrast, coming from Colombia, Guillermo Vasa embraces the U.S. as a land of relative safety and abundant opportunity. His is a typical American immigrant story—even as he patiently awaits a solution to his residency status. Fernando and Luis, both young Mexican migrants who fled home for two different types of safety, share a common sense of risk and hope for the future even as the former is more actively involved in being an agent of change. But as young men who have come of age in the U.S., one can see evidence of the notion that "every Mexican is a potential Chicano" as their identities have solidified here in the U.S. and any romantic notions of *mexicanismo* have given way to the reality that they are no longer Mexican.

GLORIA CABALLERO

Gloria Caballero was a graduate student writing her dissertation in the Department of Spanish at the University of Massachusetts, Amherst. She is originally from Cuba and migrated here after marrying an African American who had spent time in Cuba working in an educational training program. She is also a mother who contemplates what it means to raise her children as Cuban Americans when her own values and experiences have taught her to be wary of being too comfortable with life here.

GLORIA: I was born in Santiago, Havana, Cuba. I married a man who was born in Harlem, New York. I used to be an English teacher in Cuba, an interpreter, and he was part of this huge project there to teach and retrain teachers of English to their knowledge of the English language since traveling abroad from Cuba is so hard.

LOUIS: *Was it hard to leave Cuba to come here?*

GLORIA: It was hard because it takes two to tango. It was hard for me on the part of the Americans because I was a member of the Young Communist League. They were afraid I was going to come here and kill the president. We married in Cuba, had our first child in Cuba, and that was part of the whole problem. [My husband] pretended to be here when he was in Havana. And on the side of the Cubans, it was hard because you were de facto leaving your country for an enemy one.

LOUIS: *So what did you have to do to convince the United States that you weren't going to be a threat?*

GLORIA: It was amazing. He had to go down to Cuba to talk to the folks in the Interests Section, and they gave me this interview that was horrible.

Gloria Caballero in her office at the University of Massachusetts, Amherst.
Photo by Louis Mendoza.

He was outside and I was inside with the baby. They wanted us to produce some proof showing that the baby was an authentic baby, you know, that he was the father and I was the mother and I was not marrying just to leave Cuba. It was a very sad and horrible interview.

LOUIS: *How long did that process take?*

GLORIA: Six months. When we moved we came here to Massachusetts, to Brookline, because he was a professor at a university in Boston. At the time when he went to Cuba, he was living in Montreal, but he kept his job at the university teaching languages. So we moved to Brookline where his mother was living. We lived there three months until we got this call from Milton Academy saying they needed a Spanish teacher. He said, "Well, my wife just arrived, she's Cuban." And they said, "Well, we want you both." We ended up working there two years. In '99, I applied to come here to the U.S and arrived here in 2000.

LOUIS: *What have been your impressions of the United States?*

GLORIA: I was not impressed at all. I don't know if I came here already influenced by all the information that we were getting in Cuba, but when I came here not even the snow impressed me. But the waste and the abundance of things! I came in '97 right after the hub of the Special Period in Cuba and coming in and seeing all this plethora of food in stores. You have rows and rows of Cheerios. I remember the first month I would get dizzy in the car because I was not used to being in a car. In Cuba you bike a lot. But here everywhere you went, you had to take the car. We ended up working for two years at Milton. They are rich people, very rich, the Ivy League, and food was wasted, and everything was so much that it was grotesque. I had to appreciate the fact that we were given that job, that we made good money, that our kids were in a safe environment. I came here shaking because of the proliferation of arms, weapons, and drugs in the streets.

>*LOUIS: Do you have ambivalence about being here where the culture's so different from Cuba's? What do you think has happened to your identity?*

GLORIA: It's funny, I've been back to Cuba four times, and every time I go back I feel bad. I can no longer live there. I have changed and the country has changed. Once out of there, you become more Cuban than the Cubans who remain inside. It's nostalgia first and the fact that you grow up in a very united, extended family. I came here alone on my own, my two kids and my husband, and I played Cuban music, music that I took for granted, the old-time music. That's my music in the house. I cook the Cuban way in my house. We don't eat McDonalds or any kind of chain food. We don't go to malls because there are people out there who aren't getting paid properly, so we buy stuff in thrift shops and Goodwill to get clothes, hand-me-downs, and yet when I go back to Cuba they expect me to go with gold chains. And yet I'm living the Cuban way up here in the country of abundance and waste because you get to understand that there's so much poverty inside this rich country and so many people left behind.

>*LOUIS: Is that also true of you politically and ideologically?*

GLORIA: Oh, yes.

>*LOUIS: Are any of your ideas about Americans challenged by living here?*

GLORIA: That's an interesting question. I don't know. I came here focused on my kids, and everything else I disregarded. Nothing surprised me because I came here prepared and not with big expectations. I gave up everything in order to focus on my kids and our growth here. I'm not a chameleon, but I go with the flow that favors my philosophy of life. There's a lot of bad things, but good things mostly. You just have to adjust.

LOUIS: *What is your kids' understanding of their identity?*

GLORIA: They know they're Cubans. Well, Cuban Americans, that's what we are called here. But of the ten years that we've lived here in the United States, we've physically been here six or five years, because we travel, and that's been good for them. They know they're Cubans, but they also identify with the Spanish culture and the Portuguese culture. We lived in Lisbon for a while. We go a lot to Montreal. It's hard to finger point and talk about identities, about identifications, because you have to survive. We're survivors, and when I talk about identity, it's sort of putting chains up, you know?

LOUIS: *Do your kids know Spanish?*

GLORIA: Yes, that's their first language. My husband speaks Spanish too.

LOUIS: *Do they go to schools where that's reinforced?*

GLORIA: We live in Holyoke; that's 42 percent Puerto Rican population. That's a lot. And in public schools they are well above 80 percent of the population. It might sound like the segregation of public schools because you have then the private schools, collegiate schools, and charter schools. We have one of those, and they don't get stuck with the metaphor either, being called Latino. We are much more than that.

LOUIS: *Do you feel you have experienced anti-Latino sentiments?*

GLORIA: I have felt anti–Puerto Rican sentiment in Holyoke. This is an example from my reality and in Holyoke, if you go to a downtown area, that's mostly Puerto Rican. That doesn't mean that you don't find African Americans or Caucasians or even European Americans. Holyoke is on the side of a hill, so the higher you go, the whiter it gets. So it means that where I live, I live sort of in the middle; the white population does not relate to their Puerto Rican neighbors. They won't communicate, or if they see that they're changing a tire or there's something going on the car, they call the police. Because they think it's inappropriate, or they're afraid of something. I think when there's something different from the white culture it poses a threat. I can say it's anti–Puerto Rican sentiment because that's what I see. And the city, well, they clean this area, but they don't clean that area. They have no schedule for garbage collection and they do in the other area.

LOUIS: So what are your hopes for your children?

GLORIA: What I pray for every night is that life allows me to see them become good citizens. That they can do something for a more just society and that they be part of that whole project and that they be open-minded and inclusive and make sure that they do the right thing. Not what they can do but what they should do. I hope my children contribute to a better understanding of what the world is because they've traveled around, they've seen different cultures, by introducing a new way of talking, a new rhetoric, a new language about what peace and justice is.

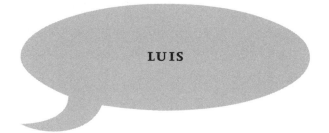

LUIS

Luis was a graduate student at a university in the northeastern United States. We met at another local university where he was working as a tutor. He came to the U.S. from Michoacán. He asked me not to use his last name.

LUIS: When I hear those politicians talk about immigrants being criminals and all the bad stuff that they say about us, I would just like them to know what it takes and how hard it is to live in a place where you have no food, where the circumstances and your situation just push you to survive somewhere else. I wish they could understand that. They have these ideas, and they only see immigration from the exterior, but the ones who live it are the only ones who can truly understand what it's like. And it is sad, because there are a lot of people who have come to this country running away from poverty. What kind of human tells you to just put up with the circumstances and let yourself die?

LOUIS: *Where did you come from?*

LUIS: I was born in Michoacán. I came to the U.S. ten years ago, when I was about fifteen years old. First I lived in San Diego for a month. I thought that I could make it by myself. But then I realized it was too difficult. I couldn't do it, and I went to live with an aunt in California. I lived with her until I finished high school, and then I went to Fresno State, then to Michigan for my master's, and then I came here for the Ph.D.

LOUIS: *Do you remember the decision to come here?*

LUIS: Yeah. [Clears throat] There were many reasons. One of them was because I am gay, and my family is a traditional Mexican family. It is so, so taboo; it is really, really bad. I was living in this society in a family, and all I would hear about gay people was really bad. I grew up thinking that it was a sin. That I was going to go to hell, a lot of bad things. And then you realize, okay, what am I doing here, I am not accepted by my family; it is the people I love, but I felt like I didn't belong. That was one of the reasons. The other reason is that I didn't have money. In Mexico, yes, education is free, but you get to a point where you also survive according to how much money you have, and I didn't have money. Sometimes in my family there wasn't food. As a teenager I had to work there, and I was frustrated with life because I had to go to school and then go to work full time, so I was frustrated with that. Poverty and the desire of going to school and not having money to do so, plus the sexual discrimination in my environment, pushed me to come here.

LOUIS: How did you get over here?

LUIS: The first time I tried with one of my friends. I have friends on this side, so they got me an ID of this guy before coming here. We were in Tijuana. We got drunk, and we decided, okay, let's go, and I try with this ID that they got me. But that didn't work, because they got me at the border. The first thing they told me is, "You have to say, 'I am an American citizen.'" That didn't work because of my accent. They put me in the jail for five days, and then they sent me back to Mexicali. I didn't know anybody, and I had to go from Mexicali to Tijuana to find help. But in jail I met this coyote who told me, "Okay, when we are out, just hang out with me, and I am going to help you." So that is what I did. I hung out with him in this hotel in Tijuana. A lot of immigrants live there, and there are just a bunch, a lot of people just waiting for the opportunity to cross the border. So I lived there for like a week with them, and one morning they said, "Okay, they are ready, so we are going." It was a Monday, I don't even remember what day, but it was very early in the morning, like 2:30 in the morning, they said, "Okay, let's go," and we went. There are mountains we went through, and then we crossed the river, I don't know, everybody got lost, and I got lost there too. I didn't know where to go.

And I remember they said to me, "Just follow the path and wait for us. We are going to look for other people." They never came back. I was there, all day, part of the night, and I was so scared. I said, "Oh, my gosh, what am I going to do?" Someone said to me, "Okay, you see that light? That is where San Diego is, a little light." Well, it was impossible for me to get there. I just followed the trail, and I got to where I couldn't walk anymore. There was so much vegetation around me that I couldn't move. I tried to climb the trees to say hello to the helicopter for them to rescue me, but they couldn't see me. And so I continued to move, and I got to a point where I heard the noise of a truck and it was *la migra*. Well, I started to scream, "Hello, help me." It was that bad. They got me and sent me back. They put me in jail for one night and then back again to Tijuana. And in jail I met another guy, and he said, "Who are you with?" I didn't have anybody. I was alone. And I went with this guy, and he told me don't worry, just sleep. In this hotel, it was a very, very bad hotel, but that is where people live. He told me, "If I help you cross the border, are you going to pay me? How are you going to pay me?" And I told him I had the money, and I was going to pay him. He was a good man, and he said, "Okay, don't say that, don't even tell anybody that you have money, or they are going to kill you." And so I didn't tell anybody.

The money was in my shoes. It was like $500 just to cross the border, and the next day another kid my age told me, "Okay, let's go," and he was helping people cross one by one, and you know at the end there were like two vans full of people. It took us like three hours or so. We crossed where there were some factories. The plan was for us to pass like if we were workers. And so we crossed, and a *migra* helicopter was there watching people. We jumped and just started to walk, just like if we belonged. The plan was to get lost among all the people, so they could think that we were workers. Eventually, after a while, I got to San Diego. My friends were waiting for me there.

LOUIS: *Was education always part of your plan?*

LUIS: Yes and no. I wanted to finish high school, but then I ended up working in the fields. And to work in the fields—oh man, it sucks.

LOUIS: *What kind of crops?*

LUIS: Tomato and the rest of them. I ended up working in a restaurant washing dishes, and it was the worst thing ever, so I said to myself, "Okay, you have to do something else." That is why I decided to go to the university. I knew that if I had to work I had to get fake documentation, so I decided I may as well go to school. When I was at university, I started to talk more English and I knew how to survive. I got a job tutoring other people in math or science or things that were not hard labor, and I said, "Okay, at least this is not being in the sun all day long." I have been fortunate, because in my university years I have encountered a lot of good people who have helped me, and it is through them that I am here, because I had nothing.

LOUIS: Do you keep in touch with your family at all?

LUIS: I have communication with my mom by phone. With my *tía*, the one who lives in California. I talk to her every once in a while. But, again, due to the fact that they do not know that I am gay that puts a barrier between us.

LOUIS: You can't tell them about your life?

LUIS: Right. And now I go to the university here, but last year, unfortunately, they found out about my status so they said bye bye.

LOUIS: How did they find out?

LUIS: The government sends these letters to the employer. I went to talk to a lawyer and he said, "Okay, in all of your history, in your lifetime that you have been in school and working, it is because these people, your boss, the person who hired you has given you the chance to continue working and studying. When an employer gets these letters, it is his obligation to tell the employee, the worker, that this information doesn't match, and that is all he has to do. He doesn't have to fire you." This person in the university, he was not that kind and fired me. He wouldn't have been in trouble, if he just let things pass, it would have been nothing for him. So after that, I didn't know what to do again. I thought they were going to deport me. They called Immigration.

LOUIS: So they didn't just tell you bye, they actually called ICE?

LUIS: Yeah. I have a file there at the university, and everybody knows my situation. When they fired me, I lived off of giving massages to people. As an undergrad, I took massage classes—that and tutoring people. I was struggling, and I was trying to convince the administrators to give me a tuition waiver to continue studying, but that didn't happen. I have two more classes to finish with them for my Ph.D. classwork, and I will have to pay out-of-state tuition. It is a lot of money.

LOUIS: What would it take for you to get an international student visa?

LUIS: It's not possible.

LOUIS: Because you have already been here?

LUIS: Because I have been here for a long time and also because I violated the law coming here, that is what they say. If I go back to Mexico and try to come here legally, they won't give me my visa because all my diplomas are from here.

LOUIS: So immigration reform would really help you?

LUIS: Yes.

LOUIS: What does that mean for you when you finish? If someone made you a job offer, could they sponsor you, and would things be different for you?

LUIS: When I finish at least I have a tool to face the world, wherever they send me. It depends if a reform happens. If an immigration reform happens, then that could help me. If not, then nothing. So I have a lot of faith. I had a lot of hope last summer. Well, actually this June or July, when they were fighting for the immigration reform to happen, but it didn't go through. And then I got depressed thinking, and then what? But I want to finish the Ph.D. In the last instance, if I don't see any doors opening here, well, I don't know where I am going to go, but at least that is going to be a life insurance for me, because it is going to be easier to find a job with that, and it is not going to be washing dishes at least.

LOUIS: Do you feel more American than Mexican, or do you feel more Mexican?

LUIS: I don't think I am Mexican anymore, that I can tell you. I think that I live in the borders. For me the idea of going back to Mexico is so scary. I lived like fifteen years in Mexico, but I was a child and I didn't know much about the system. Now I know more about the U.S. system. I know how to survive here. I wouldn't know how to survive there. And, you know, the ideology, society, the way of thinking is so different, I wouldn't want to go back to live there. I consider myself Chicano. Even if I wasn't born in the U.S., I understand this culture. I don't know that is what I feel in my heart, because I understand both cultures now, the gringo and Mexican culture, and I am able to communicate in both languages. I have an accent when I talk, right? I would say that I am Mexican, from this side now. I don't identify myself as Mexican from the other side.

It has to do with the fact that when I was a child, I suffered this kind of discrimination there and I know that mentality warps with time, many changes. But still when I talk to my mom, when I talk to my family, they still have this mentality. And I see the news, and I read and I get informed about what is happening in Mexico, and this mentality still basically discriminates against people of a certain class a lot. So they are a society that takes into account that a lot. They judge according to how much money you have, etc. Mexicans sometimes consider Mexicans from this side a people with no culture, people with no education, with no value, because they come here, running away from something, and they are less Mexican than they are. And what I found from the Mexican population that lives on this side is a kind of solidarity, you know, and that class system doesn't exist.

> *LOUIS: There are many, many people in your situation. Across the country, I have met many people who are in similar situations and are trying to finish, and they don't know what is going to happen to them. They don't know what the next step is going to be. And they are participating in efforts to pass the reforms, because that is their only hope. I have been surprised because it seems really risky.*

LUIS: It is risky. I tell you, I have been scared to death sometimes.

> *LOUIS: So if you were forced to go back, you wouldn't even feel like you belong there?*

LUIS: I just have my mom there. She is all the family I have. I have great friends here. They are my family now, and I love them like my family. If I have to go back, I will feel like a stranger living there. So my hope for now is to live one day at a time and see what happens.

> *LOUIS: Do you allow yourself to have a gut feeling of what is going to happen with immigration reform in this country?*

LUIS: You know, I have been thinking about that so much, and it takes my energy away. It is like when you are in love and not loved in return—you think about that person so much, and that person doesn't give a shit about you. That is how I feel [laughs]. That is what I feel. I say to myself, "Don't think about that anymore."

> *LOUIS: You feel pretty powerless?*

LUIS: Powerless, yeah. I tell you my energy goes away there, and I get depressed, but that doesn't help me at all.

> *LOUIS: Do you prefer I use a pseudonym for you?*

LUIS: Well, yeah, I don't want to be found. You can use my name but not my last name, just my name, yeah, your name [laughs].

Guillermo Sánchez Vasa was introduced to me when a friend of mine in New York City was looking for a new apartment and met him as a possible landlord. He lives in Queens and owns a foreign auto repair shop, among other enterprises. Now sixty, Guillermo is originally from Bogotá, Colombia. Like many other immigrants, he spoke of full acclimation to life in the U.S. Despite having a special place in his heart for his homeland, he no longer feels like that is his home.

GUILLERMO: I was born in Colombia. I went to a special technical school in Colombia. I chose the automobile mechanical. I stayed there for three years. After that I go three years for accounting. I am an accountant and a professional mechanic. I have some businesses in Colombia. I make special furniture for accountants. But the business there is too tough. So in 1975 I have twenty-five years, and I said to myself, "In this year, whatever happens, I marry." I marry my wife, but the first year is very hard. I tell my wife, "Let me go to United States." Before coming I had a little restaurant, but I tell my wife, "Sell the restaurant because as soon as I go there I will send for you to come here." My wife give the restaurant to somebody else to sell. A friend had come here three times. He go back to Colombia and tell me, "You want to go with me? Come today." So I said, "Why not?" So we go to buy the ticket because in these days we go to Panama and from Panama to Mexico.

From Mexico I take the bus from D.F. [Mexico City] to Tijuana, three days in the bus and across the border. But after cross the border, three hours later the police catch me. I stayed fifteen days in jail. From San Diego they sent me to Los Angeles. I talked to some different people inside and asked, "What do I do?" They say I have to have $2,000 for the bail. I have to have money for the lawyer. I called my brother here in New York, never talked to the wife of my brother. My sister-in-law said, "I don't know who you is." I tried three days, called Colombia to check the number, call again here, but don't tell them what happened to me. Some officer tell me, "You don't have money for your bail, don't have a lawyer, you'll have to wait for deportation, or you decide go by yourself and you pay your tickets and no have problem." So I return to Colombia.

I tell my wife, "Don't ask me what's happened to me." After four months, I decide to come here again. This time I go to embassy and make my application for my visa and I come direct to New York. I work for the BMW shop, as a mechanic. I stayed there three years. During this three years I send money to my wife for making a different business. My wife make the application, but they don't give visa to her. So she stay. She working there, but I don't have money, don't have property, don't have nothing, so she don't get visa. After that I went back to Colombia because I lose my visa and I miss my wife, my family. Nine months later, I tell my wife, "I go back to United States." She tell me, "You bring me my visa, I go with you." So I make the application the first day for me, and this weekend I wait on the Monday, back to Immigration I talk to some people. Immigration give me the passport for my wife, and my wife's working one block from the embassy. So I go and say, "Honey, here's the visa." So we come here.

Guillermo Vasa at his home in Queens, New York. Photo by Louis Mendoza.

I am about twenty-eight at this time. I come here, and I start working again with BMW. Three years later I decide to become independent. So I open my mechanic shop. I work only on foreign cars, no American cars. I don't have papers, so I stay with no papers, very hard for the paper; they make me one application through the job, but in 1982 I have the interview in Colombia. I go with my family, and at the last moment, the people in the embassy decide don't give me the visa. They said, "No, your case is closed. You came back to United States." So I make the plan to come again through Mexico. And I came through Mexico through a coyote with my wife and my son. We cross the Rio Grande on a little boat.

It's very hard these days because I came from Colombia to D.F. and I stayed three days there for making a good connection. I come to Guadala-jara by flying, and while I have another connection, we've got to come to the border. And we make a deal for going there in the middle of the night. I fight with the guy because he wanted to get more money. I don't pay no more money because I tried this before. I cross the river, and after I cross the river, we're staying in a house—I don't know the owner, but the people who crossed me said, "The owner of this house works with Immigration, so we are safe there." After that, three days later, take another car from there to Texas. They pick up the van with fifteen people. We go to Houston. We take the flight back to New York. I started again working in the shop, and I started my business in 1992.

LOUIS: *Your children are citizens?*

GUILLERMO: Yes. My wife is a citizen, too. I make three different applications. Turned down for different things. I tell my son, "Make an application for citizen." And after my son was citizen, I ask him to make the application for me. Ten years ago I started. My application for citizen I sent two years ago, but my case is very big. The officer tell me, "Listen, I know you pass. Everything's clear, but you know your case is big. Let me check your finger-prints and I call you." I wait. That's my biggest worries. To cross the border is very bad, but you have to—sometimes you have no choice.

LOUIS: *Do you know many other* colombianos *here in New York?*

GUILLERMO: Yeah, I have maybe ten friends from Bogotá; all people who live around here. One of them is a doorman in the city. I have another guy is working as a secretary for a lawyer. I bring the sister of my wife with her husband. He opened a bookstore, right here in Queens. It's only Catholic and Spanish language.

LOUIS: Do you miss Colombia?

GUILLERMO: Romantically, maybe sometimes, but no more. When I be there for maybe one, two weeks, I miss New York because of there it isn't safe, no find job, you can't drive the good car because the people rob your car. You can't put nice clothes because they kill you. So this is a good life. That's the story.

LOUIS: What do you think about when you hear all these debates about immigration and people? Do you find that there's a negative attitude about Latinos here in the city or in the United States?

GUILLERMO: The point is that some Latinos is bad people, too. Some bring drugs. For example, so many people when meet me, ask me about drugs because I'm Colombian. So this hurt a little bit, but as soon as ask me, I tell them, "You're confused. I am different person. That's not me." I never traffic with drugs. So as soon as anybody tell me something like that, I stop and tell him who I am. Don't bother me too much. But I see the Americans don't like Spanish because some Spanish is bad people and the American get the idea that everybody is the same. But as soon as the American talk to you and you see a different person, they respect you.

LOUIS: And your children, what do they think of Colombia?

GUILLERMO: My daughter, she born here. But she love Colombia because living there is different; it's more close with the family. She stay there once, but a few weeks later said, "It's no good here. The job is no good." The problem in South America, especially in Colombia, is when you are thirty-five years old, they consider you old and you don't get job. So this is wrong. So what do you do? We stay here for a long time, and old people are working like everybody.

LOUIS: What do you think it would take for Colombia to have a strong economy so people wouldn't find the need to leave or would be safer?

GUILLERMO: Some people in Colombia love the American ideas and appreciate what the Americans do for people up there. We have good workers up there, good jobs. Not many people come here, but some people hate the Americans because here they hear so many bad news about Americans. The people there think they rob the people up there. When the people come here, back to Colombia, everything more clear. When I go to Colombia, I sometimes have a fight with the people because I try to explain exactly what's up, and the people don't believe what I say. They say, "No, you're

American now." The university in Colombia is national. It's funded by the government. All young people hate Americans because all people is poor people and never come outside the cities, so believe in what the media tells people there. Never make an exact picture of how it works in America. The American people is good people. Maybe the governments have something wrong. I love the Americans here. I love my business.

I have today from my daughter one grandson; he's eight years old. And from my son have two little girls; one is eleven, and the other is three years. They speak Spanish in the house and English outside. My ma and my wife tell my sons, "You have to take the good opportunity for learning two different languages." I am writing a book about my story. When I come through Mexico to here it's very hard. The first time, I not have too much problems. Only at the border I have the big problems. I accept everything in my life. If you accept the things, you have clear mind to find your way. But when you're angry you stop the mind. I find a way.

FERNANDO

Fernando was a student intern at a community-based organization whose work included advocating for immigrant rights and comprehensive immigration reform. I was directed to him when I called the offices looking for someone to tell me about their work. Twenty-two years old, Fernando was attending school at a local state university where he was majoring in political science. He was born near Mexico City and came to the U.S. alone at the age of fifteen.

FERNANDO: My family is all over the place. It's very common within the immigrant population that family members are here, there, everywhere. I have one brother in San Diego. It has been about eight years since I saw him. I have an older sister also. My brother is thirty-two, and my older sister is twenty-seven, and it's been about twelve years since I saw her and she lives in Tijuana. It's a difficult situation. We talk sometimes. My father left to the U.S. without documents, and he had it rough, too. He came to provide for the family, and that gave me the idea to come and join him when I decided I needed to leave home for a better life. Basically the migrant experience separated my family. I was born and my father left, and then my mother met someone else and then had my little sister. It has been six years in November since I saw my mother and my sister. So I live most of my life in Mexico up until I was sixteen and moved here. I am now twenty-two. It's been a long time that I've been separated from my family.

My father is a good person. We get along pretty well. He lives in Caldwell. He got documents in '86.[1] He sometimes does farmwork. He works in labor camps. This year he might go fight forest fires. He has a couple of trucks. He struggles a lot. Sometimes he works with potatoes. Right now he works at a *carnicería*. It is dangerous work because he does some of the cleaning, and he talks about people dying there, falling into the

machines. I worry about him. So that is my family. It was really difficult—
these life experiences. When I was fourteen, fifteen, I spent a lot of time by
myself because I was with my mother and she was a single mother. Living
in a patriarchal society it was very difficult for women and especially for a
single mother. I think that that developed my mind a lot.

LOUIS: *Where did you live in México?*

FERNANDO: Close to Mexico City. I remember this sociologist was saying we are a reflection of society and that's why we have these problems,
right? That's how I see myself. I was getting in trouble with the police. I had
situations with police brutality when I was down here. They were fucking
asses. That's also why I wanted to move here. It was really crazy. I wanted to
change my life.

LOUIS: *Were you scared when you left?*

FERNANDO: So many emotions. It was very intense. I was feeling nostalgic. Friends didn't want to see me anymore. My family was angry at me. The
police were looking for me. If I had stayed in Mexico I would have ended
up in jail or dead. I was tired. Coming to this country was like, varoom, a
cultural shock. It's a lot of change very fast. It was crazy. There was a lot of
learning, and now I have a more analytical background. I was feeling very
nationalistic, and now when I think about it, I think, "Fuck, why?" [Laughs]

LOUIS: *What did you think about coming to the U.S.? Did you have
fantasies about it?*

FERNANDO: No, yeah, I have to be honest about it. I think many Mexicans
have internalized this prayer. We have this spiritual idea about the U.S. I
thought I'd come to see big buildings and only white people. And the truth
was I did not come to see big buildings, but I did come to see white people
because I came to Idaho. I was living in Caldwell, and I would open my
door and there was nothing. There were no people, and I was used to seeing lots of people. I had a profound loss of community, but the strength and
discipline I learned helped me when it came to school. I take my studies
very seriously. I have come to see that I must be a part of building a better
world, and not only for me.

I first moved to Florida to live with friends, but it wasn't like I imagined. I had a very difficult time there. So I called my father and asked him if
I could come stay here. I finished high school here, and because he is a legal
resident, I can afford to go to the university. I became involved in social
justice causes, for workers, for immigrants, against racism and sexism,

because I need to make things better. Working with student organizations and with ICAN [Idaho Community Action Network] has been very good. In the summer of 2004 the Idaho Progressive Student Alliance [IPSA] worked on the Taco Bell boycott. In the summer of 2005 we changed university policy at Boise State University when they signed a worker-friendly contract. But even before this I began working at ICAN. We started working on advocating for the Dream Act in 2005. I had a chance to train with the Center for Community Change. At ICAN we work on immigration, healthcare, and youth organizing. We have about six thousand members throughout the state.

The truth is, I no longer feel Mexican. I've come to realize that the nationalism I once had, that which inspired the Mexican Revolution, was framed by European ideals of the nation-state. The co-optation of *indigenismo* by the Mexican government was intended to Westernize indigenous peoples and is very discriminatory. I have a grave concern for the links between nationalism and fundamentalism that inhibits progressive thinking. I can no longer accept the idea behind *México profundo*.[2] I have difficulty translating my emotions from Spanish to English, but this, too, has shaped my identity.

At ICAN we've been planning a conference with a network of community organizations. There is going to be about three hundred people, mostly college students. I am in charge of the youth component. We are doing workshops, like civil disobedience and discussions about the four levels of racism. I am facilitating that workshop. There will also be discussion about immigration and the role of youth in the Comprehensive Immigration Reform (CIR) movement. This is kind of underground, but we want people to start doing civil disobedience around CIR, but mainly we want white people to do that because we feel it will generate broader public support and show that this is not just a Latino political issue. I am really honest. I tell them I am spending time with you because I want us to get to know each other, and I'd like you to do some civil disobedience. It probably wasn't good, but I just decided to say it. And they said "Cool, cool." And actually they have been helping.

TWO

THE CRUCIBLE OF CHANGE AND ADAPTATION

THE SURVIVAL OF THE FITTEST IS THE AGELESS LAW OF NATURE,
BUT THE FITTEST ARE RARELY THE STRONG. THE FITTEST ARE THOSE
ENDOWED WITH THE QUALIFICATIONS FOR ADAPTATION, THE ABILITY
TO ACCEPT THE INEVITABLE AND CONFORM TO THE UNAVOIDABLE, TO
HARMONIZE WITH EXISTING OR CHANGING CONDITIONS.

Dave E. Smalley

The profoundness of change that immigrants experience is measured by
the contrast between the past, present, and an unknown future. But for
Latinos the contemporary immigration phenomenon should not be viewed
in isolation from the larger historical narrative of our place in U.S. society.
The intense increase in immigration from Latin America is a logical outcome of conquest, displacement, dependency, U.S. foreign policies, and free
market variables. For these reasons the interviews selected for this chapter
encompass a life marked by a fluid border and a binational existence, lives
lived in the United States for generations, and lives beginning anew in this
country. In all cases, the people who relate these testimonies have witnessed
enormous change.

What we can glean from them is the dialectical nature of change that
is motivated by contextual exigencies, in both the form of constraints and
in the form of opportunities. As should be clear in these stories, change
is a transgenerational phenomenon. And though change is ever present,
many elements of the Latina/o experience in the U.S. remain constant. For
instance, the childhood experiences of Adela Marmion reveal persistent
intracultural gender limitations and intercultural racial discrimination.
Her astute observations about social relations within and outside her community provide historical insight into Tucson's complex border history. In

a similar vein, Guadalupe Quinn, the daughter of braceros, shares the story of her political awakening in Oregon that eventually functioned as a catalyst for her to refashion her understanding of her gender and culture.

All six of the interviews here illustrate that change for Latina/os is not mere assimilation; it is not a linear or passive process of social and cultural conformity to the U.S. mainstream. Each of the interviewees, in his or her own way, has functioned as an agent of change toward the creation of a more just and equitable society. Be it as ethnic minorities or as immigrants, Latinos not only adapt as needed, in the process of building and preserving communities, raising children, and being an integral part of the labor force of this country, but also strive to change the world they live in in numerous ways. As an institutional advocate, Juan offers an inside view of how ensuring that public policies accommodate the needs of the workforce is good for the agricultural industry as a whole, even as he observes how Latinos are changing the complexion of farming in Michigan as they move from field hand to farm owner. Others contribute to social change through their union and community advocacy, through their public art, through teaching, or through utilizing their special skills in animal husbandry.

This is not to say that change is easy or that agency is always realizable for every immigrant. A common characteristic of new immigrants shared by Latinos across many generations is the value placed on a strong work ethic. While it is true that a community's work ethic can change and that no single characteristic can be said to be true of all members of a group, among many Latinos and non-Latinos alike, exhibiting a strong work ethic often assumes a moral dimension—especially in the face of racist stereotypes against people of color that often depict them as lazy and slovenly. The interviews presented here also speak to the often awkward and sometimes humorous process of cultural and social adaptation—be it legal and social mores or awareness of cultural customs and holidays. Each interviewee expresses concern for the future—for the challenges faced by the next generation. What is clear is that they all aspire not only to survival for the community but also to its ability to thrive as an equal partner in the democratic project.

ADELA MARMION

Adela Marmion, a ninety-three-year-old elder of the U.S.-Mexico borderlands, was introduced to me through a former student of mine who now works in Washington, D.C. I called her and arranged to meet with her at her home in South Tucson.

ADELA: I grew up all over. I was born in Morenci, Arizona, and my mother was born nearby in Medcalf, Arizona. She took me to Mexico when I was two and came back when I was about thirteen. I had to learn English, and learn about discrimination. Oh, did I, right away! I forgot my Spanish because they used to make fun of me because I was coming from Mexico. I was living in Agua Prieta and then Sonora. Because I was an American citizen, I could come to the school in the United States.

The music teacher loved my voice. I had a soprano voice. She was putting me in a play, and she was teaching me higher and higher notes, and she even used to tell me how to stand when I want to sing a very high note: "Think high. First you think high, and as you say the note, raise yourself and spin on your toes." In other words, the mind has a lot to do with the voice. I was in first grade, and one day I didn't want to go play at recess. My desk happened to be right by the door, and I heard my home room teacher talking to my music teacher by the door. My home teacher says to the music teacher, "What's the matter with you, you look angry." And she says, "I am, I had to change my play." "Why," she says. "I thought that you were so happy with the girl from Mexico?" "I am, but I have to put somebody else. I have to put a white girl in the lead." And the teacher says, "How are you going to explain it to the girl from Mexico? She's very excited about it." And she says, "I don't know." The way she explained it to me, she had changed my role because my mother couldn't afford the outfit. What she didn't know was that I could make my own outfit. I learned to sew on the sewing machine at seven. I could make dresses for myself and for my mother. Anyway, I thanked her for being so considerate [slight laughter]. My mother was sad, but a few days later I invited her to go to the theater because a woman from the neighborhood was putting on a play at the theater and I had a solo.

Singing has been in my life since I can remember. I could learn all the songs that were popular long before I went to school. I didn't know how to read or write yet, but I could hear a song and I would learn it. As I was singing my mother was always singing too, and it's a beautiful way to live when you sing. You have problems of all kinds, but you don't cry about it; you sing about it.

My grandmother took my mother to Mexico. I don't know what war was being fought in 1917 . . . [Louis: World War I.] My grandmother asked my mother, who was already married but had only one child, if she could go to Cananea, where she had a lot of cousins, relatives, because she wanted to get her two sons into Mexico so they wouldn't be drafted. It was a mistake. She asked my mother, and my mother had not made many good points with

Adela Marmion in her kitchen in South Tucson, Arizona. Photo by Louis Mendoza.

her mother, so she wanted to go, but my father said no. And my mother couldn't take orders, so she said she was going. The reason for her to go with my grandmother was so that my grandmother wouldn't be alone coming back. Women didn't travel alone, and so my father says, "If you go, don't come back!" Giving a woman an order is a mistake. So she went with my grandmother, and my grandmother introduced her family to all her family over there, and the older son did not want to stay because his wife didn't like it in Mexico, so he came back with my grandmother. My mother stayed over there with her brother. And when her brother joined the Mexican army my mother was stranded in Cananea.

LOUIS: *She didn't have a relationship with your father?*

ADELA: No, *mi mamá* had the brains of a mother. She had no schooling at all, but when she heard that my father was going to go over there and bring me back, not her, just me, she baptized me again in Mexico. She had me registered, so I have dual citizenship. My father still said he was going to go, so she wrote to one of her friends in Morenci, telling her that her baby had died. So my father never went to pick me up because he thought I died. Isn't it amazing what a woman can do to protect her rights?

LOUIS: *You were just a baby at the time?*

ADELA: I was two. I didn't see my father until I was twenty-two. He told me stories that are amazing. Like, for instance, he said, "I should've been more patient with your mother, she was so young." He was a lot older than her. "There's no way that I can say that you're not my daughter, because I suffered all the labor pains." The nine months that my mother was pregnant he was the one dealing with the dizziness; he was the one dealing with the throwing up and everything. I was expected in September, and he was working in the mines, five hundred feet below the earth. When she started getting labor pains, he had to get out of the mines, and he goes home just as I was coming out. My mother had called the *partera* [midwife]. I was born on the twenty-eighth of August.

My mother had it very, very hard in Mexico. She couldn't read or write, but she had a very good business mind. She even figured out how to make a living without knowing how to cook. She rented a place that had been empty and started a boardinghouse. Usually the miners would travel from one mine to another when one closed. My mother started doing the same thing. She'd go to the new mine, and the men who are there are usually without families. And then when the mine starts, they bring the family. But there was always a lot of men who don't have a family, and they need board. So my mother did that, she opened a place—a boardinghouse. They started coming in. She didn't know how to cook, but she hired somebody. She talked a lady that had a stove and had some pots and pans into making menudo and selling it that night and putting signs, so that when the people got out of the dance they would come and have menudo. The lady got drunk, so my mother had to do all the work, serving and everything. The next morning she gave her her part and then asked her if she would sell her the stove [laughter]. See what I mean, when you have to do something, you have an instinct for life and you will do whatever you have to. That's why I say a woman who has to support a child or two or three will make it always because she can always figure out ways. A man, I'm sorry to say this, but I have seen it too often, if the wife dies, the father will take the children to his mother, to his sister, to his aunt, or gets married right away, because he cannot handle the children alone. Nowadays that is changing a lot. This year I sent Mother's Day cards to several men.

Eventually my mother wanted to come home. My father was no longer in Morenci. He had gone to California. She had a car already, and the last place that she opened up as a boardinghouse was really making money. We went to Agua Prieta instead of coming to Nogales. When she left there was no Immigration, but when she decided to come back there was Immigration. This was in the 1920s. We couldn't come in because we didn't have papers, so she went and rented a house and wrote to her sisters in Clifton to send her our birth certificates. Well, it turned out that Arizona had had a fire, and all the records were burned in the fire, and she didn't have one and neither did I. She was born in 1898, and I was born in 1915, and all the records up to 1916 were burned. Fortunately there were a lot of people alive in Morenci and in Metcalf in Clifton who knew my grandparents, and so they were able to make affidavits and get us papers. In the meantime we were in Agua Prieta. She rented a house to wait for the papers, and next door was a widow who had two daughters and a son, and the son worked for the Mexican Immigration. They were a very, very good-looking family and very educated. They liked us. They were delighted with me because I did so many things, and the guy fell in love with my mother and my mother fell in love with him. They used to invite us over to have supper with them, and sometimes we used to cook the supper and take it. They had a beautiful relationship until the son announced that he wanted to marry my mother, and the mother said, "No, no, no, you cannot marry a secondhand woman." My mother was so embarrassed. We walked out. All of a sudden she had papers. She had had the papers already, but the romance was going on so she was waiting. We left and moved to Douglas.

In Mexico I was a very little girl to see so much brutality. When we were living in la Mesa del Sur a little friend that I met there and I used to love to go to the edge of the mesa and look down. On the left side was the prostitution house, and on the other side was the cemetery. We used to stand up there watching all the people coming in and out. They looked like little ants and especially when there was a funeral. One day my friend and I were watching, and suddenly we saw somebody coming out of the prostitution house in flames. Oooh, just a lot of flames, you couldn't see if it was a man or a woman. The teacher came over and saw what was going on. She pulled us away from there. We moved then to Pueblo Nuevo, where there was a new mine that had just opened up. My mother opened up a place—that's where she made most of her money—and she hired a cook who never smiled. She had a son that was already sick from working at the mine. He was a very young man, but the mine was so poisonous.

It was a copper mine run by an American company. Young men would get out of school, go work at the mine, and in six months they were already what they called *amimiados*. They were no longer healthy; their lungs were gone, and their digestion was also damaged by the gases of the mine. The son of the cook was always so sick. I was always singing and playing. He had a bench on the porch of the house, and we'd sit there all day, and at first he was very sad. I used to make him laugh and make him sing. He finally started bringing a guitar, and we were singing all the time. He was making songs for me, and I thought he was a very nice man. One day an officer came to ask the cook to go to the hospital, and she started crying so much, and she wouldn't go, and she asked my mother if she would go. There I met the girl who had been burned. She was still alive. She was burned all over, and nobody was taking care of her. Her blisters had become wounds all over her body, and nobody could turn her. My mother turned her. She was the daughter of the cook. And the guy who I thought was so sweet, so nice, was the brother of this girl. He saw her kissing her boyfriend. He beat up the boyfriend and pushed and pulled the girl and took her to the prostitution house. Afterwards, he couldn't get her out because it cost a lot of money to get those girls out of the prostitution house. That's why he was sad. It was his conscience.

And that was the first time I said, "I'm glad I don't have a brother." I've said it three times at least. I said it again when we were in Agua Prieta. By that time I was in the second grade, and my mother was working in a restaurant. The owner had a little girl my age. We used to go to school together. So we got out of school one day, and pretty soon we saw a man come running from one of the business places and behind him another man with a gun. Killed him right there in front of us. We just slipped against the wall; we were paralyzed, couldn't move, didn't even scream. I finally came to . . . I pulled her hand, and we came down to where my mother was. By that time everybody was talking about the murder, and there was somebody who said, "Well, he had to defend the honor of his name." What honor? There's no honor in killing. They explained that the man who was dead had got the girl pregnant that was a sister to the one that killed him. So he was clearing the deed, the honor of his name. That man is going to spend the rest of his life in prison, and his sister won't have anybody to help her. That was the second time that I said "I'm glad that I don't have a brother." And if you have any sisters, my advice to you is, if they make a mistake, help them, don't judge them. Everybody makes mistakes. But for some reason or another, brothers don't want their sisters to make mistakes. They want them to be perfect.

The third time I said "I'm glad I don't have a brother" is when we went to our hometown and my mother had a brother. My mother was young, and all the girls were buying powder to put on their faces. They didn't have the makeup they have now, but they did have a brand that was named Pontz Powder. So my mother put some powder on her face, and her brother comes over and scolded her, "You're always dirtying the name of the family. Why does it always have to be you?" My mother didn't say anything. My mother bought herself a dress that didn't have sleeves. Now it had all these parts over here—it had a collar like this but just a little hole here on the sleeve. There comes my uncle: "Again and again, what do you think you are?" And so on, and so on.

Then my mother cut her hair. All the young women were cutting their hair. What her brother didn't know was that his wife was cutting the sleeves out of her dress so she could be in style too. He didn't know that she wanted makeup. When I arrived in that town the first thing I noticed was that they did not have a florist. I knew how to make paper flowers and make wreaths. If somebody died they would come to me, and I never charged. I just told them, "Take it, whatever you want to give me," and sometimes they gave me more than I expected. But then my mother decided to cut her hair, and her brother comes over and, oh, he told her some awful things. He didn't know that his wife had been asking my mother to cut her hair. And my mother was saying "No, no, your husband will get mad." "No, he won't, he's very nice." Yeah, he was very nice to her but not to his sister. So she got somebody to cut her hair. She wanted makeup. Because I made flowers I had red paper, and she asked me for a piece. She would wet it with her tongue [laughter] and put it on her to use it as rouge and lipstick.

My mother became the black sheep of the family by doing the things that everybody's doing now. She was just born a little too soon. Nothing that she did was wrong, but the last straw was when she decided she had enough with the family and she was going to get away. We went to Clifton to buy a car. Somebody must have passed us on the road and immediately went and told my uncle. By the time we got to town my uncle was at the door. He said, "¿Qué estás pensando tú? ¿Qué eres marimacha?" [What are you thinking? That you're a tomboy?] And my mother said, "Pues yo creo que sí, porque soy padre y madre de mi hija, y nadie me trae una tortilla pa' mi hija" [Well, I think so, because I'm father and mother to my child, and nobody brings me a tortilla for my daughter]. And that was the first time I heard her talk back like that. We loaded up the car and got out of town. We came to Tucson.

I never went to high school. My mother didn't believe in an education for women. She was the one who needed it the most, but because she made it, she figured that women did not need to waste their time in schools. They're going to end up behind the washboards washing diapers; that was her motto. I used to beg her because when we were here she claimed that her English was not good, so if she had any business to take care of, "Mi'jita, don't go to school, I want you to go take care of this for me." "But, Mom, we are having a test tomorrow and we're studying today for tomorrow. I can't be absent today." "¿Para qué quieres tanta escuela? [Why do you care so much about school?] You already know a lot, you don't need any more." And I used to cry, "I want to go to school," and "I want to go to school." When I was in school she made me miss a lot of school, and finally she says, "Mi'jita, I'm sick, please help me. There's nobody to pay the rent or buy food; get a job, and next year you can go to school." I got a job. I paid the rent and bought the food, all the medicine for her. By this time I was fifteen. I worked in many places. I worked in a restaurant, and then I worked in a grocery store, then in another grocery store. I never went back to school, but I never stopped learning. I read books, anything I could get a hold of. And now when somebody asks about my education I tell them that I got it *en la escuela del aventón*.

Not that long ago, I was saying that to a man who's a retired principal from a school in Santa Fe, *dice*, "¿Qué es la escuela del aventón?" [What is *la escuela del aventón*?] The school that has no doors, no rules, and it's international, and takes young people, old people, all kinds, fat people, old people, poor people, ugly people, beautiful people, takes everybody, no discrimination, but it does have a big [makes popping noise], a big punch! And when this school throws a lesson to you, you never forget it, *por eso le digo la escuela del aventón* [that is why I say *la escuela del aventón*]. "Oh," *dice*, "I think we have another name." "Yeah," *le digo*, "the school of hard knocks?" [Laughter] The school of hard knocks, that's the one that gave me my education.

After I got married, we went to live in a town that was very discriminating. After I got married, my husband went to work the mine in Ajo, Arizona. There is no discrimination according to the people who live there, but there is a hill, and way up on top are beautiful houses for the supervisors of the mines, below them some are nice houses for the doctors, and a little below for the nurses, and then there is Indian town and Mexican town, so everything is segregated. They still say that there is no discrimination. My husband and I changed a lot of things there. My husband never liked to bathe in public bathrooms, and the mine had bathrooms, but he always used to come home to bathe. Somebody told him that the bathrooms that they had for the miners were segregated. He went to check it out. There are a lot of open showers, but these are for the whites and these are for the Mexicans. So my husband goes to the whites' shower, and all the Mexicans are saying, "No, David, te van a correr, no David, vente, vente para acá. [No, David, they'll kick you out, come over, come over here.] You'll get fired." My husband said, "Nobody's gonna tell me where I can take a bath." So he went in, and nobody told him to get out. The next day he went again, and the next day he went again, and about the third or fourth day another Mexican joined him, then another. It was over; he broke the rules. The swimming pools were the same way. For the whites, it was Saturday, Sunday, Monday, Wednesday, Thursday. Friday, when the water was good and dirty, was for the Mexicans and the Indians. On Saturday they cleaned the water for the whites.

The people there thought I had an education, and the principal of the school became very friendly with my husband, and he used to come over to the house and have coffee, and if nobody was looking he had a little glass of whiskey. One day I mentioned, "How do you feel having a dropout for your neighbor?" And the principal said, "What? You're a dropout? I don't believe it. Would you let me give you a test to see how much you have learned outside of school?" He graded me with two years' college, with the exception of trigonometry. I didn't know what that was. One of the things that gripes me now, and I've been hearing it since I was a little girl: English only, English only. They don't want any other languages. You go to Europe, and they speak all kinds of languages.

LOUIS: *How much have you seen Tucson change in your lifetime?*

ADELA: Oooh, have I seen changes here. There's an avenue downtown where the cathedral is, and at first the Mexicans lived on both sides of the street, on both sides of Stone. And then a lot of Scotchmen started coming in and buying on the east side of the street. And then the Mexicans moved more to the west. What they didn't figure out was that everybody was gonna go to the Cathedral. And the Scotchmen were meeting with the Mexican girls, and before we knew it Margarita Torres became McAllen, became McClain. They were changing the names of the Mexicans there. Now us in the barrios moved, because when the whites need a barrio, they go in and either buy you out or force you other ways. I couldn't believe it how easy it is to get your property. I had a *comadre* who lived on Kennedy, west of Stone, and they started sending her letters that she had to update her house to city's code. "You better go," I said, " 'cause the assessments have to be paid." She went five days after they were due, and she couldn't pay it. They took her house away. I went to check it, and I saw a lot of my area that belonged to Mexican families now belonged to the McGuinesses. I don't know who McGuiness was, but he was a wealthy guy that kept buying up property. Those were some of the changes I saw. The whites, no matter where they come from, if they want your property, they're going to get it one way or another. They move the barrios.

Have you heard the song of the "Barrio Viejo"? My husband's sister, Margaret, married Lalo Guerrero, who was a musician. He wrote a song about the barrio. That song made him more famous than he was already. He wrote it for Tucson, but he sang it in France. People cried over there for their barrios, no matter where he sang it. It lends itself for any barrio. Now there's a man who fought discrimination with music.

LOUIS: *Did you sing professionally?*

ADELA: Just in the choir but not professionally. I have sung in a lot of places that are commented on by other singers. For instance, I was with a group that made a big fiesta for the Guadalupana, at the convention center. Carmen Celia Beltrán was a woman in the barrio, very talented woman, and she wrote the story of the Guadalupana. And we did it in the community center with very fancy Mexican dresses, and the mariachi, colorful as can be. It was Teatro Carmen. Way, way, way back in the twenty-somethings, when it was open. She was so talented. She used to call me "Mi Jilguerito"—*es un pájaro* [it's a bird]. And she wrote a song *que todavía me acuerdo de ese canto* [that I still remember that song] [starts singing]:

> Y en silencio, deseando lo que nunca tendré
> Viviré añorando, cuanto cuanto te amé
> Soñaré noche y día, nuestro idilio de ayer

Y la dulce alegría que me dio tu querer.
Ahora . . . solo tuyo en el cielo testigo
Pero mucho que sufro porque no estás conmigo.
Las estrellas se ocultan cuando lloro por ti.
Y en silencio pregunto si te acuerdas de mi.

[And in silence, wishing what I'll never have
I'll live missing, how much I loved you
I'll dream night and day, our past love affair
And the sweet happiness that your love gave me.
Now . . . only yours in the sky as my witness.
But I suffer so much because you're not with me.
The stars conceal themselves when I cry for you.
And in silence I ask if you ever think about me.]

ADELA: No puedo cantar estoy muy ronca. Ya perdí mi soprano, ya no soy soprano ya no soy alto, ya no soy . . . [I can't sing because my voice is coarse. I lost my soprano voice, now I'm not a soprano, I'm not an alto, I'm not . . .] I'm not even a frog. Even frogs sound better. But I still try.

LOUIS: *You performed in* teatros?

ADELA: Yeah, and I sang at the Ford Bowl in San Diego, and I did a solo, *una* march *para el 16 de Septiembre*, and *canté en el* Organ Pavilion in Balboa Park. It's a big building open on one side; it can be heard all over town. It's a beautiful place. And then there's a Palace of Education. Allí cantamos mi hermana y yo, [she sings] "hace un año." Por cierto que nos aplaudieron mucho, mi hermana podía ser segunda, muy bonito, no le hace como comenzara yo, ella se quedaba calladita mientras yo comenzaba, then she'd get in. Nos aplaudieron much cuando cantaban, estaba nueva la canción esa, y después estábamos en una casa del novio de ella, y era Día de las Madres y todos estaban haciendo algo para la madre, unos cantaban, unos recitaban, unos leían algo para las madres. El señor Millian tocaba el acordeón y otro, uno de los muchachos, tocaba la guitarra. Mi mamá también tocaba poquito la guitarra y estábamos cante y cante. Y luego dice mi mamá, "Ay que mis hijas canten 'Hace un año,'" porque un día antes nos habían aplaudido tanto. Y resulta que no podíamos agarrar el tono. El del acordeón no nos podía dar, la guitarra tampoco, comenzábamos y de otro, y acaso que, "Hace un año," y luego decía el del acordeón, "No, no, ese no es el tono, déjeme ver déjeme ver," y luego, "Hace un año," y otra vez, otra vez, al fin me dijo, "No, no, no, ya pasaron muchos años, que se callen!" [There my sister and I sang "That Was a Year Ago." In fact, we got a lot of applause. My sister could play second for me, very pretty, it didn't matter if I started first. She would be very quiet while I started, then she'd get in. They applauded us very much when we sang. That was a new song. And then we were at her boyfriend's house, and it was Mother's Day, and everybody was doing something for the mothers: some people were singing, some were reciting poems, some were reading for the mothers. Mr. Millian was playing the accordion, and another boy was playing the guitar. My mother could play the guitar a little bit, and we were singing and singing. And then my mother says, "Ah! My daughters should sing the song 'A Year Ago,'" because the day before we got such great applause. And it happened that we weren't able to find the tone. The accordion wasn't able to give us the tone, neither with the guitar. We would start singing "A Year Ago," and the accordion guy would say, "No, no, no, that is not the tone, let me see, let me see." And then we'd start again "A Year Ago," and again, and again. Finally he said, "No, no, no, too many years have passed, they better stop." [Laughter]

LOUIS: Did you sing when you were an adult?

ADELA: No way, José! Me calló mi esposo. Vieras visto, me encontró cantando. Un profesor de música, que era compositor, era amigo del cuñado de mi esposo y era mi profesor, el nos presentó. Y ya me tenía puesta, ya habían hecho los . . . anuncios para el dieciséis de septiembre, que iba otro dieciséis. Ya había cantado una vez e iba cantar otra vez composición de ese señor. Pero me casé en junio, todo estaba listo para el 16 de septiembre, no me dejó, no me dejó, me calló, por muchos años me calló. Si íbamos a una parte, luego luego, "Adelita, cántanos esto." Cantaba uno y luego, vámanos, vámanos. Y después ya ni aceptaba invitaciones y andaba yo cantando en la casa, y también venía me platicaba alguna cosa, me preguntaba alguna cosa y me callaba, y me calló por muchos años, y después no le gusté. Entonces comenzó, me comenzó, me regaló, de eso para tocar discos. Me compró un grabador también, y me compraba discos, cada rato me traía discos, pero yo ya había perdido, se me secó, secó, secó todo. And . . . ya para entonces estaban los hijos creciendo, y la que está viviendo ahorita conmigo, quería piano, entonces le conseguí uno baratón que lo tenían afuera. Me lo dieron muy barato, lo metí a la casa, con hilo y gancho, le compuse las baquetas y le comenzaron a dar lecciones. Y me fijaba, después de que ella se iba a la escuela yo también me ponía ha ver que había aprendido, y llegó tiempo que mi esposo comenzó a notar la diferencia en mi personalidad, me tenía horcada. Don't ever do that to your wife; let her grow. [My husband made me shut up. You should've seen it—he found me singing. My music teacher, who was a composer, introduced us, he was a friend of my husband's brother-in-law, and he was my teacher. And he had me in the advertisements already for the September 16 celebration, the following one. I had sung there before, and I was going to sing this man's new song. But I got married in June. Everything was ready for September 16, and he didn't let me. He made me shut up; for many years he shut me up. If we went someplace, right away somebody would say, "Adelita, sing something." I would sing one song, and he'd say right away, "Let's go, let's go." Afterwards, I didn't accept any more invitations. I only sang at home. And he'd come and start talking to me, he'd ask me something and shut me up. For many years he stopped me from singing, and then he didn't like me. Then he started, he started me, he bought me one of those record players. He brought records all the time, but by then I had already lost it; it dried up, dried up, everything dried up. And by then my children were already growing, and the one who lives with me now, she wanted a piano, and I got her a cheap one they were selling outside. They sold it to me very cheap, and I got it in the house with rope and a hook, I fixed the keys, and she started to get lessons. And I paid attention too. After she went to school, I would try to see what she learned. And after a while my husband noticed a change in my personality. He was like hanging me.]

It's very, very, sad. Mira, todo el tiempo estamos creciendo [Look, we're growing all the time]. It would be nice if your wife and you grew up together. Sometimes you will be higher than her; sometimes she will be higher than you. When she's higher than you, be patient, don't be embarrassed, don't be angry. I haven't stopped growing. I'm still learning things. Una viuda me preguntó a mí, ya estaba viuda yo también [A widow asked me, I also was a widow by then], "When is the right time to get married?" Y le digo yo [And I said], "When you're ready. When you're through with your marriage, then you might be married." And she says, "But he's dead; my husband is dead." "Are you through with the marriage, 'cause he might not be around, but you might still be very, very married to him. If you're still in love with him you cannot give yourself to somebody else." I said, "Do you have somebody in mind already?" She said, "Yes, there is this man that wants to marry me, and he says that he can help me forget." I said, "No, no way, that's something that you have to do on your own, by yourself, and it won't be fair for him to try to help because he's gonna be competing with somebody who's not there. So you get through with your marriage first." I said to her, "What is your hurry? Don't rush into another marriage. Get free first, find yourself." She says, "I'm forty years old, I should know myself by now." I said, "No way, you don't know yourself, I was sixty-five when my husband died. I should've known myself, but I didn't." First I was my mother's daughter, and then I was my husband's wife, David's wife, Danny's mother, Ellis's mother, Denny's mother. I was everybody except me. I am now a person. No titles. I am finding that I have a mind that I thought I had put away already, that was no longer any good. Find yourself, find out who you are outside of being so-and-so's wife, or so-and-so's widow. Find out who that person in you is. And you're going to find out that it's not the same person that was married to this man.

> LOUIS: *What do you think about all the controversy surrounding immigration right now?*

ADELA: My neighbors go to Naco a lot in November to take flowers to their dead. He was telling me that it took almost two hours to cross the border coming back. Talking about Mexico, Presidente Fox, I used to like him, I thought that he would be able to do something for Mexico, but after a while I was ashamed of him. He kept making trips to Washington to talk to President Bush, to ask leniency for his people who are coming here. I used to think he should be ashamed of himself. Instead of asking Bush to do something for his people, why isn't he doing something for his people over there? I used to be angry at him, angry at the Mexicans that come over here too. En México no les importa la gente de aquí, porque no quieren a la gente de allá. Y por eso me daba a mí coraje cuando venía el Presidente Fox a mirar al Bush, asking for clemency [In Mexico, they don't care about people from here, because people from here don't care about people there. That's why I got mad when President Fox came to look for President Bush, asking for clemency].

> LOUIS: *Is that a journal?*

ADELA: Yeah, le nombro "Pensamientos." Pero verás lo que escribí para él [Yeah, I call it "Thoughts." But look what I wrote there] . . .

> *[Louis, reading from journal]*

Dear Nephew,
I have searched the attic of my mind, to see how many treasures for you I could find. My diamonds were not too bright, my gold had become foolish. My emeralds from envy had turned green, and my wisdom had gone downhill. Thank god, my wrinkles had not scared my spirits; it still works. For it is in excellent condition, and that you can have if you ever need it or want it. I also have found my pretty love box, and my old love for you it's as new as when I met you when you were age three or four. You were so brave and protective, and you still are. My love hasn't

changed either. It's still new and protective too, completely unchanged. Sorry that's the only treasure for you that I could find. But in this book I have put in the stairs to heaven so you can climb. Sorry to give you the stairs to heaven, since I am a little lame, not old. I'm taking the elevator myself. I'll see you there someday and will be so proud to introduce you as the best Arizona policeman to the greatest chief of police worldwide, chief of chiefs, judge of judges, king of kings, our lord, our father, señor de señores, Jesus Christ. We will have a fiesta to welcome you—no tamales, no frijoles, just a lot of joy, love, and more love. That's what heaven is all about.   *Your heavenly Aunt.*

LOUIS: *This is beautiful. These are like poems.*

ADELA: I wrote it for him. I put it in a little book where I put all about justice and judging. And right now I'm working on the word *fear*. So I'm making a lot of notes.

LOUIS: *Are you going to give this to your children someday?*

ADELA: What they want me to do is what I'm doing with you, to write my story. I've been telling all the people who are married to different cultures, "God said, 'Love thy neighbor.'" He didn't mean for you to love the one in front of your house. He meant one nation loving another. I had a friend who for years I heard her say how awful the Germans were. She could never say anything nice about the Germans. In the meantime she's raising her children, and the little one goes to the university. Germany sent some professors on an exchange, and one of them fell in love with her and took her to Germany. So her song has changed altogether, because they would send pictures of the children, "Comadre, mire nomás qué bonito, qué bonitos se junta la sangre mexicana con la alemana." ¿Qué bonito cambió la canción, verdad? ["Comadre, look how pretty, how pretty Mexican and German blood mix." So pretty the song changed, right?] You can live in the worst situations and still be happy. We go up and down financially, spiritually, socially, in every way. Me he fijado de los que niegan el poder de Dios [I have noticed that those who deny the power of God,] they have to scrounge for their lives. They make it, but they have hardships. And those who never deny the power of God, makes it easy. But they have to work too.

Juan Marinez works with the Michigan State University Extension Service and served as a federal liaison to Washington, D.C. From 1999 to 2002 he received an IPA[1] assignment to the U.S. Department of Agriculture and was invited to serve as Secretary of Agriculture Dan Glickman's national program coordinator on farmworkers. In this capacity he facilitated the acquisition of $20 million to assist farmworkers who had been negatively affected by natural disasters. His expertise is on Hispanic farm owners and the relationship between non-Hispanic farm owners and Hispanic farmworkers. We met at his university office.

JUAN: There's an interesting phenomenon in Michigan where Latino immigrants are becoming small farm owners. The kids start school, and all of a sudden it hits them that they're there permanently. They're great savers—wait to accumulate between $40,000 and $80,000, and that's good enough to get them a down payment on a farm in Southwest Michigan. They could then buy a 40-, 20-, or 10-acre family farm. They also would stay with family members and go back and work in Chicago until they established themselves by getting a local job and then they would farm part-time. As they make these moves in farm ownership, they bring others along with them to do the same.

LOUIS: So the notion of the land is still very important to them?

JUAN: Oh, yeah, very important. Most of them have come from rural Mexico so they know what they're getting into.

LOUIS: What is your position in the College of Agriculture?

JUAN: I'm on the extension side. I was probably one of the top administrators for ten or fifteen years in the nation as a Hispanic, and now there's a few more. I'm starting my thirty-fifth year. I spent three years in Washington as an IPA on loan from Michigan State to the secretary of agriculture. I was the first national farmworker coordinator for USDA, the first one to include farmworkers in disaster assistance. I was able to get $20 million through the agriculture secretary to include farmworkers in disaster relief, so when there's a frost or there's, let's say, bird infestation or drought, hurricanes. They never used to include farmworkers. That comes from the ag secretary, and you make grant money to the states to assist farmworkers and [those] who are negatively affected by natural disasters.

I had to fight on policy with the National Farm Bureau for this money as they were not supportive at first until we had an economic discussion on the lack of farm labor for production agriculture if farm labor could not be assisted when natural disasters occur across our land. I said, "Look, if workers don't get any kind of assistance, then next year this workforce will not show up and farmers are going to be in trouble." Very little attention gets paid to rural regions outside of farmworkers. There's also little to no talk about Latinos who now reside as permanent rural populations. The rural economy wouldn't survive if it wasn't for us who do the heavy work in rural

Juan Marinez in his office at Michigan State University, East Lansing.
Photo by Louis Mendoza.

America. But we are so much a part of the rural labor force. For example, in dairy parlors Mexican milkers now make up to 60 percent of the labor force—enough employees that today you have a magazine in Spanish for employees.

> LOUIS: *Do people think of them as a transient community that doesn't need to be addressed?*

JUAN: In some ways, yes. For example, my dad's generation contributed to that image. So, many times, you don't take actions because your head's someplace else. We had a speaker here once whose entire talk was, "You know, folks, it's nice that you want to go back to Texas, but you know what? You got to stop thinking that you're going to go back. You've got to start thinking that you are a Michiganian. You need to be thinking of what impact you can make here. Vote in Michigan." I thought he made a lot of sense. His point was that we can't be thinking that we're vagabonds or hobos or transients but that we're permanent. That's our mind-set that we need to work on, and it doesn't mean turning your back on Texas or Mexico or California.

> LOUIS: *I've met people who have a really strong sense of their rights. They may think of themselves as* mexicanos, *but they are not going to let somebody push them around.*

JUAN: Absolutely. One gentleman I'm trying to help owns a farm, and also a grocery store. A local employer pays his employees at the very last minute on an account with insufficient funds. So now what? These workers then go to the Mexican ethnic markets, because some don't have appropriate documentation. So then the grocer will cash the checks and then the employees buy groceries from him. He's told me that he has been stuck for up to $17,000 because of insufficient funds. He tells me, "Shit, Juan, what the hell am I to do? I don't want to not sell groceries to our people knowing that they need to eat. The individual I want to get is the employer who did this, but I'm stuck between a rock and a hard place." I said, "No, you're not." I said, "You need to get a lawyer." So we got him hooked up with a lawyer. He's fighting for his rights. They picked on the wrong guy because he's going to take this employer to court. I'm sure that it happens a whole lot of times. So then who is stuck with the bad checks? The small little mom-and-pop grocers.

> LOUIS: *Tell me more about the transformation of farm ownership with Hispanic farmers.*

JUAN: It didn't happen overnight. It really started with Tejanos in Michigan. Many of them had excellent working relationships with their employers, and in the process the employers also had family members who may not have the interest in continuing farming. In Michigan, 80 percent of the farms are family owned. So corporations are not as much of a problem for us. I have this map of the farm people of Michigan according to ethnicity. Michigan is a very ethnic state, and to call folks here white is really a misnomer because they really don't identify as white. Many still identified themselves by their ethnic background. It was farmers from these ethnic groups, whose grandparents were the ones who first hired *mexicanos* from Texas.

LOUIS: *Because they had a sense of their own ethnicity they weren't necessarily afraid of somebody else who identified ethnically?*

JUAN: Exactly. They could understand it; it made sense to them. The cultural clashes that we see today promoted by people like Michael Savage, Lou Dobbs, Pat Buchanan, and Tancredo are by people who want to basically claim the American identity. I'm sure if you asked them for a definition of "American" they would be hard-pressed to figure out what the hell that is. The transition of farm ownership came gradually. They knew they couldn't get loans because the banks weren't going to lend money to a migrant population, so they financed themselves.

LOUIS: *Do you have any sense of what those numbers might look like today?*

JUAN: The big numbers would be the Mexican immigrant, immigrants coming from Chicago who are buying the farms. The smaller group would be the Tejano, and the second, in the middle and the least group, would be the intermarriages. They work an array of different crops, but predominately it's blueberries here in Michigan. Michigan ranks number one in the world in blueberry production, and right now Latinos probably make up between 18 and 20 percent of the blueberry growers. I predict in the next ten years we may be up to 50 percent because of the aging of the white farmers and African Americans who also are in blueberry production. When you take a look at blueberries on a world scale, Latinos do dominate this crop. For example, the next leading producer that comes second to Michigan is Chile, and the third is Argentina. So if you look at this crop from a Latino ethnic domination of this crop, it is this population who is a major player when you factor in the American hemisphere.

LOUIS: *Is buying a farm part of an agenda when they come over here?*

JUAN: I don't think so. I think it's happening when we look at Mexican immigrants and Guatemalan immigrants, they're leaving rural areas in their countries. They're coming from rural communities, and the first kind of work that they end up doing here in the U.S., it's farmwork and/or construction. They have this sense of landownership that goes back maybe ten or fifteen generations. They come here, and they want a piece of the pie and think, "Well, if I'm going to stay here, I want to work in a farm and I want to work for myself." And they do a lot of the cultural practices that they learn in Mexico from their ancestors who have farmed for hundreds of years. All of a sudden they start thinking, "Oh, shoot. Yeah, I can make money at this."

There's one Latino farmer who has a you-pick operation, and so his farm setup is for that. By the way the majority of the people who come to pick his fruit come from Chicago and are also *mexicanos*, and when I visited the farm and spoke with folks who came with their families for the day to harvest their own fruit, I asked them, "Why did you come and pick?" They answered, "Well, because I want my children to remember where we came from. I want my children to appreciate a farm. I want my children to understand that apples come from trees. That they don't come from the grocery store." Grandmothers, aunts, uncles, everybody, the kids, come to pick, and he's got it set up so they have a picnic and they play soccer. They feel free. They don't feel this pressure of a city environment.

> LOUIS: *When I first started on this trip in Northern California, I saw some of those places, and to me they look like the kind of places where folks would go to pretend to have the experience of being a farmworker for a day, and I thought it was a little strange. But the way you explain it here is profound because it taps into a prior connection. Do many migrant farmworkers come to Michigan?*

JUAN: Oh, yeah. There is a new report that just came out, and according to this report we have close to ninety thousand farmworkers who come through Michigan. Did I mention to you that Michigan is second to California in its diversity of crop production? Therefore Michigan needs a whole lot of hand labor. In fact, just last year because of the number of raids that were being done, a lot of farmers panicked. We lost acreages of asparagus because producers didn't have the work crews needed to do the job. As a result, I think we're going to see a movement to mechanization because if Congress does not work with the industries, then the industries are going to have to move toward mechanization. Now, it's not as easy as all that. I don't know if you remember, "Hard Tomatoes, Hard Times." It took years and millions of dollars of research on tomatoes to make the skin hard enough so it would not break when they were harvested by a machine. In the process there was a loss of fruit and as well loss of taste. The customer lost in quality and character of the tomato as a result. That is why today you have a food movement of growing and selling local. The customer wants a healthier and a wholesome product for the family table. As you know, there's a cost to technological accommodation as well as a cost in nutrition. You run the risk of losing diversity in fruit as well as plants.

LOUIS: *Are most of these seasonal migrant workers?*

JUAN: That's another misconception held by both the nonfarmworker community and the farmworker community that we now have crops that are being harvested by farmworkers that traditionally were not harvested by farmworkers. For example, in Michigan we have farmworkers all the way into December who stay and harvest Michigan Christmas trees. This is a product that typically got harvested by local college kids during winter break. But now a lot of these kids say, "Hey, it's my winter break, I'm outta here! I'm going to someplace warm." That workforce that Christmas tree producers had traditionally depended on is not as available to them anymore as it had been a generation before. So now farmworkers are coming into these industries and doing the pruning, cutting, processing, and transportation. In Michigan the season starts in May, June, with our state cold crops of asparagus and other root crops, all the way into December, so in actuality we're really talking of almost ten to eleven months' employment. Not in the same crop, mind you, but moving from one area crop to another, as well as a different state location. The other thing that's happening within the farmworker population is specialization. They're becoming specialists in certain crops so that if your specialty is harvesting blueberries, you will not harvest peaches. The change is taking place among the workforce. Let's say if your skill is picking blueberries and you can make money at it, you might start picking blueberries in Michigan and then go to New Jersey and then down to Georgia. Until the next harvest season starts and the cycle starts all over again.

LOUIS: *How does all this affect the debates on immigration in a place like Michigan?*

JUAN: I think the only ones who have this discussion are the Farm Bureau and the farmworker advocates. Michigan does get pulled into some of the national debates on immigration, even though the individual who started FAIR,[2] Dr. Tanton, lives in Petoskey. One does not see Michigan being included in the national debates. For example, Lou Dobbs, what does he know? They never interview us. I don't think immigration reform is going to happen because the Democrats don't have the spine to really take it on, and they cannot even articulate it. When you take a look at immigrant destinations, it's the states with high levels of immigrants who are better off economically speaking. When you look at states where there is a deficit in immigration, their economies are doing poorly.

Guadalupe Quinn is the Lane County regional coordinator for CAUSA de Oregon, a statewide grassroots organization that works to defend and advance immigrant rights through coordination with local, state, and national coalitions and allies. I heard about Guadalupe from a friend in Texas who had worked with her while in Eugene on an academic fellowship. Guadalupe's activism is not limited to CAUSA's agenda, though her wide-ranging educational, social, and political advocacy on behalf of the Latino community complements it.

GUADALUPE: I came from Yucatán in 1951 to Ventura County in California. Most of the folks who were in that area when we first came were braceros. The Bracero Program was still going on, and we came with the sponsorship of a *tío* [uncle]. I grew up in California and was there until 1978, when my husband and I came to Eugene with some other friends. I'd never been here, and we didn't know anyone here, but we decided we needed a change. When we came, oh my gosh, there were no Latinos. What a big-time culture shock, because growing up in Oxnard where there was a big agricultural industry, mostly strawberries, lettuce, and tomatoes, there were many *mexicanos*. Here in Oregon there were almost no Latinos. Oregon is still predominantly white, but compared to what it was like in '78, there is a huge increase. According to the census, 140,000 Latinos are in Lane County, but I think it is more.

> LOUIS: *Have the economic dimensions of immigration been part of the discourse?*

GUADALUPE: Yeah. I think our work, besides talking about relevant issues that are on the front burner, like Real ID and Comprehensive Immigration

Guadalupe Quinn of CAUSA de Oregon in Eugene, Oregon. Photo by Louis Mendoza.

Reform, has been to fight the really awful bills like Sensenbrenner.[3] Besides that, we're trying to educate our larger communities and our allies about the contributions of immigrants, and we need to talk about the missing facts. Policy reports that address the economic impact are useful, because the only way we can counter misinformation is to try and educate people about the reality of the contributions that immigrants make.

> LOUIS: *How would you characterize the social and cultural climate here? I read somewhere that there was a campaign in Oregon in the 1980s focused on tourists that said something like, "Thanks for visiting, but keep on moving, stranger."*

GUADALUPE: Historically that is Oregon. The history of Oregon and the Northwest is really steeped in the white supremacist neo-Nazi movement. The Northwest is the land of the Klan, where the Christian Identity Movement has taken a foothold. It's regional; look at the folks in Idaho where the neo-Nazis and other white supremacists are. We have that here too. But we also have organizations that track the hate stuff and work on anti-bigotry. In the past the nativists were working class, because I think what happens historically is that there is a scapegoating of populations based on the need to blame someone else for their condition. In the last two to three years, the anti-immigrant movement has been really loud, proud, and very strategic. They have been able to pull in folks other than people at the bottom. There has been a real push to align themselves with folks, not just poor folks, but folks who call themselves patriots who want to hang onto "their" country. In our legislature there are lots and lots of bills that are anti-immigrant and anti-farmworker. English Only comes up regularly. Collective bargaining is always under attack.

LOUIS: *Do you find that a lot of recent immigrants get involved?*

GUADALUPE: No. It's something that has always been hard for our area. I don't think it's true in other parts of Oregon because we have a *compañero* who works in Medford. Medford is a very different community: *hay más raza* [there are more people] and more weight of organized folks. It's just like in Salem and Woodburn because of the farmworkers and the union. Here we're still very white, and the immigrant community is just trying to survive, so organizing our community takes a lot of time. We have been working with the churches because a lot now serve the Latino community. When we came in 1978 there was not one Spanish Mass in the whole county. Now there are like fifteen different churches from different denominations serving the community.

We have Mass in Spanish in all the Catholic churches. Now we have Evangelical, Pentecostal, Jehovah's Witness, Seventh-Day Adventists. There is a Baptist church on Riverway where I've been able to go and talk about our work. Since CAUSA is working on a human rights struggle here, the important thing is to work with churches and the schools and the organizations serving our communities. It's where you will find our *gente*. There are certain schools that have a large population of Latino students, so that's the best place to go and make a connection. A good friend of mine who works at the District coordinates Latino family nights once a month in Spanish. And then there are all these *tienditas* [little stores] that have come up. We used to go crazy because there used to be no place to buy anything, not even pan dulce. I used to have to go get it in Woodburn. But now there are a lot of *tienditas* and even a *panadería* [bakery]. I remember talking to a friend and saying, "You'll know our community has arrived when you see Spanish services in the churches and a *tiendita* and a *panadería*."

LOUIS: *How are the schools doing with the Latino population?*

GUADALUPE: I'm part of a group that started five years ago, called Educación y Justicia para la Raza. We were concerned with the three main school districts and the fact that our kids were bombing. We realized that we had to pay attention to the programs, really fight to be sure that the ELL [English Language Learner] stuff was okay. They don't have anything but ESL [English as a Second Language]. My son was in the first immersion program, not bilingual, immersion in Spanish, and he's already thirty. Since then they have started an immersion program in English, Spanish, French, and Japanese. But it's very elitist, and we were really upset because when we supported the immersion program our big thing was, "Oh, this will be great fun, and the kids they won't lose the Spanish." They started the immersion program where hundreds of white kids learned Spanish, and the schools kept our kids out because of the classism. They didn't want poor *familias* there looking like we looked.

In the last couple of years there is a lot of anti-immigrant sentiment. It's even among our own *gente*. I can't ever remember racism being as awful as it is right now. So a lot of the work with our folks is to address racism. CAUSA started the People of Color Action Academy. We gather our *gente* along with other communities of color to do a legislative training and take people to visit the capitol. We also do stuff on citizenship and the military to inform parents about the military. The *jóvenes* [young people] do that. Our families don't know you have to register for Selective Service, and you won't be able to get your papers later on if you don't. Our work with the *jóvenes* in the high schools is to develop leadership skills and to involve them in the struggle in whatever way we can. And to teach them to be smart because this stuff is hard and it is dangerous sometimes.

I work out of my house. I am out most of the time anyway. I am the only staff person, but I don't work alone. I am really lucky that I am pretty much connected with everything that has to do with the Latino community and our allies. CAUSA has made a commitment to work with the African American community, the GLBQ [gay-lesbian-bisexual-queer] community and campuses. I developed a steering committee of all these groups. We have a good e-network. About a year ago I put together an emergency response team to immigration raids. We have a packet to take to the churches. There was a really bad raid in Portland at the Del Monte company. We did a blitz at the churches about three weeks ago because we want the community to know they are not alone.

The media coverage on immigration issues here is awful. The radio station and the media—I've gotten into a lot of arguments with the newspaper here because they cover stuff so poorly and create a lot of misinformation. Right now our big thing is just to get information to families as it has to do with ICE. There was this 181 law.[4] Basically they want to undo that law. There was a statement from the police that they do not want to work with the Feds.

About a year or so ago when I reestablished the Migra Response Team, we talked to all the chiefs of police around the state and got them saying that they do not want to do the work of the Feds. Part of what we asked the sheriff for permission was for at least four or five of us to go into the county jail to speak with immigrants held there.

LOUIS: *So tell me about white Oregonians—about everyday folks.*

GUADALUPE: Overall, it's a pretty progressive community. They don't always get it. They don't understand privilege and the roots and faces of racism, but they care. There are the environmental, peace, and women's groups, unions. But we have a lot of work to do around educating them, promoting cultural competence. They have a lot to learn. I've worked with some of those groups for over twenty years. There is a segment of this community that are cowboys. In a small town like Junction, which isn't very far from us, they have their little Confederate flags.

These are the patriots. They want to take their country back. They want people to assimilate. So on a continuum you have the neo-Nazis here and we have a lot of white liberals who have a lot to learn. We still have a predominantly white community, but the face of the community has changed, and it has become something that for the progressives isn't always comfortable and it is something they have to deal with. They are not always good at it. In Eugene anyway we have a great mayor whom we love. She gets it. In fact, we had an awful raid around 1997–1998. The *migra* came in and raided six businesses in our area. She wasn't the mayor then, but there was a resolution made to let the *migra* know they were not welcome. When she became mayor she rededicated that resolution and her commitment to a community that is safe and welcoming for everyone, where we would not allow anyone to come in and hurt anyone. Our county commissioners suck. And our city council? Well, we have our very first Latina city councilor ever in the history of Eugene. We have the first Latino school board member. There's progress.

We have had to struggle with public safety though. In years past there was a huge issue around profiling. We have tried really hard to build bridges between the public safety folks in the county and the Latino community. It is to our advantage and the cops' advantage to have us trust them. The chief of police in Springfield has done a great job and actually hired a Latina to do some outreach. The police have made a lot of big mistakes, and we have to call them on it every single time, but that's the way it is. We fought for years for an external review board. I was on the committee that pushed it real hard, and we lost by just a few votes. It went to the voters, and they passed it. You'll see our *gente* pretty much anywhere, Whitaker, Cottage Grove. These are small towns with a fairly large Latino community.

> LOUIS: *It seems courageous that they would go somewhere with no community in place.*

GUADALUPE: Much of that is for work. Centro Latino Mexicanos, the only social service center that serves Latinos where they have day laborers, usually serves folks from Oaxaca and Michoacán. We have a small but fast-growing indigenous population. We have a couple of *compañeros* in the Salem-Woodburn area whose first language is not Spanish. They speak Mixteca. In my area we have Central Americans, but the largest number are *mexicanos*. There is an organization that I've been working with since the 1980s—CISCAP, the Committee in Solidarity with Central American People. I worked with Witness for Peace when we were doing delegations to Nicaragua. I was involved in the sanctuary movement, and I was involved with the antiwar stuff.

When I talk to young folks I tell them that I am actually doing something I never thought I would do. I come from Mexico and was raised very traditionally. My parents insisted on Spanish in the house; they didn't care outside. It was almost like growing up still living in Mexico. It was hard because the world was different outside. But in my home it was very strict, very proud, and very traditional. My parents were hardworking and honest and proud of being *mexicano*. We were taught to be very careful, very humble, to never make waves. When I came to Oregon I was married. I had a two-year-old. My husband and I were really excited about being here. I was working in the school system. I stepped into a meeting where I heard they needed someone who spoke Spanish. There wasn't many Latinos here, so I went with a girlfriend to help translate. It was actually a committee from a Quaker church here in town who were establishing themselves as a sanctuary for refugees from Central America. I listened to what they were proposing. My girlfriend said, "I don't want to do this. We'll get in trouble." But I couldn't get it out of my head what I had heard and what our government was doing. I became a citizen when I was in high school. I cared about voting but not about the government or foreign affairs.

That was the changing moment for me. I thought, "Where have I been?" I left that meeting, and I began to really start listening to the news. I began going to the meetings and said I'll help you with the families when they come. I left, and I couldn't get it out of my head. I stepped into it at that moment and never got out. I got involved with Witness for Peace, and I went to Nicaragua in '75 during the war there that the U.S. was waging on them. That was a real conversion for me to be in the mountains with the *gente*. We talked to Ernesto Cardenal, who had been excommunicated. I came back totally pissed and decided I was going to be a recovering Catholic. I read *The Gospel of Solentiname*. I began to try and understand: What was the connection between what I was taught about God and what we do in relation to God and the human beings around us?

I had so many questions. I couldn't deal with the hypocrisy. I thought, "I have to go back and understand what it means to be a person of faith." I remember arguing with my mom and saying, "You are the one who said that to believe in God means from the moment you wake up to the time you go to bed, and it has everything to do with in relation to the people you encounter every day. How, then, can I ignore the stuff that is going on and the fact that the church is complicit? And not only that, look at what it teaches—it's oppressive, it's sexist, it's racist, it's homophobic, it's classist."

What changed is that I thought if I really believed in God that this was something I needed to do. It was very scary for me because it was contrary to the way I was raised. I didn't really think I could do anything. Little by little, I found my niche. I was totally asleep during the civil rights movement and Vietnam. And then I got a job coordinating a racism and resistance program, and I became very aware of the history of slavery and civil rights and the connections, and what had happened with the Asian community with the internment. I thought, "Something's wrong and I can't fix it all, but I'll do what I can because I think we are called to do that." It has been hard for my family. I went from being a traditional Mexican wife to this nut who wasn't home fixing dinner anymore. My son is very proud of what I do. He understands why it is important. My husband too is very supportive. He could not go out and do the work in the same way because he isn't *mexicano*. We've been married thirty-seven years. It is one of those struggles even within the relationship to try and redefine yourself.

LOUIS: *Did you go to college?*

GUADALUPE: No, I was lucky to go to high school. I spend a lot of time talking at campuses, but for some of us college wasn't possible. I always tell students that my greatest classroom has been the twenty-some years I've been in the community. What I learned there I wouldn't have learned in the classroom. I am lucky. I get to do the work that I love and call it a job. I think our message to the *jóvenes* is to get what we need and give back. That's why we struggle . . . to help them move forward so that they won't forget where they came from.

VICTOR OCHOA

Victor Ochoa spoke with me at his house in San Diego, California. We sat and talked in his garage studio as the sun went down. As a lifelong resident of Southern California, he brought historical perspective to local struggles and the role of art in social movements. Victor was an integral part of the movement to establish Chicano Park and currently teaches art in the schools and continues to create public murals.

VICTOR: Here in Southern California, we consider ourselves the most crossed border in the world, and we of course always think of this as the most important border. I just experienced something really weird. I went to a wedding of one of my nephews, Victor, up in Fresno. He marries this white girl, but on my sister's side she married a white guy and so they were raised kind of white, surfers, skateboarders, etc. I really felt like a tamale among a bunch of hamburgers, you know? I felt really out of place. It was so funny because Victor and my son was there, also Victor, right, so somebody says, "Oh, three Victors. Let's have a wedding shot." So I said, "Okay, come on. Let's go." We're in the middle of the dance floor at the reception, so my son and my nephew, and they were all dressed up for the wedding and so I said, "Hey, everybody! Let's throw up some V's like for Victor." So I was going like this and these people were like gasping, all of a sudden they thought these *vatos* were gang related. I said, "No. Fool! V for Victor." "Oh! Oh! Okay, okay!"

> LOUIS: *Tell me about your family background and how long your family has been here.*

VICTOR: The issue of the border has affected me most of my life. It's a long story. Four generations. My family is from Tijuana. My great-grandmother came during the revolution, 1918, to Tijuana, so she was persecuted by that particular period of the revolution as a Catholic. During World War II my dad was a zoot-suiter in L.A. My mom was raised in Tijuana. I was born in East L.A., and then immigration caught up with my parents. My parents were undocumented so my sister and I were like the first generation born in the United States. I hadn't thought about it that way, but during 1955 it was Operation Wetback. At that time they kicked us out to Tijuana, so I got a chance to live in Mexico for ten years.

I was seven when they initially kicked us out. It was the year they opened Disneyland. They gave us like three days. I think my dad was already pretty fed up. It's been interesting to think how the different parts of my family really didn't like being in the United States. My grandmother came across, and then one of her sons gets smashed by a bulldozer in the fields over here. She never came back. She stayed in Tijuana 'til she passed away. She lived to be ninety-seven. My grandfather was a bureaucrat in Colima. When he came to the United States in 1936 he swept the casinos in Catalina Island. He told me in those times being Mexican was the same as being a black person in the South.

Victor Ochoa in his garage studio in San Diego, California. Photo by Louis Mendoza.

LOUIS: Tell me how you became an artist.

VICTOR: My mom says that I always liked to draw. She says when I was five years old all the kids were like at this picnic table in the backyard, and they gave everybody crayons and stuff. She remembers me drawing this guy with fingers and a cigarette in his hand and a suit and a vest and a hat and all the other kids were doing little stick figures, you know? It was an outlet for me.

When I was a kid I looked at the *Tijuana Siempre* and publications of comics and those kind of things. I remember the front covers. I thought of myself as a cover designer for *Siempre*. I had teachers who were from a certain period of Mexico's history. One unique thing about the way I see myself and the border is that I see artwork as a tool, a weapon, and part of the solution. I think doing this kind of work and being knowledgeable and putting it in front of people will be a way to get people to change their minds, or at least see things differently, and change the stereotypes about us.

LOUIS: Do you think that art can play a role in educating people?

VICTOR: I use art as a weapon to kick somebody in the butt.

LOUIS: Would you say that being Chicano on the border has changed a lot in the past twenty years? Do you feel like this generation's more apathetic or less involved?

VICTOR: I try to respect the upcoming generation, as screwed up as they might be. I was really surprised to see the marches in Chicano Park, to see junior high and high school kids out there. I was at the park that one day where like five thousand kids came.

LOUIS: How many murals have you painted?

VICTOR: I have something like close to two hundred murals that I've participated in making. I have three of them in Havana right now. I've got one in Yokohama. I saw a picture of it. It's partially painted over. I did one in Spain, one in Belfast.

BRENT: How do you feel when you see one of your murals destroyed?

VICTOR: I just became part of a national board that's dealing with the issue of defacement and erasure of murals. It's the same old elimination of our history, you know? Unfortunately I'm used to it.

MAGDA IRIARTE

Magda Iriarte is a secondary school teacher who lives in Hickory, North Carolina, with her family. She is a close friend of Sherry Edwards, a high school teacher in Unionville, North Carolina, whom I met when she attended an NEH Summer Institute for Secondary Teachers on Latino literature that I co-led in San Antonio. Sherry took me to meet Magda and her family just as they were finishing a Sunday lunch with a large number of extended family members at a local restaurant in Hickory. Like Sherry, Magda is a high school Spanish teacher. Her husband, Rocky, and her daughter, Hanna, were part of our conversation, which took place in the kitchen of their home.

MAGDA: My father is a horse trainer who's been in the States since 1971. We came a year after he was here. My parents are divorced, but they are still very good friends. I think that it was difficult for them to make the transition from the Colombian perception of the woman being submissive to the man. My mother came to the United States and realized that here women had a little more leverage. She's a very strong-willed person anyway, and I think it just . . . clashed. We're from El Huila. It's in the valley about six hours south of Bogotá in the Llanos (Orientales). We have a lot of family in Cartagena.

LOUIS: *Do you know what drove them to come over here?*

MAGDA: My father was in the cattle business in Colombia, but he always had Paso Finos. He had several different farms that he managed, and the horses were the *patrón*'s [boss's] hobby. He always dreamed of coming to the United States from the time he was really young. The cattle business went bad in Colombia because they started importing cattle from the United States, and a lot of the cattlemen in Colombia started suffering from that

Magda Iriarte and her husband, Rocky, in Hickory, North Carolina.
Photo by Louis Mendoza.

competition. He had a job offer here to come train horses. I think he said that when he landed on the plane he had like $15.

He came to Sparta, North Carolina, in the mountains. He stayed for a year there. At that time my parents were separated in Colombia, but when he came and he missed my mother, missed the family, he really wanted to try to work things out, and so he kept writing to her and convinced her to give him another chance. Which I guess is really good for me because otherwise I would have [laughing] stayed in Colombia and had a totally different life. We stayed maybe six months in the mountains, and then after that we move to Lexington. It was interesting because there he worked for a doctor who was originally from Colombia. A friend of his got him the job, the work visa, and had requested him to come up. So we went to this farm that this doctor owned, and the place was so overgrown you couldn't even see the barn anymore. Our entire summer was spent cleaning that place up and making stalls. We worked there for a couple of years, and he was probably riding a horse for $33 a month. It was nothing.

I was six. We struggled. He would get up at 3:00 in the morning, and to make a little bit of extra money, he would go clean the pig stalls on the neighboring farm. He would do that from about 3:30 to about 7:30 in the morning. Then he would come and he would work the horses and the farm until night. And then my mother would go to work at a factory as a seamstress. She would sew from like 3:30 until 11:30 at night. That's how they made ends meet their first several years.

After that he decided that he wanted to go into business for himself. He had been able to get a few clients, and we moved off that farm. We really had nothing. We moved into a really big old house with no furniture. We had like maybe eight, ten horses that we had to feed that were clients' horses. He found out that the type of horses that he knew best actually existed here in the United States. In the 1960s a few horses had been brought up from Puerto Rico, and he felt like he found his niche because when he first came here he worked training quarter horses. A horse is a horse. You can train it, but the Paso Finos were his passion. When he found that there were Paso Finos here in the United States, he knew that that was what he really wanted to go into. He always says that he was like *el tuerto*, the one-eyed man in the land of the blind.

He was one of the only people here in the United States at that time who had experience training these horses. They may only have had four hundred horses in all of the United States of this breed. Now there's forty-five thousand. North Carolina became the second largest state for Paso Fino horses, and he was able to be a big part of that because his knowledge really helped to improve the quality of the horses that were here. He developed a good reputation. Paso Finos are high-quality competitive show horses that are unique in that they are smooth. You're not bouncing up and down like you do with a quarter horse. And anybody knows that anything that's unique and different is what people want.

A wealthy gentleman from this area read an article that somebody had written about my father in our local newspaper. He decided that he was going to talk to my father. When he showed up there, he said, "I want you to come and work for me. I want you to come and help me set up a breeding program." My father said, "I don't want to work for anybody else anymore. I want to be my own boss." So the guy said, "What about if we do a partnership?" He didn't have any money to go into the partnership, and so the guy made him an offer. He says, "I'll buy the stock. I'll buy the horses that you have. I'll buy another two hundred horses. I'll buy the farm, and I will make you a fifty-fifty partner. Your job will be to manage the farm, to raise the horses, to sell them." It was a great opportunity for my father. That guy needed a tax write-off, and he loved the horses.

After a few years the business continued to grow and he had developed a great reputation, and eventually he purchased the partnership from the guy. The guy never thought that he would be able to do it because he said, "You know, you're just an immigrant. Who's going to let you borrow money?" It's funny because the guy who owns these properties was the head of the Farmers Home Administration at the time. My father went to him and said, "Listen, I've got this dream that I want to set up this business and I don't have any money, but I've built this business up and I need a large amount of money to buy this partnership out." The guy lent him the money to build a new barn on a new piece of property. But what was funny was that he didn't realize that my father still didn't have his citizenship. He was in the process of taking the classes—but there was a waiting list to get your citizenship papers. One day he's reviewing all these papers, and he realizes that he has given this man hundreds of thousands of dollars and he doesn't have his citizenship. He's freaking out, comes knocking on my father's door at 5:00 in the morning. He says, "We've got a problem. You've got to get your citizenship!" He says, "I'm on the waiting list." So he gets on the phone with a senator or somebody from Raleigh, and he basically moved my father to the front of the line. The next day he gets his citizenship.

LOUIS: *Do your folks ever talk about missing Colombia?*

MAGDA: Oh, yeah. But truly the United States is our home now. I grew up bilingual. I'm trying to teach my kids also to be bilingual. Our family raised us in the Colombian lifestyle. When I was dating I had to have a chaperone. Even when I met him [pointing to Rocky], I was twenty-one. It's amazing he stuck around [laughs]. We definitely were raised in two cultures. The only difference is that I will say that I feel that as a woman I had the best of both worlds. We were educated, we had the opportunity to go to college, and we were not just expected to be typical—you know, the Latin persona of the woman—you have your fingernails done, you have a certain appearance. We were one of the five Hispanic families in the whole county for years. There was one from Chile, one from Panamá. We were one of maybe two Colombian families.

LOUIS: *Did people think y'all odd?*

MAGDA: Absolutely. When we went to high school, we all had to go together. We weren't allowed to go out Friday night and meet friends and say I'm going to the football game. The only way we got to do that was if all three of us sisters went together. So it wasn't like you get an invitation to go and you're going to go with just your friends. When I went to the prom, I had to take a chaperone. My mother, who never went to PTA meetings or any other school functions, was chaperoning that prom. Everybody else is buying designer prom dresses. Momma made me one that looked like Laura Ingalls from *Little House on the Prairie* [laughs]. It definitely was different. If someone wanted to go out with us, not only did they have to have a chaperone, but they had to come and work on the farm. One guy who went out with my sister practically painted the entire barn. [Laughs]

ROCKY: The first date that I asked Magda on, I lived in Greensboro and I came up to see her, and we were getting ready to go out. She said, "Oh, I'll be ready in a little while." So her sister is outside halterbreaking babies at the back of the house. So Marcella snags me, and she says, "Come here, help me a little bit." I learned how to halter break babies, and about three hours later, Magda comes out ready to go.

MAGDA: He's sweating profusely! I was ready earlier, but I knew that she wasn't going to let him go. By the time he comes around to go out . . . I was, like, you know, you were kinda just being introduced [laughs]. It's different, but it was also a good thing. By that time I pretty much said that things would be different for me. I said before I get married, I'm living on my own. Both of my sisters married and went right to their husbands' homes. They always said that I was the most Americanized. They said that I used the church as an excuse [laughs]. That might be true. I would have said, "I'm going on a retreat, Mommy. It's through the church. It's for my spiritual well-being." [Laughs] And so I got to do more things.

ROCKY: Magda and I met through youth ministering. She worked as a youth minister for her church, and I was a volunteer youth minister at my church in Greensboro, and she wound up having to stay with the girls from my group in her cabin.

MAGDA: I'm in the room with these girls, and they're all talking about Rocky this and Rocky that, and I start to remember that name. I'd seen him the night before, and I wonder if this is the same guy. So the next day I went and I looked at his name tag, and I did something that was pretty uncommon for me: I introduced myself. We just got to talking, and you know one of the things that I always said was I always thought that I would probably marry someone Latin except for—and I know this may seem a bit prejudiced—I've not met a lot of Latin men who were really all that great of husbands, including my own father and brothers. [Laughs] There was always that machismo thing. And a lot of them have a hard time getting past that. I didn't know . . .

HANNA: That she'd end up with a white boy. [Laughs]

MAGDA: What I realized was that that's very common. It's very common in the Latin culture for infidelity to be an acceptable thing. Women were taught to just look the other way and not take it personally and not take it as like anything. It was just an understood thing you don't speak about. It happens, and that's it. I don't think I could live with that. And so I pretty much made up my mind that I would probably never marry a Latin man. It is hard to make generalizations, and now I've changed my mind as I get a little older and understand that people change. What I'm trying to say is, I don't like the generalization about Latin men anymore. I understand that that's part of our culture—but it doesn't mean that everybody's like that. I really felt like if women would be more secure in themselves and a little more assertive in what they wanted, that perhaps men would react differently.

I will say this. One of the things that I recognized from the first day Rocky and I had a conversation was what a strong work ethic he had, and that was important to me. I can remember guys coming to the farm on the way to the country club to play tennis while I'm cleaning stalls and they're like, "Eww, the flies." I'm like, "You can go." [Laughs] I just didn't respect that. Because they didn't grow up in an area where they had to physically work, it was hard for me to feel like they could understand where I came from or understand what made up my value system. They didn't understand what it took to run that business and that we all had to pitch in. Most of them spent their summers living leisurely. A strong work ethic has been an integral part of my whole life and our life together as well. Also the *ambiente*, family values, were really important to us.

LOUIS: *How do your children think of themselves?*

MAGDA: It is a very good question. I find that Hanna seems to gravitate more and more to the Colombian culture. She is bilingual. From the time she was really little, I would always speak to her in Spanish. Isabel, I realized by the time that she was three that she wasn't understanding me as much when I would speak to her in Spanish. I realized that because now I have two people in the household who would primarily speak English, Isabel wasn't hearing as much Spanish. One summer I decided that I would have a Spanish-only summer with this girl. [Laughs] So at lunchtime I'm talking to her in Spanish, "¿Quieres las papitas?" [Do you want some potatoes?], etc., and I wouldn't speak to her at all in English. She would say, "Don't speak that Spanish stuff to me." And I just ignore her. I'll keep speaking in Spanish, and she finally realized I wasn't going to change into English, and so she goes, "A-blah-blah eat. A-blah-blah-blah chips. A-blah-blah-blah now." [Laughs] And so I would say, "A-blah-blah-blah no!" That's a good try. [Laughs]. I started teaching at her school, and that helped her to feel more comfortable speaking in Spanish.

Hanna's a senior in high school and she has taken all the Spanish classes. She is now the president of the Spanish Club and has learned to do the salsa, the merengue, all of the dances, and she actually goes around to some of the local elementary schools when they have international multicultural dances, and she dances with one of her dance partners from school. She very much identifies with the Colombian culture. Sometimes I feel I need to say, "You know, you're not Colombian. Remember that I'm Colombian; you're half Colombian, half American. So you need to understand that it's good that you embrace this."

ROCKY: Some of the Hispanic kids at school will call her mutt.

MAGDA: She's probably the better one to tell you that. What has it been like for you to grow up in a family with one Colombian parent and one American?

HANNA: Well, you know, we'll have conversations at school about interracial marriages and people think it's only black and white. And I'm like, "I'm from an interracial marriage. My mom is Hispanic, and my dad is American. It's not just black and white." And they're just like, "Well, I guess you are." So when they're bashing people—"Oh, that girl, she's with a black boy"—I'm like, "So? My mom's with a white boy!" [Laughs] I've never been one to say I don't associate myself with just white people because I don't think of myself as just a white person. Yes, I'm American. Yes, I was born here. But I'm very appreciative of my heritage, of my culture, and I appreciate my dad's heritage too. You know my dad's an American Indian. And they'll be like, "Oh, those Hispanics." And I'm like, "Hello, still Hispanic over here, not changing."

MAGDA: Unfortunately in our area we have predominantly one group of Hispanic people, and whatever comes in the news, whatever is negative in the news, is what people tend to generalize. If you are Hispanic in our area, the first thing that's assumed is that you're Mexican.

HANNA: And that you're a drug dealer.

MAGDA: Or if you're Colombian you're a drug dealer. So if you say, "Well, I'm from Colombia," then that's the initial response. You have to say, "I'm proud of my heritage, but where I'm from does not make who I am, it just contributes to the things that you value and what you want to pass on to your children." I want to pass on the best things of both of my cultures because I'm considered to be a person who's been blessed to have two cultures to pick from. I want my children to know that they can be strong, beautiful women and that they have the world available to them, that they are not limited by their appearance or by their education. That they can have both worlds.

HANNA: [Hums dramatic, inspirational tune] [Laughter]

LOUIS: *Have you experienced racial tension at school?*

HANNA: Yes. I've been to two different high schools. And the first high school I went to the people were just so prejudiced there. It's probably seven hundred students, and the minority are Caucasian and the majority of the people who go to school there are African American. So that creates racial tension all the time. The school that I'm at now is much bigger, but it's also farther out into the country, you're getting out of the city—so you have, I mean, serious bigots there. And they have this so backwoods way of thinking that all black people are bad and everybody who's Hispanic is bad and—

MAGDA: I think what happened with her school was that it initially was a rural school that now the county has expanded it. And so you have a lot of communities that have been developed into these outskirts of Hickory, and those communities are the ones that the people are coming in from out of state. They're executives that have traveled—their kids are more traveled, more diverse, used to more diversity, so you have this mixture.

HANNA: You have two extremes. Either you're really, really rich or you're really, really poor. Well, I guess there's a middle class there too because— but the majority at Fred T. Ford are now Caucasian. We have a lot of Asian students too.

ROCKY: And all of this is part of the change that North Carolina is undergoing.

MAGDA: It has changed in the last, what do you think, about twelve years? I'm sure here in the South you have people who want to hold on to the heritage and the southern drawl. But there's a difference between that southern drawl and the real hick . . .

HANNA: It's like they're proud to be from the South. I understand that. But what the South did in the past—yes, it's history, and it wasn't a good one. But for some reason, they feel like they have to hang onto that to be proud of all of it. I'm in a public speaking debate class and half of the kids in that class they come from parents who are flat out racist and they don't believe the same way that their parents do. Their parents hate that. A lot of those kids are like, "My parents are racist. If I ever brought a black person home, they probably would disown me. But I don't believe the same way that they do." So yes it's changing, but you still have the other half of those people.

> LOUIS: *Are people having to rethink their understanding of race beyond black and white?*

MAGDA: Yes. And oftentimes now you see the prejudice and the racism directed more toward Hispanics. A few years ago some of the factories in this area started to close down because a lot of the jobs were going to—

ROCKY: China and Mexico.

MAGDA: There was a protest in downtown. Some of the people were protesting immigrants in our area and Hispanics in our area, just making a big to-do about it. They were saying, "They've taken our jobs. They've taken this; they've taken that." And then a couple of weeks after that, they had a sit-in for those who wanted to support diversity in our community and to support the Hispanics in our community. This is a man who's got a very strong work ethic. He does not miss work for anything. When he's sick, he still goes in to work. I can't get him to take time off. He took time off that day. And he went down to this restaurant, and he sat in on this thing. I wasn't even there. I was really touched that he felt that strongly about it to say, "You know, the reason these jobs are going to other locations or the reasons you feel like you're losing your job out to other people has as much to do with your work ethic—and allowing that opportunity to exist for someone else to say, 'I'm willing to do these jobs that no one else wants to do and I'll do them at a reasonable rate.'"

We can't keep people on our farm. When I was working on our farm I wanted to hire people to come and help clean the stalls. This is a job I did when I was younger. I know how hard it is, but I also know that if I, a teenage girl, could clean seventy stalls in a day, it can be done. You have to be organized, and you have to be efficient. And you can't be lazy or squeamish. When I would call the unemployment security office, they would send some people out there. These guys wouldn't last half a day. They literally did not want to work that hard. They wanted to come in, put in an application, be turned down, and continue to collect unemployment. So my perspective from that is that if you're doing a good job at what you're going to do, I don't care what color your skin is, I don't care where you come from, somebody will recognize that, and they will give you that job opportunity.

ROCKY: The thing that also strikes me is that the jobs that they're lamenting now are the jobs from textile mills, manufacturing jobs that were in the Northeast and the Midwest fifty years ago. Those are all jobs that have moved South and continue to move on because it's an environment that the businesses need.

> LOUIS: *So the vast majority of newcomers have mostly been Mexican immigrants?*

MAGDA: Absolutely. A lot of them come, and they work—they started off in the eastern part of the state where they were working in agriculture. It has spread out a little bit more, and you see a lot of them working in the factories or in the restaurants or construction. One of the things that has bothered me is some of the conditions in which they've had to live and that they often take advantage of each other. Now, this just may be my perception, but most of them are coming because they need the work. So, not everybody is coming up here with an education. They're coming with their own sense of community and they tie into that, so they feel more comfortable staying within their own community. The other thing is, they don't always understand the differences in the laws, so you see them do things like riding in the car without having the kids buckled in. So the impression that you get when you're just out in the community is that they are not taking care of their children the same way that we do. And it's not because they don't love the children.

When we came to the United States, I remember my mother driving around with my brother on the floor of the car. But those kinds of perceptions and the fact that you have people who are driving while they're drinking—these are all things that probably, where they're from, are not necessarily illegal. But here it definitely is and it has repercussions; people get hurt. That's what gets printed in the newspapers. And that's what comes in the news, and so that's the impression that the community-at-large gets when they're thinking about the effects of other people coming into the area.

> LOUIS: *Are there pro-immigrant or multicultural groups that come together?*

MAGDA: You see some of that. We have our Latino community center. They intermix people who are wanting to learn Spanish with those who are willing to learn English, and they allow them to create partnerships in which they can learn from both cultures. There's also a lot more multicultural activities that allow you to appreciate the different cultures. I find that a lot of times the people who are most open are those who are more traveled, or come from areas that are more diverse. If you've only been in this area and you've never traveled outside this area, then you can't expand your mind

enough to say, "There are other parts of the world where they speak different languages, where they have different cultures. That doesn't make them
bad." This is not about good or bad—this is different. We're getting there.
As teachers, that's part of our big responsibility, to help kids understand
that even though they're in a small area, that doesn't mean that they have to
be small-minded. To help them expand their minds to embrace what's good
about other cultures. We all have good and bad things in our cultures.

I always tell people, when I first came to the United States there were a
lot of things that just struck me as odd. We tell people this story: We didn't
speak any English and we had cats that would be dumped off close to our
farm and so one day we wanted to keep this one kitten and we begged my
mother to please let us keep this cat, but she was just like, "There's not a lot
of money." Every Friday night we would go to the grocery store—that was
our big treat, to get into the little Pontiac and go to the grocery store. She
says, "If you pick up the cheapest cat food, I'll let you keep the cat." So we
go pick up the cheapest cat food and we're all excited that we're gonna get to
have a family pet, that we're gonna feed this cat, so we feed it faithfully for
like three days. The cat won't eat. Second day, we add a little milk to the cat
food. Cat's still not eating. By the third day, we're starting to change the cat
food, put new cat food in, the cat now is beginning to take a dump into the
cat food. [Laughs]

We're very concerned that the cats in the United States are a little crazy.
I had one little friend from school, and her mother would come and check
on us at the farm to make sure we were okay. She came one day, and in
our broken English we said, "Please, come look at our cat! We think there's
something wrong with our cat. We've been trying to give it the right food,
we've done everything we're supposed to do, and it's not eating and we're
really worried." So she said, "Well, what kind of food did you get for it?"
We said, "Well, we got the right food." She said, "Well, show it to me." So
we bring it out; it's got this beautiful face of this beautiful kitten on it, and
then—and it was the cheapest cat food. Well, it was cat litter. [Background
laughter] She's just laughing. She's on the ground rolling, and we're like,
"What are you laughing about? What is so funny?" She said, "This is not cat
food." We're like, "What do you mean? It's got the picture of a cat, it's the
cheapest cat food, you know? What is up with this?" And she said, "This is
what the cats go to the bathroom in." [Much laughter]

I'm like, "First of all, in Colombia we never even had cat food." "You
just gave the cats whatever scraps were off the table." "And second of all,
that they would actually produce a product in which your cat could go to the
bathroom, that was totally out of our realm of imagination. The pets here

are held at such a high level of esteem in the eyes of the American people, even sometimes more so than their own neighbors or family. It's still a strange concept to me. [Laughs]

LOUIS: *That's a great story of cultural differences.*

ROCKY: Now you have to tell your Thanksgiving story.

MAGDA: Well, you know, Thanksgiving, it's an American holiday. So when you're a Colombian and you're getting ready to celebrate your first Thanksgiving and you really don't understand the whole process. Someone had given us two live turkeys, but I think they really gave it to us just to raise them on the farm. All we knew from all the pictures and the stories from school was we were supposed to have turkey. So we told my father, "We're supposed to have turkey on Thanksgiving Day." So he and my mother proceed to kill these two live turkeys. There's feathers in the yard, they have to hang them upside down to dry for, like, three days—it's an ordeal. This turkey must've weighed close to twenty-five or thirty pounds. One of them didn't make it; the dogs got ahold of him.

But we had another turkey. My mother cooked it—she did not know how to cook. My mother—until she came to the United States—always had a maid in Colombia. For the first year, all we ate was bologna; fried bologna, boiled bologna, roasted bologna, baked bologna. Now when I see bologna in the grocery store, I have to avert my eyes. I just can't look at it. Anyway, we were gonna have a real meal. We were gonna have turkey. We were all excited. It took them three days just cooking this turkey; it doesn't fit in the oven, it's terrible. The thing is dried up, it's awful. And we're like, "This is a lot of work, this whole Thanksgiving thing. How do people do this?" Our same friend that always would check on us, she came and she says, "Why are there feathers in the yard?" And we're just like [sighs], "We just had the Thanksgiving thing, it's a lot of work . . . "

So she says, "You gotta come with me." We go down to the grocery store. She takes us to the frozen food section, and she says, "This is how we do the turkey thing." "Wow, really? It's so much easier! [Laughs] So, you know, it was a year of learning. There's a lot of firsts that take place when you first come. I got to be friends with a little girl in first grade. And the second Christmas when we had moved out into this big house, had no furniture, freezing cold in this house, no food on Christmas Eve, my friend came over with her family and they could see that we didn't have any food. They came by just to probably bring some cookies or something. They decided that they were going to go out to the grocery store and buy all the makings for *arroz con pollo* [rice with chicken] and some of the traditional Spanish meals. We come back to the house, and my mother and them make the food, and they stay with us all night. In Colombia you really only start celebrating around midnight. We all played cards all night, we danced. That was the epitome of somebody going out of their comfort zone to be kind. They could have spent that night with their family doing the very traditional dinner. Instead they really put themselves out there. I'll never forget that. They made us feel welcome.

> LOUIS: *Did your family take a step down economically when coming here?*

MAGDA: Absolutely. My father always had the mentality of being his own boss. He's always had that mentality that, "I'm going to have my own business," no matter what it takes and he would do whatever it took to build up his own business. I've always admired that. Both he and my mother worked; it wasn't just him, I mean it really was a family effort, they did what they had to do. In the end he still brought himself to that same level of being his own boss and really realizing the American Dream. I know it sounds cliché, but I think if you've always grown up in this area, you probably don't appreciate some things. Like being able to leave your house and be relatively sure that you're gonna come back that night, and that your college isn't gonna have a bomb in it or you're not gonna be assaulted. In most cases, we live in a very safe country, and for the most part, we enjoy rights and privileges that a lot of people take for granted until you've gone to a third world country, lived that experience. I wish everybody had a chance to do that. They might change their perspectives.

I think it just takes time for a community to accept and embrace change. You see a lot of that happening in the high schools. That's why what Hanna was talking about is really important. Their attitudes are going to be what's going to shape the leadership of our communities tomorrow. I tell my kids that being bilingual has opened many doors for me. When I was in high school and when I was in college I did not take Spanish, because I thought, "I'll never use it." How foolish was I? And my mother always said, "Take Spanish, take Spanish!" and I was like, "I'm not taking Spanish, I'm Americanized." I knew how to speak Spanish, but I wasn't comfortable with the grammar. In high school I'm learning about conjugating verbs, about things you're already speaking, but I did not know how to write a letter in Spanish. I was intimidated. But as I matured, grew wiser, started seeing the changes in our community, all of a sudden I'm getting jobs translating manuals and documents, and I really didn't have any formal education, other than what I'd taught myself. Then it dawned on me: this is something I need to do.

Twenty-some years later, there I am, forty years old, in college, taking the Spanish classes my mother always told me to take so that I could teach Spanish. And she was like, "I told you so." She was right. Our community changed. So what I tell my kids is, "You can't be left behind, because those children coming in here with their parents speaking Spanish, they're going to get educated, they will compete for jobs against you. And if you are not willing to learn another language you're going to be a step behind. You need to be as competitive as they're going to be." That's the part I want to instill in them.

I'm really thinking about the kids in our community. I want to tell them it's not gonna matter who your dad is. If for some reason—God forbid—you no longer have that family business to go to, or that family money to fall back on, and you're just out there on your own merits, what are you going to bring to the table? If you never worked hard at anything, how are you going to start doing that as a twenty-something-year-old? You got to start working on that now. We're in a society where the kids are so used to everything coming so quick. They get easily distracted or easily bored when something takes longer, or they struggle with something. I've worked in childcare services, I've worked on the farm, in restaurants; I've had lots of different types of jobs, and as an adult I've had a lot of job offers just from the fact that I speak two different languages. I don't want to have to tell my kids, "I told you so!"

MARIANO ESPINOZA AND ALONDRA KIAWITL ESPEJEL

Mariano Espinoza and Alondra Kiawitl Espejel are former executive director and the assistant director of the Minnesota Immigrant Freedom Network (MIFN), respectively. We spoke in their offices in St. Paul, Minnesota. The MIFN is a young organization that grew out of the need to raise the visibility of and respect for the new Latino immigrant population. It was founded in the wake of the National Immigrant Workers' Freedom Ride of 2003 and the Minnesota Freedom Ride of 2004, held in the tradition and spirit of the civil rights Freedom Rides of the sixties, to call for humane and just changes to America's immigration laws.

> LOUIS: *I would like to hear your perspective on the current climate around immigration and the challenges you face advocating for the education and human rights of immigrants.*

MARIANO: It is really, really sad to hear all the debates about immigrants and immigration from politicians and people who are against us. They close their eyes knowing that we are here.

ALONDRA: To me, it's as rational as math. Take the Dream Act. You need people to work. It's a mathematical equation. This plus this equals that. But people don't wanna see that. They're invested in keeping the same sick system.

MARIANO: This country has built a system where the upper class doesn't have to work. They don't have to clean toilets. They don't have to cook because they are professionals. Most service jobs belong to nonwhite people. Yeah, white people are also affected, but most of the workers are immigrant workers or people of color. This country has created this monster where so many Americans believe they are a superior class, and they don't

Alondra Espejel and Mariano Espinoza of the Minnesota Immigrant Freedom Network.
Photo of Alondra taken by Louis Mendoza. Mariano's photo from MIFN office archives.

see how they benefit from an immigrant presence here. As long as we go to different countries to get the cheapest resources and labor we are going to continue to have these problems, not only in this country, but all over the world. If we pass immigration reform here, it won't change conditions that make people leave their home country.

LOUIS: *Do you believe it's possible to create meaningful change?*

ALONDRA: We're taking baby steps through our organizing. If we just look at Minnesota, one of the struggles has been that Spanish-language radio hasn't been friendly to these discussions. We have these contradictions within our own so-called community that are preventing discussions and mobilizations from happening.

LOUIS: *Why is the struggle for immigration reform important to you?*

ALONDRA: I read this quote by Che Guevara a while ago that talks about how deep down inside the revolutionary is really doing all that he or she is doing out of love. That really defines it for me. Because you care about people, and when you're happy and you're good and you're cozy and you have food to eat, you wonder, "Does everybody else have it the same that I do? Is everybody else enjoying the same privilege? Is everybody else able to be happy like I am at this moment?" Part of it is because a lot of my life was living this precarious line of not knowing if we were going to have food, not knowing if my parents were going to get deported one day to the next. It was constantly being in that really weird place of having privilege because I got to go to college but not being free enough to live a life free of struggle and challenges and racism and people not knowing how to pronounce my name. Or having to learn English when I was ten and crying because my mom wasn't here. I would pretend that I was sick in the mornings so I wouldn't have to go to school. All those memories were so deep down inside that I really wasn't able to cope with them until I was in college, where I was introduced to Chicano Studies classes, classes about Cuba and Puerto Rico.

These classes helped me understand my family better. I remember my grandma. When I was young, she was always complaining. When I was little I was like, "God, Grandma, quit complaining!" Now I realize that it was her social justice values where she wasn't going to take no for an answer if she didn't think it was the right answer or if she didn't think it was fair or just. Whenever we went to the town plaza and saw the Raramuri or the Tarahumara Indians asking for money, she would always approach them and be like, "Here, meet them, this is our people. This is who we are." She would give them money, and then we'd go off on our own way. I didn't know what those things meant. Now that I'm older and I reflect on it, I'm like, "Wow, I can see where this is coming from." Those are the things that I have to constantly reflect on and think about and put into conversation with who I am today.

There are issues with my brother that bring up the racism within the Latino community for me. My brother is a lot darker than I am skin-wise. So I know that when I was in high school, one of the reasons I was able to survive is because I could blend in as a white person. If I didn't want to be this Mexican girl, I didn't have to. I could just blend in. I didn't have an accent. Everybody my whole life has reminded me, "Oh, it's great. You don't have an accent." What do you do when you grow up with white people? That's the only accent you can pick up. So I am very aware of my white privilege as a Latina. I try to talk about it as much as possible because I don't think people talk about it enough. I'm very thankful that I had that experience because that keeps me in check when I do organizing because I know that in my life I may have succeeded in a couple of areas, but that doesn't mean it's going to be like that for everybody.

Both of my parents were from Chihuahua. My mom came here as a single mom when I was ten. She sent me first, and then everybody else came along. We came straight to Litchfield, and it was because my aunt and my uncle had come here in the '70s and '80s. They went to California first to try to find jobs, but they ended up in Minnesota helping a farmer with his farm. My uncle was milking cows. They were able to get their citizenship in the 1986 amnesty. Then what happened was when I was in my mom's stomach, she crossed the border, and she had me here. And then she had my sister in Arizona. She went back and forth. She came to Minnesota with my aunt. After a year she was like, "No, I'm not really liking this Minnesota winter stuff. I'm really lonely and depressed. I'm going to go back." So she went back, and I grew up with my grandma. My brother was born in Mexico, so we had to get his papers later. Eventually I had to get the papers for my mom because she didn't have any when we came.

LOUIS: *How long have you been working with MIFN now? What makes it rewarding?*

ALONDRA: First as a volunteer and a board member and then later an employee, I've been here a total of maybe three years. The reward is the hope that you're building a better world, one by one. The idea that you're connected to a civil rights struggle that goes back five hundred years. I didn't see this before, but now I see that I may dedicate my lifetime to this work, and I may not see needed changes. Before, I would get so frustrated because I'd be like, "God, I want to see the change now. Why aren't things changing?" My teachers would have to remind me that the struggle is long, and it's going to be years. Now I get it. So is this work challenging? Yes. Is it hard? Yes. Is it rewarding? Yeah, because at night I can go to bed and feel okay about what I did today. I can feel good about not being just one cog in the machine but actually trying to change the machine.

MARIANO: I came in 1991 because I had a brother here. I was looking for better opportunities. When I came, my daughter Denise was a newborn. So it was very difficult for me to go to school and work and have a daughter in the family. My brother was here, and he told me if I wanted to come here, I needed to learn how to drive and learn English. My mom's brother was the first person who came to this country, in 1957. The whole family, everyone, on my mom's and dad's side, everybody, has always been back and forth. My uncle, who now is retired, he gets a social security check in Mexico; he was a professional before he came to this country. He worked for a few months at a hospital cleaning. And then he got a job in a printing shop. He always likes to tell that he spent his whole life in this printing shop with a union job back in the fifties and sixties. He said he was making almost $20 an hour. He met my aunt from Brownsville, Texas. He was the person who helped all my family come to this country. They're the only family who has been able to have a stable life in this country. They have papers.

I came here looking for a place to work and have a better life. It was not really a difficult decision to come because since I was very young I wanted to come to this country. You hear and hear everyday that you have to go to *el norte*. You have to go to the U.S. if you want better opportunities. So I was always in my mind thinking about the U.S. But I didn't know that the jobs that we have in this country are really, really hard. I was not expecting to be working as a dishwasher or as a room cleaner. First, because I didn't know the language even though I went for two or three years to school to learn English. It was not the same. Once I got to Minnesota, I never in my life had pictured myself having two full-time jobs. It was really painful. I worked at the Radisson Hotel in Bloomington. It was a huge hotel where sometimes they had banquets for two, three thousand people. Sometimes two or three dishwashers had to clean all the stuff. After two, three months my back was killing me. Sometimes you have to weigh if this is really a better life because you're killing yourself.

Every single full-time job that I had was a union job. I came to Minnesota, and I was able to get a job really easily and quick. It was good pay since I didn't have experience. I was making like $10 an hour. I think that was unusual for seventeen years ago. I was in a union for seven years at my janitorial job. My brother Uriel started at the same hotel but got elected to the Unite HERE Union, the janitor's union. They were looking for a bilingual person. My brother told me about the job. I didn't believe in the union. One day I lost my job due to a bad experience with *la migra*, so I decided to take the job with the union. Little by little I realized that I was helping a lot of people. I was one of the first Latinos at this janitorial company, so I was able to bring almost every single person that I knew who wanted a job. Every time the company needed a worker, they asked me. I was even negotiating the salaries for the workers. We always were fighting for more benefits.

The first day at my job at the union, they sent me to the storage room. That was going to be my office. And all the other guys had nice offices. Even twenty years ago the janitor's union had probably 40 percent Latinos . . . and a really high percentage of other immigrants, Somalis and Hmong. But they didn't have anyone who was fluent in Spanish, Somali, or any other language. It was the same group of officers running the union for almost twenty years. I had a lot of challenges there. My experience with the union was not always the best experience. Two weeks after I got hired, I was told to organize the Mall of America. I didn't have any experience. People from D.C. came because the Mall of America was the target for a national campaign. That was when I first met people who really believed in unions and believed in the workers and our right to fight for better benefits and salaries for our families. A few months after, I asked to be sent somewhere to get trained.

I went to Chicago and then to Fairfield County in Connecticut, and that was when I decided I didn't want to work as a janitor anymore. I learned a lot about organizing workers, organizing for social and economic justice issues. I came back to Minnesota and told the union that I was going to work for the international union. I got transferred to the international, and I stayed in Scotsford a few years. It was one of the most rewarding times in my life because with a group of organizers we were able to organize undocumented workers by the dozens. We won contracts where workers were making minimum wage, no benefits to almost $9 or $10 an hour with healthcare and vacation for the first time ever. It was really, really good. I came back to Minnesota in 2003, and I asked the union to hire me again. They did. It was the same situation, the same people. Nothing had changed.

This is the bad side of me for the union. I started to talk about workers' rights to union workers. I was mobilizing to have dignity and respect in the union. We had the Immigrant Workers Freedom Ride. Three months after I arrived, we had union stewards in eighty-seven buildings. And just to give you a perspective on the Twin Cities janitorial market, we have more than two hundred buildings that are over two hundred thousand square feet in each of those buildings. So there are thousands of workers. I was trying to create a movement inside the union. We went on the Immigrant Workers Freedom Ride, an effort from Unite HERE that included faith and community groups from Minneapolis. Within six months of returning, the workers were very active.

This is one of the things I started to do. Under the contract agreement, you have to go to the union office to file a grievance. So we switched the process. We elected stewards in all the buildings. The worker was fixing or trying to solve the issues in the building with the supervisors. Very soon the companies were telling the union that I was not allowed to be in the buildings anymore. They were asking them to get rid of me. One of the biggest companies was pushing really hard. In December 2003 I found out that the union was having elections for president and other elected officers. All the officers were friends of the president. The workers were not informed, and I knew that was against the law because we went through the same process in other places in the country. I told the workers that they had the right to elect their own officers.

I got terminated in December 24, 2003. The election was going to take place January 3, 2004. So the workers organized really quick. The day of the election, a group of workers went and challenged the president, and they were able to postpone the election. They filed a grievance against the union with the international union. It was a big deal here with the labor movement in Minnesota. I was one of the so-called bad people within the labor movement because I was organizing workers. When we came back from the ride, the *Star Tribune* was planning to profile six immigrants. I was one of them. It was serious. We got the front page. The story was originally going to be, "SEIU Leading the Way." But they changed it to "Organizer Got Fired for Organizing Immigrant Workers." So the story really pissed off a lot of people, especially the union.

The voting extension went all the way to D.C. It was a national case, and the international unions got involved. I was banned from unions. This was at the end of 2003 and January 2004. We had just come back from the Immigrant Workers Freedom Ride. We had all these people willing to do stuff, so this is when I decided I wanted to fight for workers and their families. Quito Ziegler and I started MIFN. We didn't have money for more than six months. We didn't have support from the labor movement. But now we have very good relations with the unions. Workers are the ones who have been able to make changes. The executive board of the union had only one Latino or immigrant person and fourteen white executive board members. The white population of the union was probably 5 percent. Now it's the other way. When you tell people the truth, you also make enemies because there are people living comfortably, and as long as they get their paycheck and they don't have to worry, they're not accountable for anything. They are living *la vida loca*.

LOUIS: *Has the mission of MIFN changed from the beginning?*

MARIANO: At first we were just advocating. Now we have moved to developing youth leadership. We were advocating for immigration reform and legalization for all people. Everything has changed right now. This is one of the biggest problems that we have with people who believe in immigration reform. We don't know what immigration reform is. We are advocating for something that we aren't clear about. Everybody is living in his or her own world. Until we have one proposal that comes from the people most affected we can't all come together. I disagree that we just need to ask for legalization. I think we need to ask for citizenship. We live here, we work here, we pay taxes. The problem is not the people; it's the laws we have.

LOUIS: *Is it any different from the '86 amnesty?*

MARIANO: With that amnesty you got the papers but not the citizenship. This disenfranchises people from voting. We have a lot of legal residents who are not citizens. I think we need to demand to have the same rights. I know that this is going to scare a lot of people, but the anti-immigrant people are really clear with their demands. They don't want us here. They want to build the wall. We are only asking for legalization. In a legislative process, you have to negotiate. And we are starting our negotiation already in the middle. We believe a lot of people will be happy just to get a green card.

LOUIS: *What gives you hope and what gives you nightmares about this kind of work?*

MARIANO: I think our hope is students, young people. I believe that if we are able to have more conversations about what it is that we want as a community, we are going to be in a better position in the future. We are trying to do that with the dream curriculum—develop consciousness. We are not trying to train others to organize right now because we don't have the capacity. I believe that to make collective changes, you have to start with yourself. If you know that some things are right and wrong according to your principles, you are going to start acting with other people.

ALONDRA: I think that for me the hope is that this immigrant discussion is more widespread, it's in the news, on TV, and on the radio. It provides an opportunity for people to engage with social justice issues. It's the door of opportunity to organize and talk to more people about why they're unhappy with their situation and what we can to do to change it. We had three or four marches in the last year, and then we had the big forty-thousand-people march in St. Paul. To me, that is hope. That's people connecting to the issue and doing something about it. The seed has to be planted, and it has to be nurtured, and we have to start somewhere. Every single person counts. Every single discussion counts. People come and go in this office, and it makes me feel a certain level of responsibility to stick around. I would like to do other things, but I know that if you want to make some real change, you have make a multiyear commitment, and you have to build the leadership that's going to take over when you're gone.

MARIANO: Hopefully, what people learn here is going to be used later. I think one of the biggest challenges is with the educational system. Every social movement has relied on young people to make changes.

THREE

AN EMERGING SENSE OF MUTUALITY

TÚ ERES MI OTRO YO
[YOU ARE MY OTHER ME]

The Mayan concept of *in lak'ech*, approximated in the epigraph, has its specific manifestation in Mayan culture but is in many respects a concept that has corollaries in cultures around the world. This notion of reciprocity and mutuality can be found in Western civilization in Christianity's "golden rule," doing unto others as you would have them do unto you. In this chapter mutuality and reciprocity assume particular importance because the interviewees each speak to their role as facilitators of change in their midwestern communities.

Not insignificantly, while both Minnesota and Iowa have had a Latino presence since the early twentieth century, primarily as workers actively recruited for the agricultural and railroad industries, they have also experienced an intense surge in Latino immigration in the past twenty years. Melrose, Minnesota, and West Liberty, Iowa, exemplify small-town communities whose economic stability has depended on this influx of immigrants. Numerous times throughout my trip, I heard stories about how local communities have changed and about how the younger generation no longer wants to perform wage labor in fields and factories. In pursuit of better opportunities for social mobility they often move to urban areas for an education that will give them access to white-collar work. A paradox has resulted from this phenomenon: The economic viability of these small towns and the way of life of an aging white community have become dependent on new arrivals, who are often actively solicited to live and work in these towns. This occurs even as townsfolk grapple with the cultural changes that accompany the new arrivals.

To state what might not be as obvious as one would think, the local leadership of small towns makes an enormous difference in determining whether a community receives newcomers with open arms or suspicion.

The process is uneven, of course, as generational differences between youth and elders often emerge, with the latter often being more rigid in their attitudes toward cultural difference. But this, too, is uneven. What we learn from these interviews is what facilitates and what impedes a sense of mutuality. As mediators and facilitators of change, all four of these interviewees seek to find common ground and dispel the unwarranted fears of the host community. In "The Meaning of Mutuality" the psychologist Judith V. Jordan asserts:

> In a mutual exchange one is both affecting the other and being affected by the other; one extends oneself out to the other and is also receptive to the impact of the other. There is openness to influence, emotional availability, and a constantly changing pattern of responding to and affecting the other's state. There is both receptivity and active initiative toward the other.
>
> Crucial to a mature sense of mutuality is an appreciation of the wholeness of the other, with special awareness of the other's subjective experience. Thus the other is not there merely to take care of one's needs. Through empathy and an active interest in the other as a different, complex person, one develops the capacity at first to allow the other's differentness and ultimately to value and encourage those qualities that make that person different and unique.
>
> When empathy and concern flow both ways, there is an intense affirmation of the self and paradoxically a transcendence of the self, a sense of the self as part of a larger relational unit. The interaction allows for a relaxation of the sense of separateness; the other's well-being becomes as important as one's own. This does not imply merging, which suggests a blurring or a loss of distinctness of self.[1]

Although Jordan is referring to individual relationships, her analysis provides important insight into social relationships as well.

The tactics that each of the interviewees in this section use to bridge differences are premised on (1) the idea that difference is just difference—that they need not be placed in hierarchical relationship to one another nor serve as the basis for fear between communities; (2) that being a facilitator of change requires a willingness to place oneself in an uncomfortable position; and (3) that there are core values that people share—as workers, as human beings, as members of the same community, and as immigrants or descendants of immigrants, that can be tapped into to cultivate a sense of reciprocity. Moreover, they are guided by a shared belief that there exists a moral imperative to promote equitable relationships between majority and minority groups and that justice as a value is not the prerogative of any one community. The similarities, more than the contrast of perspectives offered here by whites and Latinos, by community volunteers, a police chief, city councilperson, and a labor educator/organizer provide fertile ground for hope that a humane and just solution based on our common humanity is possible.

John Jensen is the chief of police in Melrose, Minnesota. He was one of several people introduced to me by George O'Brien, a retiree and former two-term mayor of Melrose. It was during O'Brien's tenure as mayor that the influx of Latino immigrants began. His leadership and open-mindedness to Melrose's newest residents had a tremendously positive impact. He was the catalyst for the formation of Communities Connecting Cultures, a nonprofit immigrant service organization whose single part-time staff person is paid for by the Jennie-O processing plant. Jensen and I met about midday at a small coffee shop in downtown Melrose. As a town leader, he sees his role as that of mediator between longtime residents and immigrants.

JOHN: I was just telling George it was kind of busy for me this morning, because I was helping at the church fishing clinic over in Sauk Centre previously, and then I had made arrangements to meet with you, and then we were going out to Elena Cruz's graduation party later this afternoon. We've known the Cruz family since probably 1983. Got to know their dad through the police reserves, and then through dad they had kids who were baby-sitting age. So there are seven Cruz kids, and we used all but two for overnight baby-sitters. I believe the Cruzes and Carbajals were the first Hispanics to move into the community.

Just a wonderful relationship with the Cruz family, and the Carbajals also. Ozzie, Osvaldo, but everyone calls him Ozzie, Carbajal, he was on the police reserves with us when he first got out of high school and then when he got out of the military. Now he's chief of police in Belgrade, Minnesota. I think for the most part we didn't see the big influx in the Hispanic community until the days when the stock market was going through the roof. Through that economic growth, especially in the St. Cloud area, there was a labor shortage. A lot of people who were working at Jennie-O migrated to St. Cloud to work for $12 to $15 an hour and left a void in the Jennie-O workforce, and that would be about the time we started to see a large influx of immigrants coming here.

LOUIS: How do you think they found out about jobs here?

JOHN: Well, in large part that had a lot to do with Dave Carbajal and his wife. They still have roots in Mexico. And then after that there was a fair amount of advertising done. We've got a large population from Michoacán. I think the word got out that there are plenty of jobs up here. I think it just rolled from there.

LOUIS: From what I hear, Latinos are 20 to 25 percent of the population.

JOHN: I would say it is close to that.

LOUIS: How long have you been chief of police?

JOHN: I started to live here in 1983, and I have been the chief of police since 1998. I'm originally from St. Paul. I was looking for a job, and this one opened up, and I moved here and have kind of set down roots.

Melrose Police Chief John Jensen. Photo courtesy of John Jensen.

LOUIS: How would you characterize the way in which people have accepted the change?

JOHN: You know [pause] I would like to think it went smoother here than other places simply because we did our homework and we talked to places like Willmar and Worthington. I hope that we learned from some of their mistakes. And I think that really helped us. I don't think there's total acceptance. Just under the surface there may be a little resentment; in some cases, a lot of resentment.

LOUIS: What is that resentment about? Jobs? Cultural change?

JOHN: I don't think it is so much about the jobs. More about cultural change, because everyone does things a little different. We had some instances where people butchered goats in the garage. When they were done they would wash out the garage and the blood would run into the street. I asked people, "What is the difference in that and when we butcher deer—except that we usually already have them gutted when we bring them into town." We don't get nearly the complaints anymore.

LOUIS: Do you think there is a difference in age groups?

JOHN: I would say yes. We have had high school seniors who have probably been going to school here for eight years. I'm not quite sure we have the first one who started in kindergarten and went all the way through to twelfth grade, but we are not that far away. It's the same thing everywhere. A lot of time prejudice is learned. Sometimes it comes from home. Kids don't have any preconceived notions, but it might be what they hear at the supper table, and it carries on. I would definitely say the older people have issues. With the older people it is the fear of the unknown, the inability to even carry on a conversation. I don't think that will ever change. It wouldn't make any difference whether it was a Hispanic or an Eastern European who spoke Russian.

LOUIS: How would you characterize your relationship with the Hispanic community?

JOHN: Fair and good. The biggest thing is establishing a trust. There has been underreporting of crime because they feel like if they do report it, it might bring Immigration into the picture.

LOUIS: Has there been much interaction with Immigration officials here?

JOHN: Very little. The only time Immigration has come up is when there have been major drug enforcement cases and they've come to assist, to help with interpretation, and also the resources they can bring as far as a database to see if people have been in trouble someplace else. We haven't had any raids here like Worthington did with Swift or anything like that.

LOUIS: *Has English been an issue?*

JOHN: Yeah, up until a couple years ago we were spending annually $5,000 to $7,000 on interpretation services. I think we were down to about $3,000 last year. Part of that is because we have not had as many incidents. I can honestly say that we haven't had anything that you can characterize as hate crime or racially motivated crime or bias crime. I'm somewhat surprised by that.

LOUIS: *It seems like Melrose has done a very deliberate job of trying to do things right and be sensitive. Why do you think Melrose is different from other places?*

JOHN: [Sighs] I don't know if we are that much different. We've got good people in place. Between Sister Adela, George O'Brien, John and Peggy Stokman, Ana Santana, the Carbajals, Salvador Cruz, before he moved to St. Cloud—a lot of people who have set higher expectations, higher standards, gone the extra yard to make it easier for people to assimilate. I think that handful of people right there is one of the biggest differences. Our Catholic church has done a lot.

Another thing we had going for us, for four years or so we had a police officer by the name of Pete Ortega. We came to know Pete because he was in a law enforcement class at Alexandria. One of our reserves introduced us to him. He came down, got on our law enforcement program. Pete's family were immigrants from Mexico. Pete was naturalized. Bilingual. Tremendous asset. We were lucky enough to keep him for four years, so again we had our own built-in interpreter. Somebody who had actually immigrated from Mexico. His parents were agricultural laborers, went back and forth for several years. Pete grew up in the Willmar area. In the police department he helped us. Now he is a state trooper. That was huge. Someone to build that trust. You hear stories—they say that law enforcement in Mexico is somewhat corrupt, and I've heard it enough times that I tend to believe it. You know, the fear that we're not going to have our hand out.

LOUIS: *Would you say that the acceptance of things goes for some of the surrounding communities as well?*

JOHN: I know that there are families living in Meire Grove and Green-wald. Not quite sure about Freeport, Sauk Centre, Long Prairie, Avon area. I don't think there's any in St. Joseph's or Elrosa. But as affordable housing becomes available I think they are starting to spread out. I haven't made a count lately, but there are a large number of families that are owners of homes here.

> LOUIS: Some small towns have been passing all these ordinances against renting houses to immigrants because they feel like the national debate hasn't gone anywhere, and so they are trying to make all these local laws. What do you think of these laws?

JOHN: They are saying we want you to work here, but we don't want you to live here. Makes no sense.

> LOUIS: It's been a source of division for some small communities in different parts of the country.

JOHN: One of the things that I think that's helped here is that they've actually moved into neighborhoods. They are not all in a trailer court. One thing we learned from Willmar, where 90 percent of the Hispanic community is all living in the trailer park down there, is that it leads to isolation, and it's somewhat detrimental to the Hispanic community because there is no real need or opportunity to learn English. If you live here and both neighbors on either side speak English—you want to communicate like normal neighbors do. I think that's helped a lot.

> LOUIS: What would have happened if these people hadn't come in and taken the jobs at Jennie-O? Would other people have come in and taken these jobs?

JOHN: You know, I don't know what would have happened if they hadn't been so readily available. Jennie-O would have had to increase their wages to make it more attractive. I imagine they would have had to become more attractive wage- and benefits-wise.

> LOUIS: Is there any kind of unemployment problem?

JOHN: There's a hiring sign down by Jennie-O for hiring right now—it comes and goes. Jennie-O pays around $9.50. For anything higher without any skills I think you would have to move to town. About the time a lot of Hispanics were moving to town the housing market for a home was 40 and $50,000. But two people working qualified for an $80,000 home, so the price of a $40,000 home went up to $80,000 because that is what the market is ready to bear. I thought that was somewhat unfair. Now with the downturn in the housing market you can't give them away. The housing bubble occurring on the national level has also had an impact here.

A lot of Hispanics spend a lot of the money in town. The meat markets, the auto supply stores. There are a couple of Hispanic-owned businesses. Some of the older people are a little bit afraid of the unknown. Take Main Street here. A lot of Hispanics live in apartments above the businesses because they can walk to work. They don't have a backyard. They don't have a front yard. There are five or six guys living up there. So in the summertime, where are they going to be? On their front steps. Hang around, talk, socialize. You get a sixty-, seventy-year-old lady see five or six Hispanic guys. When she walks by there's a smile and a nod. It's about all they can communicate. When people see that they ask, "Why do they have to hang out there?" But I tell them, "Just like with any other five guys living together, it probably feels crowded, and they prefer the open air." Little things like that that people will work through.

> LOUIS: *It seems like you all have been very proactive and not pretended it's not happening.*

JOHN: Well [pause], if anybody needs to be held accountable for illegal immigration it seems to me it is the industry that's hiring them. But holding industry accountable is just a small part of the large picture of the immigration issue. Industry and employment are a major reason people immigrate to the U.S., but the collateral issues that go with it are huge.

PEGGY AND JOHN STOKMAN

Peggy and John Stokman are a retired couple from Grand Island, Nebraska, who recently moved to Melrose. As they drove me around town, it was readily apparent that many people in the community knew them and liked them. Sometimes I referred to the speaker as "P&J" instead of as an individual; like many couples who have been married for a long time their thoughts were in sync. Often John or Peggy would begin a sentence and the other would finish it without hesitation.

P&J: We used to live in Minnesota long ago. We chose Melrose because we wanted to live in the vicinity of St. John's, St. Cloud, St. Paul, for the university and culture and things. We liked the connection at St. John's, and we went there and asked the priest who was director of Hispanic Studies which community he would recommend. He recommended Cold Spring and Melrose, and we looked at homes in both communities. Each community was about twenty minutes' drive to St. John's, but there literally were no Anglo advocates here. Cold Spring had a program of outreach with Casa Guadalupe, so we knew there was an opportunity to make a difference here. Basically, we knew that in retirement we wanted to serve and involve ourselves in this type of outreach. It's been a real rich and meaningful life for us.

LOUIS: *What do your children think of it?*

P&J: Oh, they are supportive.

LOUIS: *Do they wonder what is going on?*

PEGGY: We have to watch that they don't feel jealous or slighted, because, you know, the needs are great and are right here and our children are sort of spread all over.

P&J: But our children, we raised them with some of the same values. Several families are learning Spanish. They've been to Guatemala, and so they have an appreciation for what we're doing. But politically we are in different places. There are several of our children who do not share the same philosophy with us on immigration. They say things like, "They've done illegal things, they need to go back home." That is not a comfortable thing for us at all. But you know what, that's where they are. And for us this issue has such a face. Maybe we'd think differently, but this is about people we love and we know their goodness.

JOHN: The rents are horrendous. It's such an atrocity. The city is so concerned. Some of the owners have just been terrible. Everybody knows it's an injustice. Just terrible. You just see lineups of people on Saturday and Sunday mornings at the Western Union. They are sending money home, and that is part of why they are here—to support their families back home.

PEGGY: Things aren't 100 percent pro-immigration here. People don't talk to us because they know where we stand.

LOUIS: *Really? I've heard mostly pretty positive things about Melrose.*

P&J: Well, we think Melrose is better than Grand Island, where we came from.

JOHN: I think to the credit of the Hispanic families here they have been good neighbors. They buy old homes and fix them up, and as people see that, they value them as neighbors and respect them. So I think that with integration a lot has happened already.

LOUIS: *Do you think that the youth are more accepting of immigration and the change?*

P&J: Well, let's see if we can find somebody to talk about that. I think it is pretty cliquish. That's a good question. We are not involved with the school. But I think that the Hispanics go around with the Hispanics and the Anglos go around with the Anglos.

LOUIS: *Has the church been pretty good in the community at promoting acceptance?*

PEGGY: Oh yeah, it has. A great number of people here go up to Sauke Centre. They have a Prometido Prometiera, I think—an Assembly of God Church in Spanish.

JOHN: What has helped is that every Sunday for the last year we've had a

12:30 Spanish Mass. That creates a following. We have Sister Adela Gross here, and she has been great.

> *LOUIS: What other ways do you see a coming together of the communities? Do people see them as making positive contributions to the economy?*

PEGGY: Oh, yes.

JOHN: People are buying the homes. I think there are minimal homes here that people are selling for prices that are pretty decent because there is enough of the Hispanic population buying them.

PEGGY: And the grocery store. They shop here. I mean the truth of it is—I don't know whether people realize this, but this town was hurting before people came here. We will probably have a raid because our dear governor ran on that, and we were given $17 million for that. I think some parents complain that there are too many Hispanics in the school and their kids are not getting as good an education. Others love it because it is more diversity. There are about eight kids at the Catholic grade school, so they are very much the minority. But even those things are kind of positive. If people are not acknowledging that our town is better because of them—they just have blinders on. It's obvious. And I think everyone would agree.

JOHN: Even the use of this park. It's a beautiful facility, but the use besides this Hispanic population is very little.

JOHN: George O'Brien, the former mayor, he's tremendous. He's been advocate number one. He's gone the extra mile. He's reached out.

JOHN: All these second-story apartments on Main Street are occupied by Hispanics. There are three or four buildings on this street and that street. They would be empty if it weren't for them. The people who own those buildings are collecting rent.

PEGGY: People are happy to have people who are bilingual because it helps with business. We are lucky we have some nice small homes that probably sell for $60,000, $70,000, $80,000, which is affordable, and most of the realtors have a Hispanic person on staff. We don't have a lot of respect for Jennie-O's, to be honest. They do not contribute to the community. They really are not good citizens. A lot of people have trouble with them. People are just having terrible problems.

JOHN: Here's the English Learning Center. We started this.

PEGGY: The owners of Klaphake's [a turkey farm] contacted us and asked us if we knew any good Hispanic people because they have had it with these Anglos—their irresponsibility and their bad morals. They contacted us and said, "Do you know any good Hispanics?" So part of the agreement when Arturo got hired there was that he would learn English. We worked in partnership with Klaphake's. During the second year Arturo moved into second place out of four employees. So they have been so pleased with him, they hired a friend of his. Now they are taking a chance on a second person. And they've been so, so, so thrilled.

> LOUIS: So you've been an inroad for the Hispanic community in that you helped them get jobs?

PEGGY: Well, you know this is how I feel—you work in partnership—even with my limited Spanish. For instance, with the apartments—the people who rent to them know they can always call me and I'll relay a message or complaint. The dentist in our town offers payment plans. They don't save money so in comes a big bill. In Grand Island they are not even going to look at your teeth if you haven't paid your bill beforehand, but they are willing to go over to the dental office to translate. With Klaphake's, they were willing to give Arturo a chance to work. He has been faithful for three years now with English lessons and then just got his citizenship. I think that their work ethic is really paying off—and local businesses are realizing good hard workers.

JOHN: The other area of employment is in the dairies. We have lots of dairies here, and with the dairy you can get work immediately. You don't have to go get false papers; the dairy just takes them. They don't ask any questions. But the dairy would be hard put if the undocumented didn't work here. If the undocumented were not here I don't know if the dairies would have enough employees to keep running.

Ángel González was introduced to me by Omar Valerio, a professor of history at the University of Iowa. Ángel is a program consultant and organizer with the Labor Center at the university. Born in Puerto Rico to a union family, he is a passionate advocate for labor and racial justice. As an organizer, he is also an educator who seeks to challenge people's contradictions regarding fairness and equity among workers. In 1998 Ángel assisted in a successful AFL-CIO effort to obtain public sector collective bargaining rights for Puerto Rican public employees, bringing over 150,000 new members into the union. From 1975 to 1987 he served in the army reserve, and from 1987 to 1993 in the U.S. Navy. Since our conversation, Ángel has left the UI Labor Center to work as a union organizer and lawyer for the UFCW (United Food and Commercial Workers International).

ÁNGEL: I was born and raised in Puerto Rico. I've been in Iowa now for about a year and a half. All my family is in Puerto Rico. I grew up in the San Juan metropolitan area, and I went to an English private school because my mother wanted us to learn English. She really wanted us to be able to understand the enemy so we could conquer it, because Puerto Ricans have this issue with colonial Puerto Rico and imperial United States. That was her purpose as she stated it.

I came to the United States the first time when I was eighteen. I joined the army reserves and spent three years at Ft. Bliss, Texas, and Ft. McClellan, Alabama. I went back to P.R. [Puerto Rico], and the only job I could get was as a shoe salesman. It wasn't very good so I figured I would go back into the service. I spent six years in the navy, and once I got done with that I figured it was not a very good life. My brother had gone to Penn State and liked it so figured I'd go there. I studied labor relations. I've always been interested in issues of social justice and always bet on the underdog.

My father was a lifelong union member for the power company in P.R., and when he went on strike we were hungry. That's the way it went. My mother was a nurse and things were tight for a long time. They were separated and divorced when I was nine years old, but I remember walking the picket line when I was seven. I guess my upbringing taught me to be very interested in social justice and fairness, not just in the workplace, but all around. When I went to Penn State I didn't know what to study, but that sounded like something I wanted to do. By the time I was done I had started a boycott of the Starbucks on campus. They had just started getting there, and I was very upset about the way they treated workers in Guatemala, so I started to boycott their new store. They wanted to get in and I wanted them not to get in. The United Food and Commercial Workers International took notice of that. They offered me an internship in their education department, which I took and started working with meat packers in Greeley, Colorado.

This was my summer internship my last year. Witnessing the pain and suffering of those workers was like a tattoo. I can't think of any other way to describe it. I decided there was something that needed to be done. If not me, who? I was offered a permanent position with the UFCW and was

Ángel González at the University of Iowa, Ames. Photo by Louis Mendoza.

exposed to the most horrendous working conditions of meat packers in the Midwest. Outside of meat packers, I was also exposed to a campaign in New York City in Manhattan's Upper West Side, in Hell's Kitchen. There were these eight stores that were called "Extra Ultra," and they were owned by a man by the name of Caraballo, who was a Cuban immigrant. The conditions that I saw in those work centers were so appalling that I just could not believe that a Latino would do that to a Latino. It was much worse than the *gabachos* [Anglos] ever did to us! To me it was a very lacerating, hurtful experience. This guy, a Cuban immigrant, came here through the Mariel boatlift without a quarter in his pocket, and all of a sudden he was a multimillionaire on the backs of immigrant workers.

He was forcing cashiers at his food stores to have sex with him or he would fire them. Sexually harassing everybody. He was withholding Social Security and taxes from workers' paychecks and never submitting them. He was doing everything you can think of to cheat the system and abuse those workers. There was a very big organized campaign. The union made this guy come to his knees. When I witnessed that I said, "This is the answer." The Teamsters made sure he wouldn't get any food deliveries; the community organizations made sure that no one would buy anything off of him. He was basically without supplies and without sales, and he had to give in.

It took months, but we shut him down. I say "we" because it was a big effort; I was just a witness to it really. I went on to work with Latinos in meatpacking plants throughout the Midwest, in Iowa, Nebraska, and Minnesota. Moving from place to place was great at the time. I was twenty-five, twenty-six, I didn't have a care in the world. No family, no responsibilities other than myself, and I just really believed so much it was so easy for me to do. It needed to be done, and I felt privileged to be able to do it. I was born a citizen. Puerto Ricans don't have issues with papers; we don't have issues with immigration matters, and a lot of times it saddens me to see my *compatriotas* not caring about what's happening with immigrants. A lot of times they'll jump on the bandwagon to get rid of them. It's very embarrassing and sad to see that.

A lot of people don't know where Puerto Rico is or what our condition is. I thought the fact that there are Puerto Ricans who are voting citizens in this country would be enough; but it isn't. I've been able not only to be an observer, but to participate in struggles with the immigrant community, especially in the Midwest. I went back to Puerto Rico and went to law school there. I stayed there for about seven years, working and organizing Puerto Rican workers, which was a change for me. Eventually I was offered this position here in the Labor Center at the University of Iowa. I wasn't really enthusiastic about the idea at first, but it started being more appealing as I came up and interviewed. What the Labor Center is tasked by state law to do is to educate, to serve unions of the state of Iowa through continuing education, legal rights, organizing, whatever need arises. We supply the education component.

The union's relationship with Latinos here is very interesting. It's a point of controversy for a lot of unions, not just in Iowa, but throughout the States, because Rush Limbaugh and the right-wing legacy have done a really good job of promoting separation between workers and neighborhoods. A lot of our union members in the state of Iowa and other states believe that the immigrants are taking over and they're here to take our jobs and working for less and we are going to lose what we have. It's always a very interesting balancing act to talk to angry white union members about immigrants and how they are not the enemy. Human beings seem to need someone to blame, so it's a matter of putting the blame where it belongs—on corporate America and the government. I always ask people if someone hits you over the head with a bat, are you going to hate the bat, or are you going to hate the guy who hit you? That's the question you gotta answer.

Once you sit in front of a group or lead discussion, especially among union people who have core union values like solidarity, nondiscrimination, equality, fair pay, benefits, safety in the workplace, that guide members of unions through their decision-making process. Once you've invoked those union values then you put the immigration question in context, because workers have to be seen as workers. I don't care what color you are. If you work and get exploited, that's the bottom line. Omar actually pointed me in a really interesting direction earlier in saying that in historical context that this is the way your forefathers were treated, this is the way Italian immigrants, German immigrants were treated. There was an English Only law passed in Iowa in 1917 against Germans. In 2003 one was passed again against Latino immigrants. It is a form of xenophobia and discrimination.

When I talk about immigration my job is to put it in the context of union values. Unions believe in solidarity. Workers don't have solidarity. To me solidarity is getting the guys who get hit hardest the help first, and right now immigrants are being hit the hardest. It doesn't always work. When you have a group of ten people, maybe you'll convince three and you'll lose three because they don't want to hear it, and then three will have a question mark in their head that says, maybe he has a point, maybe Rush Limbaugh is wrong, maybe Lou Dobbs doesn't know what he is talking about, maybe he is manipulating issues to stop these programs. So you got to make them aware of that.

Immigrants are just like anybody else. They pay payroll taxes, they rent, they pay property taxes, they pay sales taxes, they contribute to the economy. There is a suspense file in the Social Security Administration that is sitting there with $519 million that nobody knows where it's coming from. I submit to you that's not true. We know where it's coming from. We need it. We like it. We'd like it to continue to be there. You know how it works for immigrants: you come in, you buy a Social Security card, you go to work. Their Social Security contribution goes into the general fund, and that benefits everybody else who gets the benefits, because immigrants don't have the legal right to get it. That's a benefit in itself. They create the actual products and services; they put money into the community. In Iowa there are a lot of places that were boarded up ten years ago and now are thriving. The problem is they are not Italian restaurants or German bakeries; they are *taquerías*, they are *botanas* and *licorerías*. When the railroad industry left they left a very empty spot. Meatpacking has gone down quite a bit not because of immigrants but because of the way companies are killing animals and selling meat now. It's a different situation. Towns have boarded up a lot of businesses. What used to be empty downtowns are full of Latino businesses. The problem is that the guy whose forefathers have been in Ottawa, Iowa, for two hundred years really doesn't see himself in a *taquería*, and, well, he says, "They are taking over." He doesn't see its economic growth, that's taxes, that's revenue for the town. He doesn't want to see that because it's a change that people fear.

I tell people, "Do you consider immigrants stupid?" "Well, no." "Don't you think they want to get a better job and a better future?" "Well, maybe, well, yeah, the only way to do this is to learn English." "Now, have you ever tried to learn a different language on your own? Have you? How hard is that?" Assimilation is a process. It's a demographic process. You can't slow it down; you can't change it. I fight it every day. I don't want to assimilate. I wasn't born here. I don't belong to this country. I was born in a different country. My nationality is a different one. But immigrants don't choose not to assimilate. On the other hand, the reason that folks are creating communities where they don't assimilate immediately anymore is because the militarization of the border has made it to where people have to stay here when they didn't want to stay here. People want to come work and go home as much as possible. I know a lot of people who went home in November and came back in January/February when they had to go back to work, but you can't do that anymore, because you might lose your life in the process. You're not here because you want to be. You're here because NAFTA has destroyed the possibilities of working at home.

The fact is the majority of people who spend ten years or more here, they learn English no matter what they do. Except if you are Puerto Rican, because Puerto Ricans don't have to learn it, and they don't. Assimilation is a process you can fight all you want, but if you want to improve your lifestyle and make better money and have a better job you are going to have to change. Iowa is one of the "whitest" states I have ever been to, and reactions vary. It's very interesting. We have cases like Perry, Iowa, where they are trying to work towards reconciliation, but you have places like Postville, that they don't want them. They passed an anti-immigrant law. Tomball, for example, was a very white-bread community; now it's got Mexicans, Salvadorans, Guatemalans. You have folks that are enjoying it, like, "Man, I've got the best Salvadoran food in the state." There are also folks that are like, "When are they gonna go home? I hate them. They don't speak English. My family came here before and they learned English." We are a very small portion of the state, I think maybe 2.5 percent. We're larger than the African American population, but we are not very large, maybe a hundred thousand.

Immigrant bashing is a very productive political activity in this state. I wouldn't live in any other city. Iowa City is an academic community where people like Omar and I hang out and demand to be treated with respect and equality. It's a very diverse community with a lot of Arabs, Indians, Africans, and Asians. There are two camps. One group of folks wants to know more about immigration. They really have a genuine interest in reaching out to the Latino community. A lot of them are having Latinos in their work centers who don't join the union because it doesn't look like them and they're like, "How can we reach them?" This is a right-to-work state, so you don't have to join if you don't want. "We don't know what to do. We buy them tacos for every meeting, but yet they don't come. Can we bring a mariachi, maybe?" I tell them, "No, you need to get some people who look like them on your executive board. You may get a Latino president one of these days." They don't want to hear that. They want them to join, but they don't want them to run for anything.

Latino workers tell me, "We don't have any business there. They don't look like us. We don't have to join." A lot of times, Guatemalans, Salvadoran workers, Mexican workers, come with preconceived notions of unionism from Central and South America. They don't trust unions here. All they want to know is we don't have to belong. I don't want to be seen. I don't want to be heard. For some there is a negative experience with the CTM [Confederación de Trabajadores de México] in Mexico and executions organized in Colombia and Guatemala, and so they're like, "Aah, I don't want to be a part of that." Then you have some activists who come up every once in a while, and they see the union as an all-white thing that's against them, and they want to get away from it or actually get it decertified.

They would rather be invisible. For example, Davenport has had a Mexican community since the beginning of the twentieth century, late 1800s. They came with the railroads; they came with the meatpacking plants. You have a large community in Marshalltown where there is railroad money, but then those dropped off in the '40s and '50s, and the new surge came in the late '80s, early '90s. Then you have folks in Davenport whose families have been there a hundred years, a very large community. Their experience is totally different from the experience of the new immigrants. They are assimilated; they belong there; they grew up there; they were born there; their parents were born there. They have the Latino fire, but they don't relate very well to the immigrant experience. We have West Liberty—it's a very old community, but it's been renewed with people from Durango who work at Columbus Junction Meat Packing. It's an oasis. They have bilingual education in schools. They have a very vibrant community. However, they don't have political involvement; they haven't taken over yet, which is disappointing.

I miss the action of being an organizer, being in the trenches. Things have improved here since I've been here. In only a year and a half I've seen a lot of improvement. Does it feel like home? In a way it does; in a way it doesn't. It's interesting because I am very politically active. Iowa is very unique in its politics. I have been appointed to the Latino Affairs Commission of the state by the governor twice. I became part of the state's Central Committee for the Democratic Party two months after I got here. There is just a very big void, not enough people to fill it. Every time I turn around I get asked to serve on some committee.

The one big hurdle I have to overcome every time I do a presentation on immigration is the sanctity of the law, so to speak. I just remind them of slavery, and these are the sacred laws that were passed, and then you go into civics and how is the law passed and their hand in creating it. First thing you learn in law is that it has nothing to do with justice, nothing whatsoever. If you want fairness go and do something else, but the law has nothing to do with that. When they say, "My grandfather didn't break the law when he came from Italy," I usually say, "What if you were in a situation where people are hungry, there's no work, your family is starving, and all there is between you and a future is a little river, what would you do? If you can tell me you would sit there and watch your kids starve, then I don't have anything else to talk to you about. I can't help you." But usually they say, "Well, I'd cross any line." Well, then there you go. Are you going to let the employer exploit them? The solution as far as I'm concerned is having full labor rights in the workplace so that people can take their future into their own hands, organize through the union and take exploitative business owners to task.

There is an important role for popular education to teach immigrants their rights in this country because there are a lot of people taking advantage of them, including some of our own people. You can't assume literacy. You can't assume that there's a level of education that would allow other kinds of education to happen. They are not going to go to college. You have to use popular education methods to get the message across that you do have rights and it doesn't matter where you're from. The Constitution applies to you no matter what people tell you. It does. You have the right to the Miranda rights; rights say you can be interrogated, but no cop has the right to ask for papers. You don't have to open the door without a warrant. There is just a lot of ignorance in that respect, and the government is taking advantage of them. They knock on the door at 4:00 in the morning and say they have to open and they do. In Guatemala, if you don't open the door they'll shoot through the door. Here it doesn't work that way. But folks don't know that, and there's a lot of people taking advantage of that.

José Elizondo is the first Latino council person elected in West Liberty, Iowa's history. Now a town of about 3,500, about 49 percent of the population is Latino. West Liberty, about fifteen miles outside of Iowa City, has struggled to make change but has only managed to do so with the tenacity of families like the Elizondos. Along with his mother, José, the eldest of three children, owns La Mexicana restaurant in the center of town. During our conversation on August 28, his mother, María, prepares the kitchen for the lunch rush while I eat a late breakfast.

JOSÉ: With the presidential campaigns, everybody is talking about immigration. They put everything else on the back burner; they think everyone wants to know about immigration. I can't quite stand it, to be honest. I have so many campaign managers who come by who try to set things up here. They stop by to try to get a little perspective on how to get Latinos to vote. That is one of their main goals. For me when they come and argue with you about immigration and what you feel about putting a fence up, you are really not trying to get my feelings about a candidate. A lot of them don't understand why I try to switch the conversation to healthcare and education, which are the main reasons we come up here anyway.

What I always try to tell people is, you need to remember what your parents or grandparents did and not forget. What I have noticed in the Latino community is you get a wave of Latinos coming in, the kids go to school, they get highly educated and get so Westernized that they forget where they came from. When you see a group of Latinos that are coming here looking for work or looking for food or clothes, I have seen many turn their heads. I am not one to do that at all.

LOUIS: Do you think your mom fostered those values in you to be close to your community?

JOSÉ: Yeah, and from growing up here. I was born in Muscatine. I am thirty-two. I was taught that someday it may happen to you, so you just can't turn your back on anyone. On Thanksgiving we will open up the doors, and if we see young families, we invite them in to eat, because we know they are so far away from their homes.

LOUIS: When did your family come up here?

JOSÉ: They are second generation. My mom was born in Weslaco [Texas], and my father was born in Mexico, Tamaulipas. They told me that he just pretty much walked over.

LOUIS: What brought them to Iowa?

JOSÉ: My mother was a migrant worker. My father was also a migrant worker. Both my parents did not finish grade school. They went up to the third grade, mainly because, like in any other culture, the family got sick and they had to help. When they got married, they moved to Chicago. My dad had a vocational training degree in electronics and took a job as a cab driver and my mother would not only work in the fields, but clean hotels, clean houses. They got together and said, "You know, we have got all these Latinos coming up, but there is no food." So they packed up a station wagon

José Elizondo at La Mexicana restaurant in West Liberty, Iowa. Photo by Louis Mendoza.

and started going house to house selling tortillas, jalapeños, cheese, whatever they could get their hands on. He would go to Chicago to pick it up and bring it over here.

LOUIS: Why did they settle here? Did they work in the nearby fields?

JOSÉ: Yeah, and Muscatine was very close by. There are a lot of tomato fields in this area. There were lots of Latinos around here at that time. He felt a little more comfortable here, because he was a businessman. He also would bring in big-name bands from Mexico to play on Saturdays. That really struck the community. People would have worked all week and not have anything to do, so my father would send for a band, pay out of his own pocket, and only charge like $5, and you got to dance from 8:00 at night to 1:00 in the morning. After that he would open up the restaurant to sell menudo.

LOUIS: They started off by selling food wholesale?

JOSÉ: No, house to house, and then they opened the restaurant and the store. We were the first store in town. I began working with him when I was five. We got to the point that we were selling all our products to Hy-Vee Econofoods all through this area, all the way up to Cedar Falls, all the way down to Keokuk. When Father passed away, we kept it for a couple of years and then we sold it. I am more into working with people than I am working with business. I am really good at getting people together and coming up with solutions. And that is where immigration reform comes in. It seems the more you criticize the way things are, the more someone tries to stop you, and that just makes you want to do it more. We had troubles here when we first opened up the restaurant with people actually blocking our doors, saying you don't belong here. This was in 1978. My father was always getting pulled over; they would check his card, take everything out of the car in front of everybody. But Dad was so good at meeting people. He got to know sheriffs, lawyers.

LOUIS: He won them over by not being negative?

JOSÉ: Pretty much. It got to a point where every time a police officer would stop him and start taking his car apart, a sheriff or somebody would show up and ask them what they were doing, and they would say, "Well, he doesn't have a permit." So they would actually sign a permit right there. They understood that he was a businessman. When we opened up the store it became the center of town where all Latinos would come and talk. Mother got into becoming a midwife and helping other Latinos when they got here. We did it because we cared.

LOUIS: When did you get elected to the city council?

JOSÉ: Two years ago. First Latino ever elected. There was another Latino before me, but he was just temporary. He was just like a little puppet. He would argue about an alleyway that he wants to pave for the Latinos, and a lot of people, especially Mother and Dad, were like, "Why don't you do other things besides just paving?" It was just thinking so small. Years go by, nobody got involved, everything was somewhat quiet, everyone was numb. They understood there were a lot of Latinos. They understood it was a different culture, but everybody had been assimilated. But with the new wave of Latinos coming through, everything seemed to change. People start thinking more about other issues.

This was about '95 or '97. The "recorded" Hispanic population now is 49 percent. Some people don't understand why I wanted to be on the council. Well, half the town is Latino. Since I have been on I have gotten a chief taken out of his position for being too rude and not understanding Latino culture. For instance, there was a time when he was interrogating a child about not being in school in front of his house. Of course, the father and mother are going to run out and defend their son. Well, then a nightstick comes out, and these parents are on their knees on their front yard. When I got on there, it took me four months of constantly badgering him, bringing it to the council, getting everybody else involved. What I had to go against was my tires being flattened, a loss of business, people making rude remarks, just about any rumor you could think of was brought on me. The chief even confronted me. Growing up here, you have a whole different attitude when you are confronted, and you sometimes have to switch that off. As someone in power I had to not only switch it off, but I had to call the mayor, I had to call the city manager, and I had to call a couple other people. And this all started from a young kid being interrogated without the permission of his parents. You can't have that kind of abuse of power.

When they got rid of him, I was in charge of hiring a new chief. We made the new chief take classes in Latino culture, and we are making them all take Spanish. They go to MCC, Muscatine Community College, and they take those classes. What they couldn't understand is in the Latino population, we take it, we take it, we take it until we explode, and when we explode it looks negative to everybody else, but in our eyes it's justified.

We have done something, and I saw it when I was a kid. I was maybe four years old; we had a restaurant on the corner. There is a Mexican bar down here, and rumors I heard from my parents and others said that the police would routinely go in and grab one person, take him away, and go have their way with him just to remind him of who was in charge. One day they got fed up and when a police walked into that bar someone turned off the music and put the jukebox in front of the door. Everyone was just standing there, and the door was locked. The police officer called for backup, and state troopers and the sheriff's department all came in.

LOUIS: *A standoff at the bar?*

JOSÉ: A big one. After that it all changed. Everyone got calm. It just switched. One of those things you never talk about it, but it was done.

LOUIS: *What is the overall population now?*

JOSÉ: Recorded, about 3,300. It has been steadily growing. The factory here, West Liberty Foods, and the chamber of commerce went down to Mexico and brought people up. They also told Latinos, "Go get some more family members. We have got jobs." Before you know it, there is a large migration.

LOUIS: *I am really fascinated about the story of your parents starting their business.*

JOSÉ: My parents really didn't want to be working in a factory or being told what to do. Anything you needed, my dad was always there. He got the title of Don José because if you needed help, he was going to help you if he could. Because of that example, I have helped people locate jobs, cars, apartments, pay their gas bills, anything I can do.

LOUIS: *So what are the schools like here? Do they accommodate the new immigrants?*

JOSÉ: Quite a bit now. They have ESL classes. They teach just about anything that they need. No one got the money to keep it going, but they actually started a dual-language program. The kids that have done that took it in elementary school are now in middle school heading to high school and know perfect Spanish. And the ones that only knew Spanish, know perfect English.

LOUIS: *Do you see a generational shift in attitudes among whites here, or is it that the old folks are somewhat afraid of the change and younger folks are different?*

JOSÉ: I have noticed that a lot help as much as they can. If you are raised in a community like this and you have got a university about ten miles away, you tend to be more open. We try to tell everyone it is about respecting cultural difference. Remember what your culture is, and learn about mine.

The best way to know someone's culture is to dance with it or eat with it and enjoy yourself. When we were kids, the *quinceañeras* [coming-of-age parties for fifteen-year-old girls] were packed with our friends. My sister's *quinceañera* had over eight hundred people. We put it in the paper, saying, "Never experienced one? Come down and experience it." We put it in flyers in Iowa City and Muscatine, you name it. Dad told everybody on his routes. There were whites, blacks, Laotians, Chinese, Japanese, everybody. My sister's court was all mixed-race.

> LOUIS: *Do a lot of whites come in here to the restaurant?*

JOSÉ: Actually, most of our clients are white.

> LOUIS: *So what do people in the area do for work? You mentioned West Liberty Foods.*

JOSÉ: That is a turkey processing plant. It got taken over in 1994–1995, got turned into a co-op. All the turkey farmers in the area bought it. Then we have got Muscatine, which has many, many factories. Then there is Columbus Junction, where they have Tyson Foods.

> LOUIS: *Have there been any local ordinances passed to deal with immigration?*

JOSÉ: Not here. But in Marion it's happening. They are becoming a new technology center. They had a lot of Latinos there, and then somebody was running for office. He thought maybe if he brought immigration up, he could win, so he got in contact with ICE and with marshals to try to figure out how to bust all the Latinos there. It was getting to the point where they could almost pull anybody over. I know they called area mayors and councilmembers to join. But everybody declined, said no way. Our city manager is African American, and he was like, there is no way. Once that starts, who's next? The lawsuits would have been immense. As a result growth has almost come to a standstill in Marion, and prices have tripled to quadrupled because Latinos won't go there. Now they are starting to feel the sting, and they didn't quite understand how cheap it was to have labor come in and get it done in a day and a half, compared to a month.

> LOUIS: *Do you think the Latino vote was responsible for getting you elected, or was it just your ability to talk to both or multiple cultures?*

JOSÉ: To be honest, everybody knew me before I even ran for election because of my work with the kids. There were times where I would have this whole area full of kids. It got to the point where I just opened up an arcade just to keep the kids in there. I had trouble with that—police coming in, checking kids for weapons. I said screw it, and I closed it down and joined the library board, thinking maybe I could make a difference there getting some kids to come in. I was on that for six months. I told myself, "This isn't working. I need the big enchilada." So I quit that when a spot opened up for city council. I waited until the last minute and was like, okay, I know business is going to go down, and I am going to be threatened, but I jumped into it headfirst. I'll see about running for reelection. It is time-consuming and really, really hard. You are not only dealing with major issues, but the little issues. Now that Latinos know that they have someone to speak to, I get asked to address every single problem.

> LOUIS: *Do you think the future for Latinos here will ultimately get better and better?*

JOSÉ: Much better, with everything that is happening in this town, with everybody becoming part of the local culture and getting high-paying jobs and all their kids going to college, coming back and giving to the community. It's opening up doors for others.

> LOUIS: *Do you think Latinos are going to finish school and stay, or are they going to move to the big city?*

JOSÉ: I have seen a lot move back to Texas or Mexico. The employees I have are Salvadoran, Honduran, and Ecuadoran. We're becoming more diverse.

> LOUIS: *Do you go to Texas?*

JOSÉ: We used to go there every year and stay for a month. We would take three trucks to Chicago to pick up supplies, and my dad would go one direction and I would go the other. We would deliver a month's worth of supplies and go on vacation. The teachers would give us all our books, because they knew, the Elizondos are leaving, so give them a bunch of homework. I loved it to be honest with you. You would wake up out on the ranch, and you hear the roosters crow. You smell fresh flour tortillas going, a little Mexican music going on the radio, which you couldn't ever get up here. Your parents are jabbering away with family. You get up and you are just respected and you are loved, and, you know, you get to eat, and the next thing you know, do your homework.

> LOUIS: *That's a beautiful way to describe the love of extended family.*

JOSÉ: Yes. My brothers and I are all with non-Latinos. My brother married a German. My fiancée is German, so sometimes we get dirty looks as interracial couples. Sometimes some in the Mexican community look and wonder, but then they understand. My fiancée's family is very accepting. In high school I could never meet any parents. There was no way, even though they knew me from football or elsewhere, that I could meet them as someone dating their daughter. It was, "Come get me here, come over here," you know, the high school thing, which after a while kind of wears on you, and relationships don't become strong that way. So you end up having a lot of girlfriends.

   LOUIS: *What made you so outgoing?*

JOSÉ: When I was very young my dad and I would pull up to a field, a tomato field, and he would say run out there and tell him what we have. So there I am running into the fields to sell tacos and burritos. I would get the order and run back, and Dad would make it. For me it was no big deal; it was just what Dad says to do. My dad would make me speak to store managers and store owners, so here I was, eight, ten years old, making business deals in English. When we walked in there, pulled up to the store, he would say this is the person's name, this is what we need done, be right back. And I would run over there, grab the manager, and sit down with him, and say here is what we have for you. My dad would take all the boxes in and put them away. Then he'd come over and shake hands, like he made the deal. As soon as he came in, I stepped in the shadows behind him.

   We would wake up at 4 o'clock in the morning, unload the truck and reload it to rotate everything, then I'd go to school. The teachers knew I would be late for the first class, so I would always get a gym class or study hall and then go in and do my homework and afterward go to football practice and then come home and unload the truck again and sit there with him, talk about what happened. Come the weekends, I was with him. Heck, I was driving the backroads by the time I was twelve because he would be so tired. He was like, "Don't go over 20. Don't tell your mother." So there I was just driving the van home full of merchandise. You feel kind of good. As soon as you get home Mama takes you and sets you up with food and everything and sits down and talks to you about your day. In that sense it was perfect. When you hang out with your other friends you realize it is not the same. They bicker at their parents or don't want to go home for dinner. My dad wasn't much on saying how pleased he was, but he would always tell Ma, "Oh my, you should have seen your son today. He sold all this and this." After Dad passed away, she started telling me stories.

FOUR

CONFRONTING THREATS
TO COMMUNITY

AVERAGE PEOPLE AND THE AVERAGE COMMUNITY CAN CHANGE
THE WORLD. YOU CAN DO IT JUST BASED ON COMMON SENSE,
DETERMINATION, PERSISTENCE, AND PATIENCE. *Lois Gibbs*

The conversations included in this chapter speak to the ways in which
Latino communities have responded to persistent and intensified threats
to their well-being and the process, rewards, and challenges of organizing
collective action in their own defense. They are, of course, only a representative sampling of issues and responses. Taken together, though, they demonstrate how urban-rural-suburban and border-interior communities share
very tangible risks to community integrity and control of their environment,
be it from encroachment by developers, local ordinances premised on the
view of Latinos as an economic or social threat, or the building of the border wall. In fact, in some cases all three of these issues conspire to threaten
community well-being.

Each community has its own organizing philosophy and varying
degrees of infrastructure. As might be expected, organizations in urban centers contend with competing forces within and outside the community and
more refined discourses regarding urban renewal and community development. As different as they might be, however, the Resurrection Project and
PODER both have at their core community self-determination of land use.
In contrast, the rise in local anti-immigrant ordinances and the plan to build
a wall along the entire U.S.-Mexican border have spawned coalitions of legal
groups·and community organizations to mount court challenges and efforts
to intervene in the public discourse on border security that has made the
establishment of a border wall an essential first step for conservatives before
they will initiate discussion of comprehensive immigration reform.

In the interviews with Yolanda Chávez Leyva and Rogelio Núñez, we can see the way the border wall has spawned fierce anti-Mexican sentiment and given rise to rampant opportunism and corruption, which has, tragically, led to a decline in civil discourse and a rise in fear, the use of intimidation, and a distortion of what it means to represent the best interests of the community. Finally, in a context in which Latino youth are being criminalized and anti-Mexican sentiment has become a popular political wedge issue in local elections, a certain nostalgia for and wariness of a Chicano movement arises, which speaks to generational tensions surrounding strategies, perceived co-optation, and what community control means as well as how that is determined. Collective action is nevertheless seen as crucial to community well-being, even as it is also clear from these and other interviews that community organizing today will not look like it did in the past.

Raúl Raymundo is the executive director of the Resurrection Project in Chicago's historic Pilsen neighborhood. I met him on a late Friday afternoon in his office. The Resurrection Project's mission is "to build relationships and challenge people to act on their faith and values to create healthy communities through organizing, education and community development."

RAÚL: From my perspective, if you live in places like Iowa, Nebraska, the heartland, if you will, you better be welcoming immigrants, because they are the ones who will be paying for your Social Security. The population is aging, and they are taking care of your future. There has been research comparing the economy of Chicago with the economies of Detroit and Cleveland, particularly during the '90s and especially the late '90s when they were booming, and why Detroit's and Cleveland's economies didn't prosper as well as Chicago. Number one reason: immigration. In Chicago, Latinos primarily but immigrants in general reversed the decline of the population.

Latinos are all over now. Pilsen, along with southeast Chicago, used to be the key port of entry for *mexicanos*. This community has always been an immigrant community, even going back to the turn of the century. It was built by Eastern Europeans. This used to be Czechoslovakian, Croatian, Lithuanian, Bohemian, Polish, German, so there are about fourteen Catholic churches in this neighborhood. And every church was an immigrant, ethnic parish. I would love to have been a fly on the wall to hear their conversations back then.

You still have tenement housing here. But the difference in this community, as opposed to other communities where it got just devastated, is that the population was replaced by *mexicano* communities. This city has been a working immigrant city for many years; it was founded on that and developed a very strong foundation of support organizations. So there are a lot of coalitions, networks, nonprofit organizations, social service agencies. It used to be that in the suburbs you didn't need services, you made it, you were well-off enough to leave the problems in the city. That has come back to bite them in the ass, because now that you have a whole demographic shift in the region a lot of these cities and municipalities are not ready to adapt in the schools. The challenge of serving the new population, in this case Latinos, has become a big issue.

LOUIS: *Is there an effort to gentrify now that people want to move back into the city?*

RAÚL: Oh yeah, we are in the path of gentrification. But you know gentrification is like a double-edged sword. It is not about pricing people out, as much as it is about why people move. You have got to have development to progress. We are an organization that is doing a lot of work in that area, and that is what I call natural displacement. There is no way in hell that everybody who wanted to could live here. That is why new communities get formed. People leave for different reasons; people leave because of poor schools, safety, and so forth, and then others are priced out, so there are multiple reasons for it.

Raúl Raymundo in his office at the Resurrection Project in Barrio Pilsen, Chicago. Photo by Louis Mendoza.

The city has come through a tremendous renaissance. A lot of development has taken place, and a lot of development is unaffordable. So on our end, we are trying to create what I would call balanced development. The private sector is going to do what it is going to do. We have to figure out how to create opportunities for existing families to remain in the community by creating affordable housing. And that is sometimes what people fight about, you know, they say, "We want to preserve the community the way it is," and I am like, "Well, sometimes you don't want to preserve it the way it is. I don't want the gangbangers on the corner. I don't want to preserve that."

So you have to figure out why you are creating that opportunity for balanced growth, but you know the other thing that is going on is that the face of affordable housing has changed. Before, in the '90s, affordable housing meant making affordable housing for working families. Today, affordable housing is for teachers, civil servants, college professors, as if we solved the problems of affordable housing for the working class. We haven't; people just got priced out. But it is easier to tell the decision-making official, the people in the suburbs, you know, we need to provide housing for the local schoolteacher instead of the local busboy.

LOUIS: *How did your family get to Chicago?*

RAÚL: My dad came here in '68. He was the pioneer of the family. Like many immigrants, economic reasons was the motivation. In fact, he tells me it took him almost a year to put together money. He had to borrow money in the end to get out here. He was one of the lucky ones in that the person he dealt with over there was placing people, so he actually had a work letter, so as soon as he got here he would have work. He came from Mexico City. He was able to put his visa together and take the bus up here. He tells me his last meal until he got to Chicago was at the border, because he didn't speak any English. When he got into the Chicago downtown bus station he tells me that he was going to step out and he heard this loud noise and he immediately ran back into the bus station. Before he left he was being told by folks, "Why are you going there, the Vietnam War is on?" and all this stuff, and he thought the buildings were falling apart. He had never heard the rumbling noise made by the elevated trains.

LOUIS: *What kind of work did he come to do?*

RAÚL: Factory, renovating tires, and they did the blades for the large agricultural tractors that cut the wheat. When he got here, he showed his letter to a cab driver, who took him to the factory. He met with the owner around two o'clock, and he said, "You can start tomorrow." And the owner said, "You just got here?" He said "Yeah." "Well, where are you going to stay?" He said, "No clue." So he put him in touch with two other Mexican workers, and they put him up for the next year and a half. [Laughs]

LOUIS: *Was he single at the time?*

RAÚL: No, we had all been born. I was born in Mexico City. I think he must have been like twenty-eight. All six of us already had been born.

LOUIS: *Did he share with you any sense of what was going through his head as he was leaving his family behind to do this?*

RAÚL: What was going through his head was survival. There was no way in hell, he tells me, that he would be able to survive and support the family of six kids in Mexico City with what he had. So that was really the reason for doing this, taking a big leap. My dad served as the branch from out of which other people came. I have a lot of family in Mexico, and I have a lot of family here too.

LOUIS: *Where do the values come from that drive your social justice and community empowerment work?*

RAÚL: My parents and my faith, particularly from my mom. My dad has been a workaholic all his life, so he wasn't really around other than providing. The set of values that he provided are his hard work ethic and providing for the family, but he wasn't around much to participate in community stuff. After thirty-plus years at working in this factory, it dawned on me to ask him what his hourly wage was when he retired. And it was $12.25 after thirty-plus years of working in the same factory. But it's not the hourly wage; it's the number of hours they put in. He was working sixty to seventy hours a week.

My mom, on the other hand, also worked. She *is* the pillar of our family in terms of involvement, community stuff, made sure we talked to the teachers and did all sorts of things to keep us in check. Early on I recall she told us, "You are never given things; you have to fight for them." One of the biggest fights was for the high school in the neighborhood. I was in grade school at the time. The school I went to was the high school that got built, Benito Juárez High School. There is a whole history behind that high school with the struggle for it being built, but what I can remember is my mom telling one day that I wasn't going to go to school, that people from *la lucha* [the struggle] are boycotting and so forth, so a lot of it comes from that.

The other part is I grew up as a Catholic, but the Catholicism I grew up with was very rigid. When I went away to school I started learning about other traditions and why they do what they do and even questioning my own. It wasn't until I came back from Carleton and decided to live in the neighborhood, and my mom, the good Catholic woman that she is, said, "Where are you going to go to church?" I said I don't know that I want to go, but out of respect for her I said, "Okay, Mom, where?" And I did. What moved me was the epiphany I experienced when the pastor was preaching from the pulpit during the homily about a young man who just got shot across the street from church. He was asking, what are we going to do about it? Are we going to pray the problem goes away, or are we going to do something about it? And I am like, whoa, he is right, you know. That inspired me to participate more in the parish, teaching ESL classes, doing other stuff. Before I knew it I was deep in, and one thing led to another, and I, along with this pastor and a few other laypeople, cofounded the Resurrection Project.

I became a born-again Catholic, because I realized now as an adult the broadness and richness, if you will, of Catholicism. That you can feel this way and think that way, and there are people in the opposite extreme as well, so as long as people respect my thoughts and thinking, then I do the same. There is nothing wrong with questioning my faith. And this particular pastor comes from the school of liberation theology, which is building justice among earth, and I like that. The church is not perfect; there is so much junk going on. To me faith is virtuality, it's people, community, it is celebration, it is doing good for others. Not what the pope says, not what the bishop says.

> LOUIS: *I saw an article recently about the publication of the diary of Mother Theresa that said she was full of spiritual angst, wondering about the existence of God. She had enormously big questions that bothered her for the last fifty years of her life, but she kept doing what she did.*

RAÚL: I think that's the difference between faith and hope. For me faith is you know what is going to happen, you just don't know when, but it is there. I am not wishing for it, I am not hoping, I know we are going to do right. We are going to succeed. This is the motivation behind a lot of this stuff we do. The organization itself has been just phenomenal. We were founded in 1990.

> LOUIS: *Did your involvement arise from your reintegration into the church?*

RAÚL: Yeah, with the values that I had through my parents and family. The faith part came afterwards in terms of discovering that it is a powerful force that moves people. There is a reason why people act the way they act, believe what they do, the faith that they have in wanting to do something for others. Today we work with a lot of parishes, and some participate really good, some don't. It is all about leadership. There are some priests, I tell you, I wouldn't even want to talk to them. They are just lousy leaders, both spiritual and otherwise. Then there are some who are really inspirational, and they do a lot.

LOUIS: *What is the parish name?*

RAÚL: St. Pious. It's a Dominican order. There's an interesting story in naming the project Resurrection. When we were getting the effort off the ground, we were in the church basement. Names like Nehemiah, Esperanza, and the Phoenix project came up, and then this old man in the chorus said, "Resurrección." There was silence for a moment, and then the realization that, yeah, that makes sense for what we are trying to do. That is how we baptized our name. When we launched our project, we had a baptism ceremony in which we had about eight hundred people in the parish, the mayor, and some VIPs attend.

LOUIS: *What is your primary purpose with the project?*

RAÚL: Our mission is to challenge people to act in their faith and values, to build health in their community. We do this through economic development, organizing, and education. Before we built the first home, we did a lot of work in relationship building among the parishes. You know, these parishes are very close to each other, and in the same community, instead of being an island to themselves; how do you create more community? As we continued, other challenges surfaced, day care, for example. We have built over three hundred units of housing. We have built two day care centers. We have health outreach programs. In the next four years, we plan to do more than what we did in our first fifteen. We are gearing up to do a senior project—seventy-five units. We also do rental housing. We own and manage over 150 apartments in the neighborhoods we work in. We have broadened our scope of work. We do a lot of advocacy and organizing around immigration. We had over one hundred people go to D.C. to lobby. Down in Springfield, we are part of a coalition that is moving some legislation. Right now, we are doing *derechos*, which is educating many of our families that are undocumented as to what their rights are. That is how to prevent getting arrested; second, what to do if you are. It is just a matter of time before reform passes, so we are preparing ourselves for it.

There are three major areas of the organization: community organizing, leadership development components, and our community development efforts. We are gearing up to start an exciting project. We are going to be creating a college dorm in the neighborhood. We are converting a convent in the neighborhood into a college dorm for local area high school students, a majority Latino. Unfortunately very few go on to college. Of that few who go, a majority of them commute to local universities, so we're putting together a conducive living environment for them. It is going to house about eighty students.

LOUIS: *How do you finance all this?*

RAÚL: We are a nonprofit organization, so we have to raise money from different sources—obviously from the philanthropic community, foundations, corporations, banks, individuals, and then we manage some government contracts. But what we have been doing more and more is earned income opportunities, earned income operations, like the management of the apartments. We also do commercial stuff. We are building a branch for Citibank here on the corner.

LOUIS: *How long have you been the executive director?*

RAÚL: Since 1991. I was one of the cofounders. We made an offer to a candidate to take the job, but he turned us down because it was an organization that was fledging. The leadership said to me, "Why don't you do it?" I was like, I am just a kid still. I was three years out of college, still trying to find myself. I told them, "I have to finish my graduate degree. I am not interested until then." Then they came and asked me again, and their confidence in me made me seriously consider it. Lo and behold, I took it.

I just had a twentieth college reunion and talked to some colleagues who have been through three or four careers since college. They ask me, "Why the hell aren't you doing something else? You could be making more money. Why do you still do it?" I tell them, "I get up in the morning, and I look forward to going to work."

LOUIS: *Tell me a little bit about the Latino community here.*

RAÚL: Chicago is a microcosm of the Latino community around the country. The majority of the Latino population in Chicago is Mexican, probably 65 to 70 percent; the Puerto Rican community comes second; Central American is probably third; and then the Cuban community and South

Americans. Chicago is three million people, and 33 or 32 percent are Latino. If there are more Latinos now in the city, then you are talking a million and a half in the region, not to mention the ones who aren't counted.

LOUIS: Are there any interethnic tensions among Latinos?

RAÚL: I think there is some, but I don't think they are deep. The tension comes in how sometimes the public officials make it. For example, the mayor appoints somebody to a cabinet post, and people ask, why didn't you appoint a Mexican or a Puerto Rican? The Latino community in general is pretty solid behind comprehensive immigration reform. There are very few Latinos who are out there saying the opposite. Chicago is a very, very progressive immigrant working-class city.

I should qualify what I just said because even though there is a lot of receptiveness from the business community for the recognition of the contribution of immigrants, there are still a lot of people who don't want us, like Carpentersville. We as a community have got to stop preaching to the choir and start getting out of it. We only have one Hispanic congressional representative. I don't want to talk to him anymore about comprehensive reform; he is on board. I need to talk to the black congressman, I need to talk to the white congressman. The immigration marches that happened a year ago here in Chicago and across the country did a lot for putting our face out there, but at the same time it would have been a lot more powerful if you saw a lot more black and white faces.

Rogelio Núñez is the executive director of Proyecto Libertad, an entity well known in the Rio Grande Valley for its advocacy and legal services on behalf of immigrant and working poor communities along the border. I went to the Proyecto offices without an appointment one afternoon and asked to see Rogelio. I gave a brief explanation of my trip, who I was, and mentioned that my friend Raúl Salinas had recommended that I speak with him. That recommendation made all the difference. Rogelio immediately set aside what he was doing and spent the next couple of hours with me explaining the challenges his organization faces in the increasingly militarized border region.[1]

> LOUIS: *I understand that the plans for the border wall have really hit a nerve.*

ROGELIO: Sí ha habido. There's been a good response from some of the immigrants themselves. We do legal work, and we got cases up the chingao. And then we do community organizing work también. Some of the people we work with, mainly undocumented, are participating a lot, and como aquí there's a couple of local colleges where some of the students have responded really well, which is good, verdad, porque entonces ya se conectan al trabajo este. And then some local community, more in the world of businesspeople, que usually at this point it's hard to say que they'd be your allies pero they are. From their perspective it's not good for the border. There's been different forums where you see all of us together. Chingao, está interestante, 'cause they wouldn't come to anything else.

I've worked with some other groups here in the sur de Tejas, with other nonprofits. We do different services, but mostly their client base is immigrant families. Y todavía trabajamos con la comunidad inmigrante, you know, so we want them to come out and participate. "Que va haber una marcha, que va haber una protesta." And so we kept thinking about, well, that's good, we'll turn in five thousand to ten thousand letters to the senator's office on comprehensive immigration reform, but they're all immigrants, and they don't vote. So on the wall thing, agarramos una onda this campaign, this five-month campaign that's gonna draw together fifteen thousand signatures of registered voters. Tenemos some folks who went out and accessed the voter records of every voter in the counties for the last three or four elections. We'll go door-to-door with the petition and say, "Here is this wall, are you for it or against it? What do you say?" The idea then is that you're tapping a group of folks who aren't participating in any of these issues, maybe working-class raza, working-class and middle-class professionals who are not politicians, who are not activists, who are pretty much going to work raising a family, but who we think we can then engage in a dialogue. I say we keep preaching to the choir, man, le digo a la palomilla. Nothing against los camaradas de los imigrantes, "Ya no los quiero ver." "¿No pero por qué?" We need to bring other folks to the table, be they immigrants or residents or citizens, verdad. Aquí, pues 90 percent of this whole world is mexicano.

Rogelio Núñez of Proyecto Libertad in Harlingen, Texas. Photo by Louis Mendoza.

LOUIS: Has immigration enforcement intensified locally?

ROGELIO: What is here is not your average raid, verdad. Aquí es house to house, they've got the orders to deport, ya traen, ICE [Immigration Control and Enforcement] has got you a list of people and they're just going door to door. They just set that fear, porque no nomás llegan uno o dos. We've had two people who've called that have been detained now and are going to be deported, they're from El Salvador. Llegan nine or ten agentes, man, dressed in their anti-riot, black stuff, todo, their rifles and everything y tocan la puerta. Pues chingao, it creates fear in the neighborhood. I mean people don't wanna come out. Of course we've always been saturated with Border Patrol here. But after 2001 they're all over the place.

LOUIS: Was there a period when it seemed that everybody looked the other way?

ROGELIO: I want to say que estaba calmado . . . there were folks who would get deported. There was a time when they would do what's called "baggage letters." You would go to your hearings, you have no remedy, your case is denied, you know there's no appeal process, entonces, okay, we're now ordering you removed from this country. Pero te daban un ninety-day baggage letter, which meant you have ninety days to gather your stuff and get yourself out of this country. Ahora no. It's a federal offense to cross the river illegally, it's against the law. When you do that, they can throw the book at you, they can detain you, they can incarcerate you, they put a fine on your bond. The next step to really intensify it some more is to begin to say, sabes qué, we're just going to detain everybody, especially the *mexicanos*. Before they would just say, "sign here" and throw you back. Now we're going to detain you. You've got Pearsall, Raymondville, Port Isabel, Laredo. They have enough beds, and they're building more. Aquí van hacer mil camas más en Raymondville.

And they're doing time, tiempo largo. Vi un chamaco el otro día, twenty-year-old Honduran guy, he spent casi los nueve meses en Pearsall until his wife was able to pay the $500,000 bond. The judge reduced it to $1,500. He's been here for four years, pero, lo perscaron when he was going up north, and so they put him in immigration proceedings. Pues a donde, nosotros, we handle over a thousand active cases in a year. When I come to the office paso por el expressway, there is a brand-new Border Patrol station that was built three years ago. The parking lot just full of cars; it's massive. We've got a bus station down the street. They're over there every day, every day, todo los días están two or three vans waiting for the bus to come in.

Now you go to restaurants, and these agents pues tienen que comer. So they go into these places where people are working.

Que a la cinco de la mañana they've already talked to the local P.D., the local sheriff, the local highway patrol. They come in with vans, agents, helicopter y todo. Nobody knows what's going on, luego amanecen, and then the word starts going out, and then some of the folks were trying to get in there. They wouldn't let their lawyers in, you don't know what's going on, the kids are at home, desmadre, man, desmadre. I do know they're picking people up and putting them in detention and then at one point deporting.

I belong to the National Network for Immigrant Refugee Rights in Oakland. I go to those meetings, también surge allí, porque allí conectas, and there's people. Pero aquí no te hallas. I just have not had that here. Y luego lugares are not the best in terms of el nivel de intelectualismo. There is a big fight down here on the border. We're dealing with this, all kinds of issues with immigration, all kinds of issues of poverty. We've got the worst rates in the world, como dicen, in terms of poverty, pero las universidades, desgraciadamente. Ninety percent of students are from Hidalgo County. They all live at home. They all come from working-class, poor families, below the poverty guidelines. They use their financial aid to sustain the household. Sixty or 70 percent of the starting freshman class in Pan-Am and Brownsville[2] drop out. So allí está el otro pleito. Students struggle. La mayoría no tienen computers en la casa.

I would never trade living here. Estamos bien jodidos, man, bien jodidos. Fifty-five has been a good year, pero as I'm looking at the coming fifty-six I don't know if we can turn some things. Todavía estoy watchando el chingado debates y esta bola de cabrones. It's just disgusting to hear these sons of bitches talk the way they do. It's jumping on the bandwagon. It's always us versus them. Local raza leadership is lacking. When I was in Kingsville in 1978, you know, of course ya habiendo estado bien metido in the Chicano movement. The Raza Unida Party was where I grew up. We fought for bilingual ed, and we fought for this, and we fought for that. There was some money that came down, me acuerdo. Había dinero, no, pero all it created was what I called Chicano bureaucrats, who'd never been part of the struggle, who got a good job.

We now have 1.2 million in the four counties aquí. Ninety percent are Mexican origin. You divide that up by first generation quién nació aquí. Then you look at your school districts; 99 percent of the school districts are brown. You look at the superintendent all the way down to the teacher; you look at the city school board, county, pura raza. The graduation completion rate is horrible. It's horrible. Nobody says anything, nadie dice como que, no one says anything, todos you know . . . and you know there's going to bring this program and train these teachers and we're going to do this thing and da da da da . . . zerito . . . pero anyways, así estamos.

> LOUIS: *Where is immigration on people's radar screen? Is there a "them" versus "us" attitude?*

ROGELIO: That's why I like this campaign that we started with registered voters. I wanna say que siendo ciudadano, again cause you're going to have a different generation, if they've made it, si no te está buscando la migra, or you've made it, you're a legal permanent resident or you're a U.S. citizen. I don't see them getting involved, occasionally sale un tonto chingao en el radar screen del Letters to the Editor that says that we should put up a fence and electrify some people. You'll get a few that respond . . . but nothing that becomes organized, that says we're going to have these meetings, que va haber una reunión de concerned citizens.

That's sad. El año pasado there was an incident in my hometown, San Benito. We had a good basketball team that was competitive with the district. Tocó de que in one of the home games. It kind of got out of hand. The fans got involved beyond what they should've. A fan went down and cussed out the other coach, and security comes. Al final they had to clear the basketball court of fans so that they could finish the game. The sports writer for the *Valley Morning Star* wrote a really strong editorial saying que the worst fans were in San Benito. Then of course letters to the editor saying que, "Who does that Lairo Jaimez think he is?" In his writing he said, not only was that a bad incident, there were two other incidents where those fans got out of hand. The first was a game against Los Fresnos in Brownsville, to the Brownsville school, and one was Weslaco. And the Brownsville schools and the Weslaco schools had immigrants on their team. So the fans were saying, "Hey, call *la migra!*" and "Y vállanse pa' 'tras pa' Matamoros!" I see that as a potential for conflict.

I spent some time, I wrote a real nice letter, I indexed it with some material. We had this training guide, launched with the network called *Bridge: Building a Race and Immigration Dialogue in the Global Economy*. It was a curriculum that takes you through a popular education model y te lleva with different topics on immigration. History 101 for community folks. So I made some copies of this and said you know that these kinds of comments are derogatory, they're not good, we need to address these issues and nip them in the bud. I sent a copy to the writer and I cc'd it to the school board president. A lot of response, que dijieras tú, "Mira Rogelio, pues que bueno que me mandaste esto. Y no es de, no lo mandé de pleito." I haven't created some pleitos in a long time, pero the idea was, why don't we do some training? We were willing to offer our office. No te vamos a cobrar; we just want to do the training so that people can at least begin to understand this idea of immigration and what it means. These are our students in their classes, and they'll hear these comments. Nada, zero, period.

I'm very disappointed in the leadership of South Texas. Now there's leadership in terms of some things. Por ejemplo, you know there's programs that fund-raise for scholarships. We have some wealthy raza. I don't mean millionaires yet, pero maybe some, you know, wealthy—meaning que ya están establecidos y they're doing good. We do have sort of a sliver of solid middle class, but there's some segment of corruption. Every sheriff here has been indicted and is in prison.

LOUIS: *Was it down here that Border Patrol agents were recently indicted for smuggling immigrants?*

ROGELIO: Yeah, these were Border Patrol agents that were smuggling. Luego out of the Raymondville detention centers, which they got two thousand detainees there. Mueven prisioneros, from wherever they're going to move them. Just this past week they caught these guys taking these immigrants in the vans, verdad, por que this is a private corporation that runs the whole thing. And they try to move them past the checkpoint without any paperwork. They had about twenty-seven people in the van. Yeah, we find county sheriffs in Hidalgo County, Zapata County, Webb County, todos, they're all part of allowing the drug traffic to flow. I think the local politics reflect a lot of the national politics, ya el que tiene dinero puede correr, el que no tiene, no corre.

LOUIS: *Does local law enforcement cooperate with ICE?*

ROGELIO: They do. We actually got the local P.D. in San Benito to pass a policy to say that they wouldn't do that unless under extreme circumstances que they needed to verify the identity of whoever they stopped. And they actually signed it. The Cameron County sheriff's office, también, cause we did a campaign against them stopping folks. Hidalgo County has a policy that they will not cooperate on this whole idea of stopping you for a state violation and calling Border Patrol, but in some places I think they do. What they do is if you're caught for any infraction and put in jail, just about every morning all the jails are checked by Border Patrol. So say they caught you last night for a DUI, verdad, andabas tomando, they caught you and you're an inmigrante, and you're in jail. En la mañana viene el Border Patrol, and see what you're all about. Well, if you're undocumented, it's a different story. Like I said, it's interesting in South Texas.

I worked with some folks in Mississippi in the Delta that have the same historical evolutions as in South Texas. If you didn't know they were black and we're brown, you could just muffle our voices and cover our faces, you know . . . from the schoolhouse to the jailhouse. We have the same. There's the detention center. That's the other one that where also folks have gotten riled up about, besides the wall. It's two thousand beds, and the county of Willacy, where it's at, just approved another $50 million bond, to build a thousand more beds. They're minimum wage jobs, they're dead-end jobs, but, yeah, raza needs jobs. I keep telling folks those are local decisions. These are your county judge and county commissioners. If we were able to como decía organizar locally and put the pressure on these guys and say, "Sabes qué, no!" we might have some impact because it is a local decision. There's nothing that says, "Wait a minute, what's the quality of what we're bringing in?" We could turn some things around; we could run candidates and get 'em involved in the political process, pero, nada tampoco. That's not happening. I read something that says we're worse off economically now than we were twenty-five years ago. What we're lacking now, even though in different parts of the country there was different degrees of what the Chicano movement was, at least we had that to hang on to. Kingsville was a hotbed for the Chicano movement; a lot of the Chicano leadership in Texas went through Kingsville. I strongly believe that it created a major impact. We don't have that now. How do we connect it to a new generation?

You have media forces. Me acuerdo cuando estábamos en Austin, we were doing this research with immigrants in Austin, todavía no había los what I call the immigrant infrastructure that's now providing them with everything that they need from their community in Mexico. Porque now, my thinking is, como el inmigrante is a resource to organize 'cause the media takes them to things that are insular to them. They can see novelas; they can pretty much access what they need. They're not looking for us. They don't know we even exist. There's a few moments when I come across inmigrantes who say things like, "¿Pues ustedes están todos aquí? ¿Por qué están tan jodidos?" Well, you've been here all your lives, and you're all here in poverty. It's a challenge to live in South Texas.

YOLANDA CHÁVEZ LEYVA

Yolanda Chávez Leyva is a professor of history at the University of Texas at El Paso, where she also directs the public history program. Over a wonderful home-cooked breakfast on Saturday morning I interviewed Yolanda in her home about her work with El Paso del Sur, an emergent organization founded to resist the urban renewal plans crafted by the city's political and business elites, which involved redevelopment of the downtown area and the adjacent historic Segundo Barrio. The plan was developed and subsequently adopted by the city council without input from residents. It involves the displacement of numerous people and a redesign of the neighborhood that would destroy the barrio's structural and historical integrity.

YOLANDA: El Paso del Sur formed in May of 2006. The Paso del Norte Group's plan was announced in March of 2006, and everyone was really excited because the way that it was framed. It was going to redevelop downtown, and like so many other cities, our downtown is really vibrant, but it used to be vibrant in a middle-class kind of way. Now it's very vibrant in a working-class way and shoppers from Juárez are the main shoppers. If you go to south El Paso, where the bridges are, you see thousands of people every day crossing to go shopping in downtown. So a lot of stores sell very inexpensive goods. There's a growing Korean business community here the past twenty-five years.

LOUIS: *What makes it affordable to come shopping here, as opposed to over there?*

YOLANDA: It's specialty items, but also it's regular things. When I walk across to Juárez, there's always families carrying like a hundred toilet paper rolls, and then stuff like electronics. All that stuff is much cheaper here.

Yolanda Chávez Leyva, Professor of History, University of Texas-El Paso.
Photo provided by Yolanda Chávez Leyva.

And the clothing in downtown is super cheap. So there was this big deal about "we were going to redevelop downtown, put money in downtown." But once David Romo started to investigate it, because he's done a lot of journalistic work, he discovered a map that was marked "Not for Distribution." He wrote a newspaper article for the alternative online newspaper, the *Newspaper Tree*, and it's called "Not for Distribution." He was really shocked to find out the real plan for El Segundo, which was to build condos, to build very luxurious kinds of stores, and to put a Wal-Mart and a *mercado*. It's the same old story of wanting to displace a living community and sell the culture. Just like Olvera Street in the '30s. Once that got out a few of us historians said we have to do something, we can't let this just happen.

We got together, and we drew in artists, lawyers, activists, the director of the Farmworker Center, and we started meeting and trying to figure out what to do. Our demand has always been to scrap the whole plan and to start over with input from people in El Segundo because people in El Segundo have not had input. In the summer of last year, what the city did as public input was to have a series of meetings. This is how disrespectful the city is . . . they had tables with games, and each game board represented a certain street in El Segundo. Each group could decide what to put on these streets, as if people weren't already living there, as if it was just empty land. There were no people from El Segundo there. It's such a huge conflict of interest with Robert O'Rourke, who's the city councilman that represents El Segundo being the son-in-law of the developer behind the plan. The ethics board said, "There's no conflict of interest there." Now he's started to recuse himself from any votes having to do with the plan, but what that means then is that El Segundo doesn't have anyone speaking on their behalf.

LOUIS: What was their time line for implementing this?

YOLANDA: They passed the plan Halloween of last year, and Paso del Norte, which is the group of businessmen, developers, civic leaders, and politicians behind the plan, they started buying buildings in downtown. It goes way beyond just El Segundo. The developer, Bill Sanders, is the founder of a company called the Verde Group. They have a plan to do binational development all the way from San Diego/Tijuana down to Brownsville/Matamoros, and they have this map where they're going to develop both sides of the border with Mexican businessmen. The Verde Group wants to redevelop El Segundo and also downtown Juárez. But in New Mexico, in Santa Teresa, which was a very small community, they have a plan to build a big city at Santa Teresa and connect it to a development that's called San Gerónimo, which is empty right now. They're working with millionaire Mexican businessmen, and the Verde Group has offered to build the international crossing privately. That's how much they want to do this. But in between Santa Teresa and San Gerónimo is the neighborhood of Lomas de Poleo. That's why Lomas de Poleo is suddenly something that they want. Most people, if they've heard of Lomas de Poleo, they've heard of it because of the femicides, because that's one of the areas where lots of women have been found [dead]. When I look at it chronologically, when the women started to be found in Lomas de Poleo was the same time that they started to try to take the land from the people in the early '90s. To me there's some connection.

LOUIS: Why pick a spot like that, or even El Segundo? Is it because it's central?

YOLANDA: Lomas de Poleo is on the periphery. There's not an infrastructure that can be used as a foundation, but it's the proximity to Santa Teresa, New Mexico. Sanders owns Santa Teresa. And in his plans to develop that area, he's even gotten incredible water rights from Bill Richardson [then-governor of New Mexico]. The things that are happening at Lomas de Poleo have been happening for four years. Under Mexican law, if you go live on a piece of a land and you're actually living there and developing it, and no one comes and tells you, "Get off, it's my land," after five years you have legal claim to it. That's how Lomas de Poleo is. They even got permission from the Zaragoza older generation to be there. In the early '90s, the Zaragoza family, which is one of the richest families in northern Mexico, decided that they wanted the land back, but the courts keep ruling on the side of the residents of Lomas de Poleo. What's happened in the past four years is that the violence against the residents has gotten stronger and stronger to try to force them off the land. They put a barbwire fence around it so when you go to work or you come back you have to go through a gate where there are armed guards pointing guns at you. It's that level of intimidation.

Initially the guards were there to scare people. Then they started to bulldoze the homes while people were gone. You go to work, and you come back and your home is demolished. Then they started using arson, and two little girls got killed in one of the houses that were burned. A couple of years ago they actually beat one of the activists to death with machetes and shovels. On Monday of last week, a professor from Juárez took forty of his students, and they were going to meet outside the fence, and they attacked them, including a pregnant woman. They're hiring lots of gang members to do this stuff. When the house burned down with the two little girls in it, the police said it was an electrical short, but the Zaragoza family had already taken the electricity out, so there is no electricity there. They literally took the poles, the wiring. They de-electrified the place. The mayor of Juárez was connected to them business-wise. So he was saying, "Oh, there's nothing wrong."

> LOUIS: *Is there a connection between border security and border development?*

YOLANDA: I think it's definitely connected. The Santa Teresa crossing is connected directly to NAFTA. The guy that owns the land where San Gerónimo will be developed is a guy named Eloy Vallina—he's on the board of Verde Realty, so they're all very connected. He's also the owner of companies that log, including illegally in the Sierra Tarahumara, and they're displacing indigenous people in the Sierra through logging. They're ending up in Juárez, so it's displacing people everywhere.

> LOUIS: *Is there discussion about what's going to happen to people when all this happens?*

YOLANDA: There's no real discussion about what's gonna happen to people. They were talking about tens of thousands of people being displaced, and they're mostly renters, which makes them more vulnerable. In El Segundo it's mostly renters. In Lomas de Poleo it's home owners, people who physically built their homes themselves over time. People are being scared into selling. One of the guys that was a very vocal opponent, he owned a tenement building across from the church, and the only people that lived there were his elderly mother and him. They came and did an inspection and tried to take his mother, saying that it wasn't a good place for her. He's trying to sell it now because they took him out of his home.

LOUIS: *Tell me about the historic quarters of El Segundo.*

YOLANDA: Rudy Acuña [renowned Chicano historian] was here giving a talk a couple of weeks ago, and I was telling him about this. He said that to him El Segundo represented the heart and the soul of Chicanos all over the U.S. To me that's true on one level. For most of the twentieth century El Paso was the largest port of entry for *mexicanos*. Families all over the U.S. trace their U.S. roots back to El Segundo, because it's always been a place where people come and stay for a little while and then move someplace else. It's a very historic barrio in terms of immigration, in terms of *mexicanos* all over the U.S. A lot of the buildings here are very connected to the Mexican Revolution and to the pachuco era. Lots of people were born there that were poets out of the Chicano movement, probably one of the two most well known musicians of the pachuco época, Don Tosti, was born there, so it's produced a lot of people, and to me it's still important as a receiving area for immigrants.

LOUIS: *How big an area is it geographically?*

YOLANDA: The part that they want to demolish is 160 acres. Downtown and El Segundo are separated by one major street; they're contiguous. They're trying to make it sound like El Segundo is downtown. They are doing interesting things with words. Last fall the city came out with this thing about, "We're not demolishing anything in El Segundo." That's because they renamed the part of El Segundo that they're gonna demolish as not being El Segundo. They started to call it the Golden Horseshoe. Golden in terms of profits, 'cause the shoppers from Juárez will go down this street and then turn back and shop going back, so they're like, "We're not demolishing El Segundo; we're rebuilding the Golden Horseshoe." It was never called that before the city decided to call it that.

LOUIS: *Are they trying to seduce a new class of shoppers?*

YOLANDA: The Wal-Mart makes sense to me because it would be right on the border. But I've never been able to imagine who they think is gonna go shopping at these luxury stores they want to build. El Paso wants to be a tourist town. El Paso always talks about, "We want to be like San Antonio." That was the justification for putting the forty-foot conquistador statue at the airport, to draw tourists . . . somehow. [Laughs] That's why as part of this development plan they want to do the *mercado* to sell arts and crafts. The businessmen in Juárez didn't like the idea of the *mercado* too much—"Who would come to a fake *mercado*? Just come to Juárez, and come to a real *mercado*." And they want to do this mixed-use housing. They're trying to do what they've done in other cities, build condos.

> LOUIS: *So have y'all had any luck getting residents in El Segundo involved in all of this?*

YOLANDA: Yeah, but it's been a difficult thing for obvious reasons. *Pues* people are scared. People don't trust the city. People don't think they can affect the city in any way. The main medical provider in El Segundo is part of the downtown plan, and people have been denied medical care for vocally opposing the plan. They have a lot to lose if they're involved. But people are against it if you talk to people. I've talked to hundreds of people in El Segundo. There's a lot of absentee landlords. The city has never really enforced housing laws in El Segundo, but now the city is saying, "Look at this crummy housing." But the people who are home owners, there's multigenerational families there, they're very scared. The city's offering them nothing for their homes. In October of 2006 the city agreed not to use eminent domain for two years, so they have a moratorium on eminent domain in that area until 2008.

> LOUIS: *What is the strongest leverage you all have in trying to affect change and policy?*

YOLANDA: The strongest thing we have going is that the city has broken a lot of federal laws. They didn't do an environmental study. The city has done a lot of things without following procedures.

> LOUIS: *What does the rest of the city think about this?*

YOLANDA: Many people I've spoken to base their opinions just on what the media reports. They think it's going to be a great thing, because it's presented as a great thing: "We're going to build better housing for the people, we're going to develop downtown like it used to be." They think the people of El Segundo are going to be helped. Last year the city hired people from the clinic to do surveys in El Segundo to see if they wanted the development plan. They would ask, "Wouldn't you like a better house with a swimming pool?" And the people were like, "Yeah, we would." And they would come back and say, "People want this plan." We will probably have to resort to legal action. The media and the city council are connected to the developers.

LOUIS: Has El Paso del Sur tried to broaden its base of support through public events?

YOLANDA: We held public events in El Segundo all last year and at the beginning of this year. We've been holding events at UTEP [University of Texas at El Paso] organized by the students, a series of gatherings called Communities Under Siege. We had speakers and films. We had a big forum that brought people from Lomas de Poleo and the people from El Segundo together. We've been trying to educate people about what's really happening, and I think that it's beginning to work. We had two hundred people on Monday, which was a great crowd.

LOUIS: Have there been any efforts to actually meet with the people behind the plans?

YOLANDA: The developers don't want to talk to us. Early last summer, during the whole game playing meeting time, the mayor tried to meet with us separately and the city council tried to meet with us separately, and during one of these public meetings, the mayor came up to David and me and said, "What if I took El Segundo off the table?" A reporter was standing near us, so he reported, "El Paso del Sur has met with the mayor." Which made everyone not trust us. All they do is lie. Our whole thing is for the people who are being affected to have a voice, not for us to have a voice. It's been very discouraging. The only media that covers it and tells the other side has been the Spanish-language newspaper in El Paso.

LOUIS: How do the debates on immigration manifest themselves here?

YOLANDA: In very interesting ways, with people with Spanish surnames talking about, "Keep those people out." El Paso is one of the safest cities of its size in the U.S., which it's really proud of. I think part of it has to do with the fact that we're under the surveillance of so many levels of law enforcement here. For instance, the *migra*'s very visible on campus. What I see are both extremes in El Paso of people who are very sensitive to immigration issues, and sensitive because they're immigrants or their parents are immigrants. Or the opposite. I had a Chicano student one time tell me, "Mexicans shouldn't be allowed to come to the U.S. anymore." I knew that his parents were immigrants, and I said, "Your parents were immigrants not that long ago." "Yeah, but now that we're here, I don't care about anybody else." Sometimes El Paso can be hyper-patriotic. We're always on the defensive since we're right on the border. Right after 9/11 I was in this immigrant neighborhood, and every house had a million flags. I was very surprised.

LOUIS: Is there no willingness to recognize the cross-border culture and kinship?

YOLANDA: They don't see that at all. We have multiple fences in some parts of El Paso, so it's pretty hard to cross. In the mid-'90s you could cross the river in a little raft within sight of downtown. People would just walk back and forth all day long. It's changed a lot. All the raids that have been going on really trap people in rural communities. There have been workplace raids. They also raided schools recently in Chaparral. There's a lot of *colonias* [unincorporated housing settlements often lacking developed infrastructure] around here, so people get trapped 'cause they can't leave their homes. They don't have access to their jobs; they don't have access to health care.

LOUIS: Is there any discussion over English Only?

YOLANDA: The only places I ever see that English Only stuff is in the newspapers, like letters to the editors that say, "This isn't Mexico!" But in reality, and I've seen it more since I moved back, Spanish is everywhere. When I moved here from San Antonio in 2001, it was a little bit of a culture shock for me because everywhere on campus would be monolingual Spanish.

LOUIS: What's the population here?

YOLANDA: About 700,000. Juárez always used to be the smaller city; now it's over two million. It's the *maquiladoras* [factories] and people being pushed out of their homes to the south because of the effects of NAFTA. Health has gotten worse here. That's connected to NAFTA. El Paso has one of the highest rates of asthma for children in the country because of the trucks going through following NAFTA.

LOUIS: What's the ethnic makeup of the city council?

YOLANDA: The city council is about half Mexican American. But it doesn't seem to matter. We had Raymond Telles back in the '50s, and that was amazing to have him as mayor. We've had a few, but like I tell you, ethnicity has not made much of a difference in local politics.

Cecilia Brennan is a lawyer who had recently moved from Los Angeles to Escondido. She joined a group of us for dinner to share insights on some of the work she's done on a pro bono basis with her firm to help challenge a local anti-immigrant ordinance. The week I was in Southern California, Escondido was in the news for attempting to pass laws targeting day laborers.[3]

CECILIA: I was an organizer in L.A. for many years doing work in Pico Union, which is in Mid-City, Los Angeles, and is comprised of mostly Salvadoran, Guatemalan, Honduran, and Nicaraguan folks. I worked with projects like CARECEN [Central American Resource Center] and El Rescate and was running youth programs and doing juvenile justice and immigration-related organizing with that community. The folks I was meeting were all Central Americans fleeing from civil war that was basically funded by the U.S. government. There was a large need for juvenile justice–related work in that community. What would happen was that the kids I was working with, from ages five to up to eighteen, right around junior high, would start getting into gang affiliations, just hanging out in the streets. Law enforcement in Pico Union—the LAPD's Rampart Division, which is infamous for all kinds of police brutality and corruption—found it was cheaper to deport kids rather than to prosecute them for criminal charges, because there was no minimum age for deportation. A lot of the kids we were working with started getting deported for just being accused of being gang members but with no real criminal charges. There was a group called Homies Unidos, founded by Magdaleno Rosas, who used to head Amnesty International, that worked a lot in that neighborhood. There was a guy named Alex Sánchez, who was an ex–gang member from MS [Mara Salvatrucha], I believe,

Attorney Cecilia Brennan at a social gathering in San Diego, California.
Photo by Louis Mendoza.

and he started doing all this organizing around these kind of issues. What Homies did was create a safe house in San Salvador because a lot of the really young kids who were Salvadoran were getting deported without even a nickel in their pocket and had no family to go back to in El Salvador. This was around the mid-'90s, '94–'95. This kind of thing was increasing and increasing toward the late '90s. And also you have to remember California passed Props. 187 and 209 and similar discriminatory legislation.[4]

So the work that Homies was doing was important. In '99 there was a statewide initiative called Prop. 21 that was passed and wasn't challenged on constitutional grounds like 187 was. Prop. 21 basically turned regular youth into gang members; for example, if you're walking in groups of three or more, with the same dress, talking the same, they can put you in the gang database and then profile you accordingly.

LOUIS: *It initiated a dossier-building cycle?*

CECILIA: Basically, yeah. Those were the immigration issues I was looking at—how it affects youth and this crossover with why people are coming here after U.S. imperialistic ventures in Central America. Then I went to law school. I had graduated from college in 1994. I was doing housing rights work with the same community because the Staples Center [sports and entertainment venue in downtown L.A.] controversy was part of resisting gentrification. There is a lot of criminalization of young people, and immigration stuff comes to play when communities are getting gentrified. In this area called the "Figueroa Corridor," between USC [University of Southern California] and the Staples Center, I worked with an organization called Strategic Actions for a Just Economy, trying to prevent this whole push of gentrification in the neighborhood and criminalizing youth.

> LOUIS: *So how does that intersect with immigration in that setting? Because they want to clean up the area, and these people are considered undesirables?*

CECILIA: Exactly. This relates to the ordinance in Escondido. Basically, it says that if you're a landlord and you're renting to folks that are undocumented, you can be criminally charged, and you can also get fined for civil law violations.

There was a report by a handful of Chicano academics that came out of Cal State [University], San Marcos, saying that immigrants are exploited in the housing context because they don't speak up as much about landlord-tenant issues because of their immigration status. The city of Escondido took the language in that report, and they say, "Oh, immigrants equal blight." So they use that report as the crux of their whole argument that the city of Escondido is under siege from immigrants, and to improve the whole city we're going to pass this ordinance.

After law school I ended up interviewing at this really small plaintiff-side consumer law firm. The day of my interview the firm got a call from the ACLU [American Civil Liberties Union] and MALDEF [Mexican American Legal Defense Fund] about taking on a housing rights case that's a crossover with immigration rights, similar to what was going on in Hazelton, Pennsylvania. The firm asked me if I was interested in working on the case and offered me the job. So I took the job for that. We put together a bunch of accessible information for people in the community.

> LOUIS: *Did Escondido model their ordinance after Hazelton's?*

CECILIA: Yeah, they're all copycats. In the end the federal court judge agreed with us and found that their proposal was unconstitutional. We took the case pro bono. It was a crossover between an individual and class case. The day laborer issue will be next. There's a kit that came out through the ACLU; it includes Hazelton's ordinance and others and the responses and briefs that were written.

LOUIS: Do you expect to see new anti-immigrant efforts keep popping up until some precedent is set that shuts them down?

CECILIA: I think so, sadly. I think that the main thing is that there's this whole rhetoric around localities saying that the feds aren't doing enough. It's so tied to these vigilante Minutemen. There are a bunch of Minutemen in Escondido and North County, and it seems like they've got the ear of elected officials. I think that part of their strategy is that even if the laws don't pass, they want to make it a very uncomfortable place for Latinos to live. And what happened in Escondido is that there were raids all over the place, like in swap meets.

ANTONIO DÍAZ,
OSCAR GRANDE, AND
TERESA ALMAGUER

Antonio Díaz and I were fellow students in the late 1980s at the University of Texas at Austin. He was a cofounder of PODER (People Organized in Defense of Earth and Her Resources) in Austin, an environmental justice organization. In the mid-1990s he moved to the Bay Area where he began working with another organization called PODER (People Organizing to Demand Environmental & Economic Rights), a grassroots organization based in the Mission District that despite sharing the same acronym is not related to the Austin group. Members work with Mission residents to find local solutions to issues facing low-income communities and communities of color. Antonio was my host when I was in Oakland. We met at the PODER offices with the other full-time staff members, Teresa Almaguer and Oscar Grande, who also participated in the interview.

ANTONIO: I met staff from PODER [San Francisco] back in 1991 at this national conference in Washington, D.C., the first people's environmental leadership seminar, and by that point we had started PODER in Austin. I was happy to realize that we were working with an organization that had the same acronym. We kept in touch over the years, primarily through the Southwest Network that they are a part of, and so when we moved out here in 1995 we looked up the folks. I was first asked to be on the board. Then I became a staff person in 1998 and made a connection through the environmental justice work, having done similar work in Texas.

OSCAR: I am the organizer, coming up on my ninth year at the organization. I was born and raised in San Francisco, in the Excelsior District, and I feel like the Mission District is my second home. My family comes from El Salvador, immigrated over here in the late '60s. My brothers and sisters,

The staff of PODER in their office in the Mission District, San Francisco. Left to right: Antonio Díaz, Oscar Grande, Teresa Almaguer. Photo from PODER files.

except for one brother, are all over here, and most of my family is in El Salvador. I got my first taste of activism doing gang prevention work, case management work, tutoring local high schools, and all that. It felt very, very stifling, like you were spinning your wheels and you were not getting anywhere. For every one success story, there were thirty, forty, fifty young people out there with no opportunities or resources to get out of the different situations that our community finds ourselves in. Some of the work that I do here at PODER has really been focused around project issues, displacement issues. We have been engaged actively in anti-displacement work since '98. I would say all the work we do could be lumped and categorized into anti-displacement from our first battle around trying to get a ground field site cleaned up and turned into a park, which was started in the mid-'90s and culminated in 2001 with the building of this beautiful park, the park that we actually use to organize out of. We had our Fiesta Navideña (Christmas party) this past Friday. There are just so few places we can get together and celebrate our culture, or get together for a meeting and figure out what we are going to do in the community. How are we going to improve it? How are we going to demand our rights? A lot of our work around anti-displacement is long-term, looking toward not just today, tomorrow, next week, but looking ten years, twenty years down the line, looking at city maps, city spaces that we can claim for affordable housing, locally owned mom-and-pop businesses, spaces for community services. In the short term what I think has gotten us a lot of visibility and a lot of trust in the neighborhood has really been our more short-term, kind of reactive work. But we have been vigilant around fighting for people's homes and businesses. Out here we have had a huge turnover in terms of evictions of residents, small businesses, primarily Latino immigrant homes. A lot of these business owners have invested all of their life savings into it or are living on month-to-month leases.

A lot of these landowners are just holding out for the next best thing. There is no security there. There is no way to plan for the future in terms of keeping the neighborhood sustainable; it feels like they are on borrowed time. So it has been our vigilance, in terms of fighting evictions and stopping development projects, that is going to impact the neighborhood. This neighborhood has been ravaged by condo development. Condos costing half a million to a million dollars; these are not for our community. Our community was built with blood, sweat, and tears when there weren't any resources, when those community development and housing resources weren't necessarily coming into the neighborhood. The neighborhood community resisted, and it was built off of the sweat of the community members. We are looking at trying to fight some of these. Sometimes we are faced with questions like, Do we get concessions? Do we mitigate a bad project, or do we just outright stop it? Because in stopping it, it is hard to mitigate. How do you mitigate a million-dollar condo? Its impact far outweighs what we are going to get back, which is usually crumbs, so we have learned a lot in terms of when we first started. Now we are at the point where it is not about community benefits; it is about community control. We would rather fight and stop the project and figure out a way that we can keep that plot of land and if not today or five years or ten years down the road build something that is truly affordable and needed in the neighborhood.

TERESA: My parents are from Mexico, from Jalisco. I have been working at PODER for six years now. I am also from San Francisco. The point when I started to become more involved was around Proposition 187. There was a big student movement revolving around calling out that proposition as being racist. I started doing some organizing work at St. Peter's Church here in the Mission District. From that experience I continued on to do youth organizing, and now I am the youth program coordinator here. Our youth program is called Common Roots. We do it in collaboration with the

Chinese Progressive Association to build more unity and solidarity with another large immigrant community that at the same time experiences a lot of the injustices in the city like us. They experience the same type of work exploitation, the same type of messed up housing conditions. Large parts of these communities also live in southeast San Francisco, where there is the majority of pollution that affects people's health, and it is evident in the numbers of asthma and cancers and different allergies that exist more in southeast San Francisco where we have the sewage plants and the garbage dumps and the factories and server farms [site where a group of networked servers are housed]. It is disproportionately higher there than in other parts of the city.

So some of the things that Common Roots has worked on include creating more awareness and education around environmental racism and how people's health is affected. The youth have created toxic tours of southeast San Francisco—that is what they did last summer—and try to work together to be more critical and figure out what are the things we need to do to create change. We presented to some of the supervisors who are on the Bay Area Quality Management District to show that as immigrant Latino and Chinese communities we are getting sick because all of the burden from the pollution. Other things that the youth program is working on are things like the gang injunction. That was just passed here in the Mission District, but that was instituted in Bayview last year. We work with youth, most of which are either immigrants themselves or sons and daughters of immigrant parents, to learn more about how legislation affects us, where there is police racial profiling and other things that are barriers for Latino youth. Right now the youth are working on creating more awareness in their classrooms.

> LOUIS: *It is pretty unusual to become that involved in high school. What motivated you?*

TERESA: There was a really strong youth movement here in the Bay Area when I was in high school. Most of us were sons and daughters of immigrant families and felt inexperienced. You know, a lot of the racism our parents went through not knowing English or being discriminated against or people taking it into their own hands to enforce 187 even though it was like found unconstitutional and never enforced. I remember at that time there were bus drivers telling people they couldn't get on the bus because they were undocumented. There was just a lot of fear, and so there was a lot of motivation for anger and the need to learn about how negatively these statewide propositions affected us. I think there was also a feeling of support in being able to know folks from other schools and being able to organize walkouts as a group. We ended up organizing a couple of walkouts of high schools, about four thousand or five thousand people, so it was empowering to be able to stand together.

>   LOUIS: *Has PODER evolved over time to do more immigrant community work?*

ANTONIO: In some ways. It is amazing to see the number of organizations and resources that exist in the Bay Area. You can barely walk around the neighborhood without bumping into another nonprofit. There are a lot of community-based, community service organizations. Part of the premise on which we were started goes back to 1991 with the growing recognition of environmental racism and people interested in organizing around environmental justice issues. People felt at the time that there was a lot of service provision, but there was an interest in starting an organization to focus on environmental justice and combining that with organizing that included door-knocking and recruiting members and doing leadership development. That is how the organization got started.

OSCAR: Some of the early founders of the organization actually were trained by the Center for Third World Organizing, so that was their model for starting this organization. The Mission District is the cultural and historical center of the Latino community. A lot of stuff that was happening in the '60s and '70s mainly provided services around unemployment or other social services. It left a legacy of, "Well, we got ours, so we are good." They just made sure these government contracts are coming in, and it kind of created this status quo—don't rock the boat; let's just divvy these services out. It leads to competition, not necessarily with groups like ours since we do organizing, but it also leads to the phenomenon of self-anointed Latino leaders that claim to speak for the whole Latino San Francisco population. It creates some tension, some friction, especially when it comes to electoral stuff. An example is when we are fighting against condo projects where developers and their lawyers have figured out how to pit community against community with the mentality that we can buy these people off by providing reasonable office space, or give jobs or donate money to your organization. And then you have us or other folks on the other side that are fighting against it, saying no, you can't take those perks. We have to be principled; we have to stick together; we have to be unified to get something better. Those dynamics become a sore point between the old guard and the new-school activists.

LOUIS: And the old guard in this case is more vulnerable to being bought out or co-opted?

ANTONIO: There is a generational shift and tensions because of it. A lot of the leadership is coming from the community-based organizations, like the Mission community organizations, MCOs—people that are rooted in their neighborhood, parent leaders in the schools. Secondly, there is this generational shift between the older generation that has been very accommodationist with a lot of the development projects, because most of them come from much larger organizations, get a lot of city funding. Everyone is tied to the status quo. A lot of the pushback against that is from the younger generation of leaders who, in many cases, are with newer organizations.

LOUIS: What are the biggest challenges with community organizing?

TERESA: I think time is always one, because people have multiple jobs in a city that is so expensive to live in.

OSCAR: Just winning the hearts and minds of people is really difficult. We have been grappling with this conversation, how we deepen the involvement of our members to provide more leadership. We have had people involved with the organization for five-plus years that have always kind of stayed in the same place. We will see them at parties and cultural events, but when it comes to political organizing, not so much. A huge challenge as an organizer is to cultivate the next generation of activists, because we tend to rely a lot on the activists we already have, and people get burned out really quick, so it is not sustainable. The other challenge is the organizer's efforts to sustain memberships.

LOUIS: What do you think it would take to really get people to care across the nation?

ANTONIO: Well, I think the national debate on immigration is an issue of political representation and political power. It was interesting in the spring of last year with all the immigrant rights mobilizations that happened across the country, an unprecedented mobilization. You were left with a nagging question: who is the Latino leadership nationally? There really isn't a set of leaders. I don't think it is a bad thing necessarily, because I think, if anything, it shows the power of a grassroots, bottom-up approach, as opposed to a top-down approach, but I think there is some level of building and then flexing that power. We do some Latino voter educational mobilization work, and every year we show the same chart that people of color are the minority. In California, the majority of voters are white folks, and it is the same in San Francisco in the Bay Area, so I think part of it is building the power and flexing it. But I think part of the problem is fear. I think that people do sense this browning of the country, and for many it is a frightening thing. You know, we are no longer the majority. We are not, and we won't be; the numbers will be decreasing. I am assuming that there is some level of fear about what the future means, what this future is going to be fifty, one hundred years down the line. You can see it in the neighborhoods where we work.

TERESA: I think economic opportunities are shrinking, and sometimes I think we get stuck on the whole Latino thing and there isn't enough class analysis. As a country, people are struggling more and getting poorer. There needs to be more discussion around how to incorporate immigrant families who are the economic base of this country.

OSCAR: One of the core pillars of our work is movement building, regional, national, international, but our campaigns are locally based, in neighborhoods. I think that is where a lot of that big national debate is materialized locally. Four or five years ago, we dabbled in it, but seeing the numbers, seeing our voice and our concerns not being represented legislatively, we have really focused a lot of attention, resources, and energy into strengthening that aspect of our work. In the short term there is probably not going to be much gain, but in the long term we are going to keep these decision makers accountable. I am really proud of the work we have been doing because it is all connected. Every issue we are involved in is echoing what is happening nationally, from immigration rights to our rights in the city. Our population is growing, but in older cities like San Francisco, New York, Boston, our people are being pushed out into exurbia where there are very little resources, where we are having to start all over. We are getting pushed out of places where we have invested so much. This is why the environmental justice work we are doing is so important because it expands the definition of environmental injustice. It's land; it's health; it's around all those things being laced together.

> LOUIS: Do you think immigration reform is going to happen, or do
> you think they are just going to keep it in limbo because it is more conve-
> nient to do that?

ANTONIO: I think it says a lot with the Democrats in control that there hasn't been much forward movement; it doesn't bode well for the future.

Once again, special interests are playing out at the national level. I think what is happening at the local level now is going to continue to lead the way. It is not as if any of the candidates have an agenda that is going to provide a path of citizenship for folks. I think what we have been seeing on the environmental end, for example, and we are starting to see with immigration, is that localities and states are starting to come up with ideas on how to deal with the issue. There can be good and bad approaches. I am willing to be convinced otherwise, but it is amazing to me, with the Democrats controlling the Senate and the House, that there wouldn't be more of a conversation about solutions.

FIVE

ASSERTING RIGHTS

THE ULTIMATE MEASURE OF A MAN IS NOT WHERE HE STANDS IN
MOMENTS OF COMFORT AND CONVENIENCE, BUT WHERE HE STANDS
AT TIMES OF CHALLENGE AND CONTROVERSY.

Martin Luther King Jr.

The Latino community's pursuit of social justice within the U.S. can be traced back to the moment they became "foreigners" in their native lands. This endeavor has assumed numerous forms, from armed resistance in the aftermath of territorial conquest to legal advocacy to remove barriers to equal rights in the educational system and the workplace, electoral participation, and community-based advocacy for fundamental respect in their communities as it is manifested in local government services, infrastructure development, and law enforcement.

This chapter begins with the recollection by José Ramón Sánchez of Puerto Ricans' struggles for social justice in New York and how that is manifested in one person's life—from welfare dependency to educational access and involvement in community empowerment struggles during the civil rights movement. As he and others throughout this collection note, being in a position where you have nothing left to lose can function as a springboard for taking risks and challenging institutional barriers. In Sánchez's discussion of the work ethos of new immigrants as it is linked to the pursuit of social mobility and the generational disillusion of Puerto Ricans and Dominicans that occurs in New York bodegas, we gain insight into why many people refer to the contemporary struggle for immigrant rights as the new civil rights movement of our times.

To be sure, many opponents of immigration would disagree by saying that civil rights should be afforded only to those in this country with legal status. Yet as many of those interviewed here make clear, civil rights are human rights, and human rights transcend national boundaries and traditional definitions of citizenship. The right to relocate across national boundaries in search of basic human needs is recognized by the *Universal Declaration of Human Rights*, which was adopted by the General Assembly of the United Nations on December 10, 1948. But in addition to the moral imperative underlying the right to survive is not only a concern about basic human dignity but also a keen awareness that immigrants are integral to the economic and social fabric of the U.S. This is a perspective not shared, of course, by opponents of immigration, who frame the issue exclusively as one of national sovereignty and security and thus declare that undocumented immigrants, "illegals," are beyond the scope of legal protection.

The interviews in this chapter revolve around the pursuit of basic rights in multiple contexts—from the fields of North Carolina, where migrant workers are changing assumptions about race and workers' rights, to the U.S.-Mexico border, where people are demanding basic infrastructure and legal protection, to Southern California, where ethical and spiritual notions regarding the sanctity of human life inspire the work of the Border Angels and others. These advocates also discuss the importance of sustained involvement, no matter how great the odds, and the media as a battleground for the hearts and minds of the American people.

I met José Ramón Sánchez at his office at Long Island University, where he is a professor of political science and the director of Urban Studies. We had met briefly a few years before when I was in New York with a mutual friend, Rodolfo Rosales. José's book, *Boricua Power*, relates his experiences fighting for educational opportunities and social justice during the civil rights era.[1] His story is both exemplary and representative of Latinos of his generation.

JOSÉ: I'm Dominican and Puerto Rican. My mother's side decided to leave the country during the Trujillo years because of the dictator's brother, Petan [José Arismendy Trujillo Molina], who ruled locally. Whenever Petan got interested in a property it was just a matter of time before he got it. My grandfather had died, and my grandmother had found out from other people that Petan had an interest in her property. My grandmother had three sons and five daughters, and she knew that when Petan came calling her sons were going to have to stand up just as a matter of pride and Petan would kill them. She began preparing to leave and sent her oldest daughter here. My *tía* Celeste worked in a beauty parlor in New York and made enough money to send for each of her siblings. Finally all of them made it here, including my grandmother.

My mother was the black sheep of the family. She always seemed to get into trouble. She never really got along with her family. My mother moved around a lot in New York because she wanted to get away from her family and because they always had bad things to say about her. At one point she got involved with this guy, and she had two more kids—my brother and sister. My youngest sister was born with Down's syndrome. My mother worked as a seamstress in the factories in New York. But once my sister was born, she had to dedicate herself to taking care of her. My sister was very tender

José Ramón Sánchez in the courtyard of Long Island University, New York.
Photo by Louis Mendoza.

and at risk of dying at any time. Once my mother stopped working we had to go on welfare. The rest of the family didn't like it, but that was what she had to do.

I don't know if you are familiar with this or not, but a lot of Dominican and Puerto Rican women go through something called *ataques*—a kind of breakdown. Anthropologists who study this say it is a way for women who are generally overworked and submissive to assert themselves. The whole family rallies around them, cooks and cleans. They stay in bed and are taken care of. So my mother had many *ataques*. Since she was in this country and estranged from her family, the medical system became involved. After one major *ataque*, she was institutionalized. They gave her shock treatments. It was pretty bad.

Although we were on welfare, my mother tried to make more money to improve our lives. She picked up bags of sewn gloves from a factory. She would sew on the fingers. My sister and I would turn them inside out. But she got into a feud with someone at the factory. This person told the welfare authorities. The piecework was illegal if you receive welfare. So they knocked us off welfare. I was already having problems in school. We were moving around a lot, eventually ending up in a place called East New York, Brooklyn. I had to fight my way through each school. In every new school you have to establish yourself. I always fought back, gained a reputation and respect as a fighter. The fighting doesn't stop though. Guys come after you seeking to establish their own reputation. I got tired of it. I was playing hooky almost every day. My mother was telling me, "Why don't you drop out?" School authorities knocked on her door all the time asking, "Why isn't your kid in school?"

At one point I applied to a school called Brooklyn Tech, but I got rejected. I always wanted to be an engineer. I wanted to build an apartment building where all my family could live, my cousins and my uncles. The whole thing about *familia*. I had dreams about this. I wanted to make a structure where instead of elevators there would be a little train inside the walls that would take everyone to their apartments. [Laughs] So stupid, but I was a kid. So you could apply to Brooklyn Tech in the eighth grade and the ninth grade. I applied in the eighth grade and got rejected—my grades weren't good. I didn't score well on the exam. When we lost the apartment and my mother got institutionalized, they put us in the homes of relatives. I ended up living with my aunt Celeste in Corona Queens, a little better barrio. I was in the ninth grade. The school I attended there was safe and good. I started doing a little better. When I saw the notice for Brooklyn Tech, I applied again. This time I got in. I didn't get any smarter. I think it was a combination of things. They accept more kids from that neighborhood, and they were responding to community pressure to admit more minorities into the specialized schools, which were basically all white at the time. When I got to Tech I realized this was my last chance for an education, and I applied myself. Eventually, I had like a 90 percent average. Angelo [Falcón] will tell you—he went to Brooklyn Tech too—I used to read the *New York Times* in the cafeteria. I wanted to catch up so bad for all those years I wasn't in school.

> LOUIS: *You became interested in the world as opposed to the immediacy of your environment?*

JOSÉ: Right. I studied engineering at Tech, and I even played football for a while. Angelo and I started an Aspira Club in Brooklyn. Aspira was a nonprofit dedicated to helping Puerto Ricans and Latinos make it through school. Their innovative idea was to create student Aspira clubs at each high school. So Angelo and I got a club going at Brooklyn Tech. We created a newsletter and started causing trouble. At one point, we wrote about racism at Tech, and they banned the newsletter. Mostly it was because of an article I wrote called "Juan the Cockroach." It was a silly parody about how Latinos come here only to get the national "boot" from the gringos, whether it's the school or the police or whatever. We protested the banning, and eventually the newsletter got reinstated. I enjoyed all of that.

In general, we felt marginalized. There were six thousand boys—it was all boys—and forty Latinos. It was run like a military school. It was a microcosm of larger society. The good thing was that we gained confidence and skills, mostly from Aspira, and never stopped trying to change things. When I was a child I used to go with my mother to the welfare center to translate for her because she couldn't speak English, and I saw the way we were treated. Each time we would spend more than ten hours there; we'd go at 7:00 in the morning and they wouldn't see us until 6:00 P.M. Then it was like, "Come back tomorrow." This experience gave me a deep sense of the nature of social injustice. I felt the disrespect in my bones.

I remember my first day in school in this country. Someone motioned for me to stand in line. I didn't know what they were saying. I didn't know any English. Some kid came up to me; I don't know what he said. The next thing I know, he punched me in the stomach. [Laughter and exclamations] This kid was beating me up, and I had no idea why. So I learned very early that there was a lot to be afraid of in this country. Back in my own country dangerous things also existed, but overall you felt safe. You felt people were going to look out for you. But in this country there was constant trepidation, like something was about to happen. People looked at you with menace.

LOUIS: *You felt like an outsider?*

JOSÉ: Outsider but also like we were under the microscope. People gave you the evil eye. The welfare experience really solidified that feeling. I even felt it in church. I stopped going to church when I was nine. My mother sent us to church, but I would take my siblings and go play. You know why we did that? Two reasons. I told my sister and brother: first, my mother sent us to church, but she didn't go. Second, it's supposed to be the place where God lives, but everybody treats us like we don't belong because we didn't have the nicest clothes and we didn't have the money to put in the collection plate. Something was wrong with that picture. So I stopped going, and my mother never knew. She would send us to church and then go back to sleep. [Laughs] It was probably her depression, though; she was living this outcast life. She felt really down, and she wanted for us to be better so she sent us to church. But I wasn't having any of that.

I give her credit for always giving me a sense that there was always some way you could make yourself better, you know, even if only a little bit. She was always looking for a better apartment. We would be like, "Mom, why are we moving? "Porque es mejor. It's got a radiator, you know?" The thing about being poor—and I tell this to my students—the deprivation is not the worse part. It's the isolation—the sense that you are not really part of the world; that things are happening but you are not part of it. No one cares what happens to you, and your world is so small. I vowed that when I got older I was going to do a lot of big things. That is probably why I wanted to go to Brooklyn Tech. It was a chance to do something in the world.

> LOUIS: *So did you grow up with a sense of dual identity, Dominican and Puerto Rican?*

JOSÉ: No, mostly PR. There were not very many Dominicans around. I grew up listening to Jíbaro music [traditional working-class folk music]. One neighbor played Jíbaro music on his guitar. We were there all the time because his lady baby-sat us. Another was a *bolitero*, a guy who plays the numbers.

> LOUIS: *When you were finishing high school, did you have plans?*

JOSÉ: I still wanted to be an engineer. I majored in the structural engineering program at Tech. I even became foreman of the structural shop. When it came time to apply to college I wanted engineering schools. Then I heard about all the strikes and demonstrations at Columbia U., and I knew I wanted to go there. Angelo told me he was going there, so I thought, "Let's check it out." I went to my guidance counselor and said, "I've applied to NYU and City College, and I also want to apply to Columbia," and he said, "No, I'm not going to submit your application to Columbia." I said "Why?" and he said, "You're not going to make it." I guess part of my experience is that I don't always obey authority. So I said, "I'm not going to listen to this guy." I talked to his boss. I said, "Look, I want to apply to Columbia. I want to submit my application." He approved it, mostly because he knew I was involved with Aspira. I got accepted to Columbia Engineering. Angelo went to the college. We joined a Latino club there called LASO—Latin American Student Organization. We did a lot of stuff. We organized a Latino recruitment program, a Latino radio show, and a Young Lords Conference. We took over buildings a couple times to advocate for Latino studies and faculty; there was no Latino faculty there at all.

We tried to create a Latino Studies Center. One time we took over a university building. It was one of the longest building occupations in the U.S. We stayed there for about a month. I was a sophomore then, and what was funny is that they tricked us to get us out. We had all these community organizations like the Young Lords helping us. They gave us food and security. The university didn't know what to do. They were afraid if they just threw us out there'd be a riot. So they contacted police headquarters. This Puerto Rican detective I met last year—he's retired from the police now and is a public relations guy—told me what happened. He said, "I went to go see the president of Columbia, this guy William McGill, who asked, 'How are we going to negotiate with them to get them out?' He said, 'Look, you are not going to negotiate with them. You are going to arrest them.' He said, 'We are not going to arrest them—that would start a riot.' He said, 'No, no. We are going to pretend they are under arrest. Then once we get them with their hands up and off the campus, we'll send them home.'" That's exactly what they did. We came out with our hands over our heads. We thought we could make a statement if they arrested fifty Latinos. They took us off campus, had all these police cars there with lights on, and they sent us home. Angelo got quoted in one of the newspapers: "We got faked out." That was the big quote: "Students got faked out." That was like '71. They won that battle. But we kept on fighting. We went back to classes and all, and they were a little afraid of us. Later, when I was ready to apply for grad school, the dean said, "Don't apply to Columbia. We're not going to accept you." I said, "Fine, I don't want Columbia."

I was also involved with the squatters' movement, an effort to put desperate and poor Latinos into housing. There were a lot of vacant apartments in New York at the time, mostly because landlords abandoned and warehoused apartments, waiting for rents to rise again. Some landlords rented apartments with no intention of maintaining them or paying the bills. After squeezing all they could out of those buildings, landlords would evict everybody and leave the buildings empty. The housing group I got involved with would locate empty, warehoused buildings. They would secretly bring them up to code. Then they would sneak families into the buildings, making them squatters. I was one of maybe two or three Latinos involved with this group. The others were all white Americans. I showed up one warm August night, and they said, "José, we're going to take the 11th Street buildings tonight, and we want you to lead the families." And I said "Me? I'm only nineteen years old." But they said, "You are the only one who can speak Spanish." They had learned that the authorities had been tipped off to our plans. We had to take the buildings then. They were afraid that if we waited any longer the authorities would put special protection around the buildings. We gathered about fifty Latino families who wanted these units.

So we are walking up Amsterdam Avenue toward these buildings that were owned by St. John the Divine. We had picked these buildings for three reasons: they were vacant, in good condition, and the church owned them. We figured the church would have a hard time kicking us out. As we got closer to the buildings, I saw police cars. They had on riot gear, batons and rifles. I asked the families, "Do you want to go back?" They said, "No, vamos palante. Vamos palante." [We're going forward.] So it's women and kids, right. We get to the first building. And I thought the cops were going to stop us. But when they saw that it was all families, they backed off. Perhaps they were afraid of bad publicity. So I said, "Let's go in." I climbed the stairwell almost to the top, and one of the other organizers who had trailed behind comes into the well and yells, "Hey, José!" I said, "What's going on, man?" and he said, "You went into the wrong building!" [Much laughter] I said, "You're kidding?" He said, "No, it's the one around the corner." So I said, "Tenemos que salir, vamos al otro edificio." [We have to leave, we're going to another building.] And they said, "¿Por qué?" [Why?] They didn't mind when I explained that this one hadn't been hooked up to electricity or plumbing or anything. The cops were shocked to see us leaving the building. They didn't know what to make of it. We were de-squatting. We went around the corner and into the right building. We took over two more buildings a couple weeks later. We made the compound into a kind of revolutionary center with a people's co-op, murals on the walls, and educational classes for the kids. We offered literacy for adults. It was all Latinos.

> LOUIS: *I can't imagine something like that happening now because of the police repression you'd face. What is the difference between then and now?*

JOSÉ: Something in the air, a general defiance in people then. There was the civil rights movement. The Black Panthers, the Brown Berets, the Young Lords fed off each other and gave people not just permission, but examples of how they can take on great powers and make some headway against them. People often think, "I'm not going to do that because what are the chances that we could succeed?" The moments of small victories I experienced is what made me think, "I'm going to give it a shot. What the hell? What's the worst that can happen?" For a period of about fifteen to twenty years, poor people in the city were also able to win small battles. All of these small victories by the poor, by Latinos and others, had repercussions for all organizations.

LOUIS: What did you get your graduate degree in?

JOSÉ: I didn't know if I wanted to go to grad school right out of college. I got a job as a network analyst. Back then it meant working on mainframes doing some of the keyboarding. That job paid me almost a full-time salary for three days a week. So I spent the two other days volunteering. I did a variety of things with no particular plan. I thought the revolution was just around the corner, so I wasn't preparing for a career. At one point, I went to City College and asked, "You guys have a writing center here, do you need a tutor?" They said, "Yeah, we need tutors, but we can't pay you." I said, "You don't need to pay me." I did this for a while, and I enjoyed it, and the students said they got something out of it. I thought, maybe I can teach. So I applied to grad school. Growing up so poor, I hadn't really traveled outside of New York. The farthest I'd been was New Jersey. So I decided to get out of the city.

I visited Chicago—I got accepted there—but I didn't like the university. I visited Ann Arbor and decided to go there. I arrived in August, four days before school began. Didn't have any place to stay. Michigan had an advocacy program for Latinos. This guy Lino ran it. I went to see him, and he gave me $100 and told me to get a place to stay. Through him I met Rudy Rosales. We created a Latino reading and discussion group. We'd go to Rudy's house and talk shit. We'd read and discuss Fanon[2]—stuff they weren't assigning in the classroom. Rudy and a bunch of us also created a Third World Coalition because we wanted the university to create Latino and African American Studies courses. At one point, we had a sit-in in the president's office. It was terrific there, especially with the support we got to do things on our own. Rudy became my big brother. I love him to death. I learned so much just being with him. Rosa, his wife, took her first college class with me. The university finally accepted the idea of a Latino Studies course. It was my second year there. I taught the first Latino Studies course there. It was an eye-opening experience since I'd never really taught a course before. Unfortunately, I didn't finish there.

I ended up at NYU. It was like night and day. I never expected that NYU would treat minority students so poorly. You'd think it would be the opposite—in the middle of New York City. I experienced a lot of racist treatment there. I walked in my first day in a Rousseau seminar, and the professor said, "You are in the wrong class." I said, "I'm registered." And he replied, "You must be in the wrong class." He couldn't imagine a Latino in that class. One time I was assigned to be a TA [teaching assistant] to another faculty who refused to use me. He didn't reject me directly. He said, "You know, I think I can handle this class of fifty-five students myself, but come at midterm and maybe you can do some grading." I had already taught a course and been a TA in Michigan—it's not like I had no experience. This guy just didn't want me near him. I came to see him at midterms, and he said, "Oh, I can handle the grading. Come during finals." My adviser told me not to worry about it. The faculty member was a staunch conservative. My adviser said, "As long as you are getting paid." I already had teaching experience. But what if I hadn't?

LOUIS: *Can you tell me about the changes you've witnessed over time?*

JOSÉ: The '65 immigration laws changed everything. People started coming from other places, and there were more Dominicans, too, especially after the U.S squashed the Dominican Revolution. I tried to get closer to the Dominican community, but by then I was more PR, . . . so I said, "What the hell, I'm gonna just stay with Boricuas [Puerto Ricans]." As other Latinos began to come to New York, I think Puerto Ricans began to feel pressure. They'd been here long enough and still hadn't risen. Every group comes to this country very hopeful. They work really hard. They accept racist and personal abuse. The same thing happened to Dominicans when they first started coming here. They started looking down on Puerto Ricans. Dominicans saw Puerto Ricans on welfare and said, "We're not going to do that. We're not going to be on welfare like those Puerto Ricans." It produced some political conflict as well, since Puerto Rican political leaders also failed to represent Dominicans very well. That was in the '80s.

One of the big transitions was in the bodegas. Puerto Ricans controlled the bodegas from the 1950s until the late 1970s and early 1980s, because they were the new immigrants here. They were pushing hard. The whole family would work there. When Dominicans came here in the '70s, many of them started to replace Puerto Ricans as workers and owners in the bodegas. Partly it was because the second and third generation didn't want to work in the bodega. They didn't have better-paying jobs; they just felt bodega jobs were too demeaning. You work fourteen, fifteen hours; you get robbed; and you get insulted. The second or third generation became more Americanized in their expectations. Sometimes they rejected the school system because it's so racist. But they lacked the skills to succeed in this society. They were not able to get well-paying jobs, but they still rejected the hardships their parents had endured. Now second- and third-generation Dominicans are going through the same experiences. They don't want to work in the bodegas anymore. They are also falling behind in education, jobs, and income. They want what Americans have, but they don't want to go through or don't think they should have to go through the struggles of their parents. If you're an immigrant, you let it roll. You have a job. You had nothing in your country. You don't care about the petty insults and discrimination that come with many jobs here. But once you are second or third generation, you refuse to put up with bullshit.

LOUIS: *Has Latino life worsened or gotten better here in New York?*

JOSÉ: Both. You have more white-collar Latinos; many have been here for a long time. But there are also new immigrant Latinos, especially Mexicans coming here from Puebla and other places. They are not doing very well. Some Latinos who have been here a long time find that space in the barrio is getting tighter. The industrial economy and its low-education jobs are gone. The city has become much more a white-collar professional and low-wage service economy. The immigrants coming here will work in the service economy but not second- or third-generation Latinos. These Latinos are blocked out of the professional economy because they do not have the schooling. As a result, many second- or third-generation Latinos move to Connecticut seeking respect and opportunity. Sometimes they find better jobs and housing. Sometimes they end up on welfare again. Often, they simply re-create a new underclass there.

LOUIS: *Is there a pan-Latino identity here?*

JOSÉ: There is some of that among young people. In fact, I see it with my daughter, who is the host of a TV show called *Latin Nation*.

LOUIS: *Are Latinos considered perpetual outsiders here?*

JOSÉ: Forgotten, more than anything. Almost every issue involving Latinos receives public attention or is defined as a minority or African American issue. Perhaps some of it is our fault. We come in so many different colors. We don't offer a clear sense of who we are as a racial group. Race is as much culture as biology. We seem to gain legitimacy to the extent we can imitate white people. People seem so afraid to stick out their necks. I say go for it. Finishing high school was my big achievement. Everything else is just salsa.

Leticia Zavala, who is with the Farm Labor Organizing Committee (FLOC) in Dudley, North Carolina, spoke to me at the Committee's workers' center, located on an obscure farm road. Though the building is impressive and surrounded by a small community of Latino workers, the battles these workers and union organizers wage against corporate farmers are even more impressive. Leticia Zavala migrated to the U.S. as a farmworker in the mid-1980s with her family. She carried her sixteen-month-old son, Fernando, with her as we spoke. Also accompanying Leticia was Angela, a former farmworker who can best be described as a *madrina* [godmother] to this FLOC office, as the building sits on land she donated and a small Mexican grocery store and restaurant she founded is located across the street.

LOUIS: *How did you come to work with FLOC and live here in North Carolina?*

LETICIA: I've known FLOC since I was a young girl. We came to the country in '86. Originally my family, my grandfather, came over here. We came from Michoacán, and our first real job was in agriculture in Ohio. That's where we met FLOC. We joined the union that same year, and we harvested cucumbers and tomatoes there. Then we would migrate south to Florida to do strawberries and citrus. We did the migrant stream for about twelve years between Florida, Ohio, Michigan, and Pennsylvania. We stopped when I started going to college at Florida. I went to school to study business administration. After that I came back to FLOC, no longer as a member, but as a staff person.

LOUIS: *Are you putting those skills to use?*

LETICIA: Yeah, in our boycotts! When I started organizing we had an office in Florida and an office here, across the street, on Angelita Lane. My job was to follow the migrant streams as an organizer with our members, and some of them were going from North Carolina to Ohio, back down to Florida. I did that for about three years. We had staff in each state. I would migrate along with them, so I would be the constant contact they had. Then we had a boycott against the Mount Olive Pickle Company, and when we won it we ended up winning the first contract for guest workers. We won a contract that covered 8,582 H-2A visa workers in the state,[3] and so we had to decide between keeping our office in Florida or opening one in Mexico in order to be able to administer the seniority piece of the contract. We ended up opening an office in Mexico. Now my migration is mainly between Monterrey and here.

> LOUIS: *Did winning the contract with Mount Olive lay out the plan for H-2A visas?*

LETICIA: During the fight we were trying to organize sixty labor camps that harvested cucumbers for Mount Olive. Half of them were H-2A workers. Half of them were undocumented workers. We were accusing the Mount Olive Pickle Company of exploiting an undocumented labor force, of using smugglers where workers were being indebted and not being allowed to leave. So the Mount Olive Pickle Company joined the Grower's Association, and it gave incentives for workers, for growers, to use H-2A workers instead of using undocumented workers. When it was time to finally talk, there had already been some talks between the Grower's Association and the Mount Olive Pickle Company because the Grower's Association was also getting sued left and right for numerous violations. They ended up both signing a three-party agreement with us. We ended up getting not only those sixty growers, but getting another thousand growers that harvest twenty-seven different crops, including cucumbers.

> LOUIS: *Obviously, there are difficulties organizing when you have H-2A workers and undocumented workers, so where does this victory fit in? Does it create more opportunities for undocumented workers to get H-2A visas?*

LETICIA: Before it would, and then after the 9/11 freakout it was becoming more and more complicated for everybody. This year we started seeing workers getting banned because they were here illegally, so it's not as possible as it used to be. There was one point where they could continue working for the grower, and they could become legal, and they had a lot more wage protection. Under the union we increased their health protection and some other stuff.

LOUIS: Does FLOC have a relationship with undocumented workers?

LETICIA: Yes, 50 percent of our membership is undocumented. In Ohio, almost 100 percent of our membership is undocumented. Here we have about a third.

LOUIS: Are there limits to how you can work with them because of their status?

LETICIA: Yes. We go around the law in everything because farmworkers are exempt from many laws anyways, and then we're in the South and we're new immigrants, and so we have to be creative in the way we organize.

LOUIS: So FLOC's promotion of the use of H-2A's doesn't feel like a tension with undocumented workers?

LETICIA: No, and we don't promote it because both systems are still not the best. But when a company says, "I'm going to offer more for my pickles so that the grower can pay Worker's Comp, free housing, and some of the other things that come along with the H-2A," then we definitely jump on it.

LOUIS: When Baldemar[4] was visiting Minnesota a couple of years ago he was telling us about the worker organizing going on in Mexico. That seems pretty amazing. I've never heard of other people doing that.

LETICIA: With the guest worker contract, it's almost mandatory and natural. We administer the recruitment part of our collective bargaining agreement in Mexico, and then we administer a lot of our Worker's Comp and follow-up in Mexico. So, yeah, we do educational tours in certain parts of the country, and we have our office down there.

LOUIS: How long has FLOC been in North Carolina?

LETICIA: Since '97. Ten years.

LOUIS: And how long from getting here to the Mount Olive victory?

LETICIA: Seven years.

LOUIS: Where do Latinos fit in the old South? It's a very black and white framework for understanding race down here, right? How've they been received?

LETICIA: Not good. When I got here, one of the things that we were working on was forming a black and Latino alliance. We started having Black and Brown Freedom Schools and education on similarities between white and black southern workers and now our immigrant workers. There was a lot of tension with black workers because of new competition on the jobs. A lot of organizing campaigns were x'd out just on the basis of, "Oh, black workers are lazy and Mexicans will take anything." In the fields as well. Agriculture in the South is still considered slave labor, so there's a lot of discrimination. The courts, the schools, just did not know what to do with people who didn't speak their language. I like working in North Carolina because in Florida and some of the states where we have Hispanics for a longer period of time, it's more difficult to organize because the charity system has matured. We can provide some services, but the services come with the struggle. It's not some bread here, some clothes, it goes with the struggle. It's like, "Here's some clothes, but you can't afford clothes 'cause you're working and your boss isn't paying you minimum wage."

> LOUIS: *Who was doing all the farmwork before Latinos started coming here?*

LETICIA: Blacks.

> LOUIS: *And blacks are still a large number of the agriculture workforce?*

LETICIA: Eighty-eight percent of tobacco farmworkers are Mexicans, undocumented farmworkers.

> LOUIS: *So is the perception of displacement real?*

LETICIA: Not in agriculture. There's a displacement in the factories, in textiles, in the packing plants, but not in the fields themselves because nobody wants to do the fields.

> LOUIS: *Does FLOC have a position on immigration reform?*

LETICIA: The big question that we ask is, "Do we support a guest worker program?" We don't. We support organized labor, and if it includes an organized guest worker program, then we support it. We believe in workers. We're fighting for legalization for all, no restrictions, fair protections in labor, and all of that. But we also believe that immigration is not something that should be addressed on its own. It's an economic issue. It's a problem that has been blown up due to the free trade agreements that we've signed, and immigration reform needs to be tied to our free trade agreement. It's not an issue of the U.S. saying, "Oh, we're going to let you come and stay." It's an issue of us recognizing that we're staying.

> *LOUIS: Are more Latinos coming here, or do you think it's reached a plateau?*

LETICIA: We're getting a lot more. We're getting a lot of people who are transferring from California to North Carolina.

> *LOUIS: What is FLOC's agenda right now?*

LETICIA: We recently launched a Tragedy Free Harvest campaign, and then it's evolved around R. J. Reynolds and the tobacco industry. Right now we're making a call for R. J. Reynolds to take responsibility for some of the deaths that are occurring in the tobacco fields and also trying to get some health protections and health benefits for workers who harvest their tobacco.

> *LOUIS: What are the causes of the deaths?*

LETICIA: The heat mainly. Tobacco is one of the most difficult crops in terms of exposure to nicotine. Harvesting tobacco is equivalent to smoking ten packs of cigarettes a day.

> *LOUIS: I had no idea it was an active agent like that in the fields.*

LETICIA: Yep! They're basically sucking it in through their pores while harvesting it.

> *LOUIS: What's the solution for that?*

LETICIA: Protective clothing but also some health benefits because tobacco sickness is something that's not curable. You just have to wait it out. It takes twenty-four hours for nicotine to leave your body, and so it's a day's loss of wages and then Worker's Comp. We have a really hard time processing it through Worker's Comp because it's just a $25 clinic visit. No medicine and stuff, so some other source of funds or something for people who are out on nicotine sickness.

> *LOUIS: Do you think that's going to be a big battle, or are they receptive to it?*

LETICIA: It's R. J. Reynolds! It's tobacco in North Carolina! And I mean right now they're fighting this child healthcare tax, and so it's definitely going to be a big fight. They have a hard time admitting that they kill people with their products. Signing a collective bargaining agreement with workers who are not their employees is another thing.

> *LOUIS: It would be an amazing victory, and it's an amazing challenge to take on. Does FLOC become the place where people gravitate to for a sense of community?*

LETICIA: Yep! We used to be in the store across the street. We used to have Gang Out Fridays when we started getting our name recognized for ganging up on crew leaders on Friday nights because they didn't want to pay their workers. We would ask people to come in on Friday after work, and if there was a worker who came in who said his crew leader did not want to pay him his paycheck, then we would all go and just gang up on him.

> *LOUIS: What did that mean?*

LETICIA: Go, pressure him, hanging around, harass him.

> *LOUIS: And it worked?*

LETICIA: We were recognized for the Gang Out Fridays. But now we have a workers' center where a lot more goes on. They give donations so they can use it for *quinceañeras*. They have their weddings, their baptisms, birthday parties. We do income taxes. We do all sorts of services. We do a lot of education around immigrant rights and police profiling, police corruption.

> *LOUIS: Has there been any harassment by authorities?*

LETICIA: We did have harassment in certain counties when we first got here. We had a wave of police corruption where police were taking money from Hispanics. They would be in a team, and one police officer would just interrogate and scare the heck out of the Latinos or the immigrants and say, "Give me your wallet." They'd get their wallets supposedly to take out their driver's license, but they would take out their money. Or they would be asking them a whole bunch of questions supposedly searching their car, and whatever they would find that was of value, they would take it.

> *LOUIS: Do you think now that you are more organized some of that has stopped?*

LETICIA: Oh, yeah, we got the FBI involved. They've busted some of the police, so there's a lot more awareness about that. Right now we're trying to struggle with this new wave of police enforcing immigration. Luckily we haven't had many takers on those proposals.

LOUIS: What's the state climate for immigration issues?

LETICIA: Immigration issues are political. I say all the time I can deal with racism in the South. It's up front. Here we get it out of people's mouths and stuff. There are people like Elizabeth Dole, our senator, who is anti-immigrant, going all across the state trying to get police departments to start enforcing immigrant law. But at the same time we go to her to see if she's gonna support ag jobs, and she says, "Anything for my farmworkers." So there's that contradiction. It's like the farmworkers are the house slaves here in North Carolina. It's not good.

LOUIS: What do you think the future holds in this state?

LETICIA: Organizing is constant, even if immigration reform passes. There will still be labor issues. We'll be organizing forever as long as there are greedy corporations. But I think the state has really developed into being a pretty respectable state for the work that's going on here, you know? Some counties are growing like five hundred times every year in terms of Latino population, and as long as we have our goals set and don't lose sight of the struggles, then we have got the potential to be a good state to live in.

LOUIS: Do you worry about the next generation's willingness to step up and do organizing?

LETICIA: During the immigration mobilization the youth were the leaders. In agriculture, all of our staff are under thirty. We've always been an organization that believes in family organizing. With our H-2A workers, they're all men, but we make that extra effort to go down to Mexico and talk to the wives and the children in order to make sure that the whole family knows what the union is about and knows how to defend themselves. Not just as a worker who is under a collective bargaining agreement, but a wife who is impacted by her husband being a union member, an H-2A worker who migrates out of Mexico every year. We're unique compared to other unions. You can't just organize the breadwinner. You got to organize their family and their church and their schools. The churches in urban communities are really good. The churches in our rural communities are very anti-FLOC, of course, because the growers are members of their congregations.

LOUIS: Have new churches sprung up, or do people tend to go to the urban areas?

LETICIA: Latino churches are opening. We have a church service here every

Wednesday, Friday, and Saturday. Some Seventh-Day Adventists use our building to worship.

> *LOUIS: Do you think that the majority of your workers still think, "I'm going to come here and work for a while," or do they expect to settle here?*

LETICIA: Our H-2A workers are back and forth. There's a few who use the system to come in and stay, but undocumented workers understand that once they're here, if they're going to make the $5,000 that they spent on the smuggler, then they better plan on staying at least two or three years. Right now we're seeing a lot of families start making plans and arrangements to go back to Mexico. This Saturday we're taking two buses to the Mexican Consulate to register children as Mexican citizens for their dual citizenship just in case.

Elizabeth García is an activist who bases her work in Colonia Cameron Park, just outside of Brownsville, Texas. Elizabeth is an active participant in the No Border Wall Movement coalition being organized in the valley. Originally from Matamoros, Elizabeth has lived in Brownsville for approximately twenty years. She runs Casa Digna and spearheads the Coalition of Amigos in Solidarity and Action (CASA) in conjunction with San Felipe de Jesús Church in Brownsville. She works part-time as coalition organizer for organizations that support *colonia* empowerment.

ELIZABETH: I'm from Matamoros originally. I've been living here for twenty years. My family brought me here when I was fifteen. I came here illegally and stayed until I graduated from high school, and there was nothing for me so I decided to go back to Mexico 'cause I couldn't continue my studies here or get a decent job. I went back and did studies over there, and then I was able to qualify under the Simpson-Rodino amnesty of '86. That's how I got my residency and eventually my naturalized citizenship. In the mid-'80s Brownsville was a very, very hot zone in terms of immigration, because all the Central American people were crossing. Now it's Arizona. I still remember going to what is called *el corralón* [the corral] in Bayview. They started that behind the bridge, the international bridge; there were just tents, hundreds of tents. Some days we would go and visit with the priest that I was working with at the time. We would see 800, 900, 1,000 people in this detention center made up of small little tents. I still remember that it looked like a corral.

There were a lot of people coming from Central America, and at that time the bishop of Brownsville was very supportive of the social Catholic teachings, so he initiated what became very popular at that time, Casa

Elizabeth García, the author, and Leide Martinez at Casa Digna in Colonia Cameron Park outside of Brownsville, Texas. Photo by Kamala Platt.

Romero, which was a refugee center for the immigrants. I was there for a couple of years as a volunteer. I remember there were a lot of people coming from up north, volunteering their time at Casa Romero. At that time I didn't know a single word of English. I remember seeing a lot of gringos and a lot of people from other parts coming to volunteer. And now that I travel a lot and I see people and I tell them I used to work for Casa Romero. "Casa Romero, I used to be there in the mid-'80s." It's a small world. People that do activism, they're interrelated one way or another. My mentor was a priest that came from Panamá in the mid-'80s. He was very good friends with Romero. His bishop got him out of Panamá because he was afraid they were going to do the same with him that they did with Romero.[5] He would give presentations about El Salvador and Panamá, and it was very eye-opening to me. When I was working at Casa Romero I met the parish priest here in San Felipe. I've been working with him for twenty-some years now.

I live near Brownsville in an area called Cameron Park. According to Census 2000, it's the poorest *colonia* in the United States. The per capita income is about $3,000. People just pray that they literally get by day to day. It was very interesting when Father Mike and the brothers [nonordained laypersons who assist primarily in secular affairs] came. This church was a small little church. We went to talk to the city commissioner and the mayor and the county judge, and they said, "You bring us numbers, and then we'll talk. People over there don't vote, so we don't care." They were plain. They said it very clear. So the team said, "Well, let's promote the vote." They went door-to-door, and from 50 votes that came from Cameron Park we went to 500 the first year that we were here. And then we went to 800, and then we promised two thousand [votes] by 2000. All of a sudden the politicians said, "Something's going on there, what can I do for you?" They came to us wanting those votes. We said, "We don't have streets," so they gave us streets. There was no infrastructure whatsoever. There were no schools. When it rained the children would not go to school for five days because the mud would go up to their knees. There was no way to get out of the *colonia*, no way.

First thing was the streets so they could access the outside world. Cameron Park used to have a bad reputation because it was out of the city limits. Nobody cared about the people here. They thought that we were drug dealers or uneducated people. But we started getting infrastructure. We started getting the vote out. All of a sudden came the attention. After getting 2,000 votes we got on the radar screen. Right now we're starting the campaign to get out the vote, 'cause 2008 is going to be very important. We're starting to plan educational meetings about what offices people are running for.

> LOUIS: *Do you think Brownsville's on the radar nationally for politicians other than a place to defend the border?*

ELIZABETH: Even with the border wall, I don't know. I went to a meeting in Seattle, and people don't hear about these issues. That's our challenge. I don't know whether or not we are on the radar on a national level. We want to be, and we're working on it. The No Border Wall group told me this morning that they're thinking of putting an ad in either the *New York Times* or the *Washington Post*. We're using YouTube and the blogs and all that, and that's how we're getting things out, without having to pay that ridiculous amount of money. The border wall is just one issue; the detention centers are another.

> LOUIS: *Is this your job?*

ELIZABETH: I work part-time with a foundation out of Seattle, the Marguerite Casey Foundation. The Rio Grande Valley is one sector here in the southeast Texas region, and there's thirteen organizations that they support financially. They give grants to organizations such as LUPE [La Unión del Pueblo Entero], Proyecto Azteca, Proyecto Digna, Brownsville Community Development Health Center, groups like that. The foundation supports Casa

Digna for them to give voice to low-income families. But they want to create a movement to build a stronger voice 'cause they can see that LUPE is doing their own stuff, and Proyecto Digna is doing their own stuff with their constituency, and now they want to bring them together to create a stronger voice to bring that political platform to 2008. So they hired me to do that, to bring these thirteen organizations together, 'cause they do excellent work on their own, but they cannot tolerate each other. It's a challenge because I've been working with these organizations for many years before, and it's a part-time job. They told me it was a part-time job. I don't believe in part-time jobs anymore [laughter]. And then I do a lot of community organizing. I have my office here, and in the mornings I work for the foundation and the rest of the day I do whatever I need to do. We started a group about four months ago called CASA, Coalition of Amigos in Solidarity and Action.

> LOUIS: *Is CASA an activist group for anything that's needed for the colonia or . . . ?*

ELIZABETH: It's all kinds of issues, but we want to concentrate on immigration issues. CASA has a little project called La Escuelita, and what we wanna do, for example, with all the raids happening is educate people. It's very sad to think about it, but here it's more like when it happens, what are we going to do? Are our people prepared for that? So we're going to have a workshop, *un taller*, to talk about those things. If you're undocumented you need to be thinking that it's not safe anymore. Who's going to take care of your children if you get deported? Give an extra key to your children when they go to school so that when they come back and you're not home because you were deported at least they can go in. Who's gonna be the legal guardian? It's very sad, and people don't want to talk about it, but we have to prepare people and have a practical plan.

> LOUIS: *Rogelio was telling me that there haven't been raids yet, but what's more intense is actually tracking people down in their homes.*

ELIZABETH: That's another thing that's included in that training. If somebody comes to knock at your door, ask who it is. If it's the Border Patrol don't open the door because they cannot force you. Now if you open the door, forget it, 'cause you already let them in and you're gone. People get intimidated, and that's the game of the Border Patrol. If you're prepared, you know what to say.

> LOUIS: *Obviously the issue of immigration has really intensified. What does that mean for Brownsville?*

ELIZABETH: The chamber of commerce is already talking about numbers because this year the sales are going down. They haven't even started the wall, but in some ways it is affecting the economy. It's like a domino effect. It'll affect schools because of taxes. We started the No Border Wall campaign about a year ago, when we first heard that it was coming this way. I had experience with the border wall when I was in Arizona, in San Diego, and Palestine with the border wall there, so I've seen and experienced firsthand the devastating effects of a wall on a community. So I start talking to people. And then I learned of other organizations that were also worried about it. We started forming a movement against the wall, and people are getting very creative in their protests—kayaking the river, doing a human chain, representing the positive way of resolving problems. There was a huge *pachanga* [party], where the bishop for the first time came to our event. It was a historic event because the archdiocese finally said something. Now we're at the stage of figuring out what to do next. The events have been good to raise a lot of awareness and to educate people. Now we're working with this petition of registered voters that are against the wall. With fifteen thousand voters that are against the border wall, maybe somebody will say, "Maybe these people deserve to be listened to."

> *LOUIS: Do you feel that a small community that is otherwise off the radar screen can really make a difference in national policy?*

ELIZABETH: It's very hard, but that's our main goal. Advocacy is not a one-event thing; it's not a six-month thing; it's not one year. It's an ongoing thing, and we need to mobilize people, every day [snaps her fingers]. That's just the way it works. Otherwise you're not going to be successful. We do see small things. Like they said they were going to start the wall here in Brownsville in July. Well, it's already November—and nothing. We've been having a lot of local media covering the events, and we have met with the Border Patrol, and we sent some people to Washington. I went there last year with a group from Arizona advocating for immigration reform. In one week we visited ninety-three offices. I did a little clip of what it is to militarize the border. The last meeting that we had was at [Senator Edward] Kennedy's office. He was not available, so he sent somebody else, and when I was about to show the clip a lady came in. We didn't know who she was. She sat in the back, and she saw the thing, and she was in shock, and she started asking a lot of questions. Later on she told us that she's the one that writes all the policies for Kennedy. She said, "You know this is where you need to bring this, because if you tell us about numbers and percentages and all that, we have that, but those personal stories . . . " This is the first time one guy actually saw how militarized the border looks, and he said, "I had no idea that that was happening." It was a successful presentation because at least an important person got to see the impact of militarizing the border. Every country deserves to protect their borders. I'm not against that; security is a good thing. But it's very different talking about security than militarizing the border.

They don't understand that the border in itself is like another country, and they don't understand the impact that this thing will have on communities here. If we can only get creative there's so many solutions to the issue. The border wall is obviously not one of them. When I was in Arizona I met this family who was a big family, like fifty members, from Chiapas. They had gone to Arizona to cross the border. Some of them got caught by the Border Patrol and sent back, and they were trying and trying to cross. In their process of coming and going, they met this guy from one of the *maquilas* [factories] on the Mexican side in Agua Prieta, Sonora, and the guy began talking to them, learning about their experiences. The guy said, "What else can you do? If you don't go to the States, what else can you do?" "If we can go back home and get the jobs that we used to have before NAFTA, we wouldn't have a need to be here," they said. So they started brainstorming, and then this guy from the *maquila* got a grant from one of the churches 'cause he learned that these people had land in Chiapas, and they were coffee growers, but after NAFTA you know everything went down. So he said, "Maybe we can send you back home. You can work the land. You can do the coffee. You can send it back here to Arizona and Sonora. We can open a small shop to roast the beans and do the packaging and do the marketing, just like Fair Trade coffee, except this is a lot better, because 100 percent of the money stays with the family." Two years later, they have no need to go to *el norte* because they own the company, they do their own marketing, they sell more than they were projecting, and now they can afford to live with dignity.

I know there's people that wanna come no matter what, but the majority moves here because of economic reasons, and if you provide them with a decent job where they can support their families with dignity and give them what they need, I guarantee you they won't need to come. I talked to one guy, and he said, "When we left our homes, we died a little bit leaving our land. We didn't want to leave." That's true for almost everybody. We need to develop creative ways of dealing with the root of the problem, which is economics.

PASO DEL NORTE CIVIL RIGHTS PROJECT STAFF

Briana Stone, Gabby García, Paulina Baca, and Valerie Noce, the deeply committed staff at the Paso del Norte Civil Rights Project, sat down with me in their offices. They spoke about their human rights work in the El Paso area, which involves a range of legal and advocacy services on behalf of individuals. They also spoke about their efforts to effect policy reform, as well as why they do this seemingly endless work.

LOUIS: *What does your family think about you doing this kind of work?*

BRIANA: They support it, but they think I'm nuts. They're very apolitical, and they don't really feel like it's going to make a difference. They support what I do and they understand why, but it's not something that they would ever want to be involved in. They want me to do criminal law and make tons of money.

LOUIS: *And you?*

PAULINA: My story is kind of similar to Gabby's. I was born here in El Paso, but I was raised in Juárez my whole life, until four years ago when I moved here. I started doing this because I grew up in Juárez and I saw horrible things going on there: police brutality, the youth, and the women that they killed in Juárez. I think that's where it all started. I moved here and started going to college, and I majored in political science. I got interested in issues that are of concern to women, and I think that's why I like this job so much. I find it very rewarding.

LOUIS: *It's interesting how many people have this Juárez-El Paso connection. It sort of embodies the old idea of continuity across the border. Do you think that's under danger of being drastically changed with immigration enforcement?*

The staff of Paso del Norte Civil Rights Project, El Paso, Texas, at an organizational fund-raiser. Left to right: Paulina Baca, Briana Stone, Gabriela García, Valerie Noce. Photo from Paso del Norte files.

VALERIE: It's breaking up families. You know, when your mom's deported, and she's forced to sign a voluntary waiver of departure, and you can't see her, it's definitely affecting it. Then that means, who's going to take care of that child now? The mom or dad needs to find jobs in Juárez, and that affects the economy. It's a domino effect.

PAULINA: I think the people in the border have various types of identity. Like for me, I don't feel I'm from Mexico or the United States. I feel like I'm a mixture of both. What happens there affects me here; what happens here affects me there.

LOUIS: What does your family think about you working here?

GABBY: [Slight laughter] Very similar. My family has lived all their life in Mexico. They support what I do, but there's a lot of skepticism: "I like what you do, but it's not going to bring that much change." So it's sad sometimes.

VALERIE: I grew up in Northern California, in the San Francisco suburbs, and then I went to college in Santa Barbara. I studied psychology and Spanish. That's partly why I'm here, because I wanted to be able to use my Spanish. I joined Jesuit Volunteer Corps, and once they heard I knew Spanish, they're like, "Oh, El Paso!" I was like, "Great." I was looking for like a more international experience to broaden my perspective on social issues, and once I heard about this placement I thought it was a good opportunity to learn more about civil rights and give back to the community here.

LOUIS: Has it been what you expected?

VALERIE: I didn't know what to expect. I'm getting deeper and deeper into the issue here, and it's really enlightening. It's hard to go back home, though, 'cause you know you can't understand here unless you come here. I'll try to talk about it with my parents, and I feel like I can only get to a certain point until I'm just like, "You actually have to meet these people that you're hearing about in the news. The news is just showing you one side of things." It's been eye-opening, and it's only been three or four months.

> *LOUIS: What kinds of cases do you take on here?*

BRIANA: Well, we're the only civil rights staffed office in town that does litigation. We're the only place to call. [Slight laughter] Whenever you read the papers, something's going on. A lot of times we'll just call the reporter and say, "Can you give me that family's number?" Mostly it comes to us. Every once in a while we do track it down, but you can't get away from it really.

VALERIE: Now that there's connection with other community organizations, they'll call us and say, "Hey, we have this family here. This happened to the dad. Is this something you can help out with?" And if it is, then they'll call and do an intake with us.

> *LOUIS: Do you think that when a policy is getting enforced in a way that's violating people's civil rights that it's intentional? Or is it bad implementation?*

BRIANA: We see a range of situations. I think that a lot of problems that we see stem from a lack of training. And that has to do with things related to immigration enforcement, but it's also related to all kinds of other things. Police brutality is another major issue that we try to confront, and a lot of times the department doesn't properly train their officers. They think they're doing the right thing, and they have no idea that there are these limits on their authority. I really think that that comes into play with the immigration enforcement issue as well and just civil rights generally. Civil rights, human rights, police department, sheriff departments in Texas, New Mexico, and I venture to say the country, they don't properly train their officers on the limits of their authority and on their obligations under the law when it comes to those issues. It's like, "We'll do what we're doing until we get caught, and then we might talk." And then you have to eke out this kind of small little victory in a policy change. The ideal would be that because they take this oath to uphold and protect these rights and because this is the foundation of what we agree to here in the United States, then that would be a primary part of their training, and it would be a thorough and important part. But what you see most of the time, not all the time but mostly, is that what happens with law enforcement agencies when it comes to immigration enforcement and civil rights generally, they'll go through the Bill of Rights, "the Fourth Amendment says . . . blah, blah, blah," and then they might do one hypothetical, and that's kind of the extent of it. And then they have it on a CD-ROM should you want you want to refer to it in the future. And you know from teaching that that is not the kind of in-depth discussion that will lead to a really rich understanding of human rights and civil rights and how it comes into play in the field. Some of those moments are really heated, and if you don't have that really rich understanding it's all for naught. So I think there's that, but to be honest there are really awful people running departments and in power all over Texas and all over the country, and there are times when I really believe that they're not kidding, they mean that, what they're saying and what they're doing. They're happy to be able to do it until somebody will stop them.

PAULINA: Here we have a big immigrant community. Your rights in Mexico are not the same rights you get here. So you have a lot of lack of education in the community. So people can keep on violating people's rights, and people won't know who to call or where to go.

LOUIS: Does anybody do educational work around people's rights?

GABBY: I think we all do in the VAWA program.[6]

VALERIE: We're working on that too, especially in conjunction with immigration raids. Now we have this immigration task force of different community organizations in El Paso, that we've started meeting here monthly and talking about the needs of these immigrants during the raids, and one of those was education. So I had a conference call a couple of weeks ago, about a Know Your Rights presentation that's happening in other parts of the country like Colorado, and we want to bring that here more because this is where it's really needed, on the border. I've had people calling in just saying, "I want a presentation. Who can do this for me?"

GABBY: Have you spoken with the Border Network for Human Rights? They're more of a grassroots organizing organization that focuses on human rights issues, especially as they relate to immigrants on the border. And we make really good partners because they focus on organizing and education and we do litigation and education, so we often partner up. They're actually one of the plaintiffs in our Stone Garden immigration raid case that has been the big case here lately. So they do Know Your Rights stuff. The ACLU New Mexico does it in southern New Mexico, but they don't really come to Texas because of the rules. I think our ACLU local chapter is probably going to start doing stuff like that.

LOUIS: So you work in different areas in the office?

BRIANA: Yeah. The VAWA program sort of runs itself. Officially I supervise both of them, but really she [Gabby] does it. And some of the same kinds of things that we deal with in the litigation part of what we do come up in the VAWA program because it's the same mentality that's rampant throughout law enforcement agencies all across Texas, and it has to with immigration. But it also has to do with violence and domestic violence in families and the way that law enforcement officers treat victims of violence and fail to follow procedures and how this impacts our clients, who have this sort of compounded problem of not only being undocumented in the United States but also being victims of domestic violence and basically held hostage because of their status and of the relationship that they're in.

> LOUIS: Through the litigation, are you wanting to change policy or ensure that policy is enforced and improve the way it's implemented?

BRIANA: Where there's good policy we want to make sure that it's being followed, and when it's not, then we intervene. Unfortunately there aren't so many of those situations, where there is already good policy. Mostly what we deal with is there's not policy at all, or your policy itself is unconstitutional [laughter], so we identify specific cases where it's sort of not necessarily an isolated issue but something that we can use as a platform to attack that policy or that lack of policy in the negotiation for settlement. Or if we're going up to trial the idea is to get a judge's order or get the defendant to agree to implement a new policy, do some training with our officers, do training policy, and continue that education and make sure that it's being enforced.

> LOUIS: Is most of your work focused on law enforcement agencies?

BRIANA: I wouldn't say most of it, because we do civil rights broadly. We also do a lot of disability rights stuff. That usually has more to do with municipality and private businesses and doesn't have anything to do with law enforcement most of the time.

> LOUIS: Where is the interface between human rights and civil rights?

BRIANA: To me civil rights are also human rights. But there's this whole other world of social, economic, and cultural rights that in the United States we're really just beginning to be able to talk about and still haven't really found a way of, I don't think, fully inserting them into the legal realm, certainly, but also just in our public discussions.

> LOUIS: So civil rights in the framework of existing laws, in terms of what's allowable, how to treat people, what are people's rights, and human rights often transcend civil rights?

BRIANA: I would characterize civil rights as human rights, but they're just a specific kind. Because we've taken the language of civil rights and made it something very Americanized based on the Bill of Rights and our Constitution and civil rights movements, we understand civil rights to mean a specific thing. But in the human rights framework in general, civil rights are broader in a lot of places than we understand.

And I think there's also a difference that I notice in the people we have as clients and whom we interact with in our work, between people knowing their rights and being willing to speak up about them. I think that a lot of people know that what's going on in their community is not okay, but they're not necessarily willing to come out and say anything about it because of the fear and because of being targeted. So mostly what we find is that this will go on and go on and go on until somebody who has status gets caught and is willing to come forward and be a plaintiff, for example, or speak out about it. Then that one person sort of becomes the spokesperson, or it starts something that people feel more shielded, and we'll see a mixed status group come forward and be willing to speak on it. But it really often will start with someone who's an LPR [lawful permanent resident] or someone who's a citizen who gets caught up in whatever the enforcement issue is who feels like they don't have as much to lose and will come forward.

VALERIE: Even people who call on the phone, I have to tell them, when I'm doing intake, this is confidential, because sometimes it will come up, "What's you're status?" in their incident, and a lot of times they're like, "Wait, can I share this with you?" They're scared. They don't know who we are, they hear it from a friend, call this office. And I understand that, 'cause if you're not educated on it, you're gonna be protecting yourself.

PAULINA: I think the state of fear might even apply to the students in UTEP. If you are a Mexican student coming to UTEP you don't want to call attention to yourself, so if there's a march or anything you might prefer to not go in case further on you have the opportunity to be a citizen or a permanent resident.

GABBY: We've definitely had people ask us when we invite them to events, "Well, is this going to impact my application? How will this look?" So it's a real issue. When you're doing this kind of work in this community, it's not even just about immigration, because there's a strong culture of retaliation and intimidation, even as an Anglo. We know people who have been targeted for some of their work. It's just part of the culture—retaliation, intimidation, and fear.

VALERIE: And another thing is, because people are fearful, they're not reporting crimes. This is why it affects whole communities, because crimes in the whole community aren't being reported because undocumented people are afraid to report anything they see.

> LOUIS: You've mentioned that the sheriff's office cooperates with ICE, but what about the police department? Does it have a policy?

BRIANA: Locally our police chief that we have now has been real outspoken against cooperating and has gone to Washington with coalitions that we're actually members of to talk about border reform or immigration reform. In general the police department does not do that kind of thing. However, the police chief that we have now is fairly new, and so there are some isolated incidents where officers are doing things that are not following policy. So things still occur, but it's not a broad-based strategy like it is with the sheriff's department. Problem is that when people talk, they don't necessarily differentiate, somebody's knocking on the door, and they're taking people away, and it doesn't really matter, and we cannot trust these people. Keep your head low. Don't talk to anyone. El Paso's crime rate went down recently, and they trumpeted all over, but there's no way to know how much that has to do with unreported crime because they get statistics by reported crimes, not committed crimes. So it has this really troubling effect of making people feel safer when really they shouldn't feel so safe when people who have a criminal mind-set know that too and target those who are vulnerable.

> LOUIS: Is trying to reform the sheriff's policy of working with ICE big on your agenda?

BRIANA: Certainly. That was sort of our first big case that we had when we started was with the El Paso County Sheriff. Operation Linebackers was what they were calling it. That was our first case that we did out here. We ended up settling that, and they did this broad-based immigration training for the entire sheriff's department, and later on the county passed a resolution, and so did the city. So things have really calmed down a lot in El Paso, but the sheriff has been the sheriff for like eight zillion years . . . fifteen years. He's retiring, and he was the one behind all this stuff locally. So he's retiring, and now we're facing this election. What are there, six candidates at this point? Some of them are former ICE agents. So we're starting to get involved to the extent that we can without violating our nonprofit rules with educating people about the candidates—all of them, not one specifically—and making immigration enforcement and civil rights key issues in the election debate. We privately have some ideas of some of the people who might be better than others, but really once people hear their views on those issues it'll be clear.

PAULINA: We're working with Border Network for Human Rights on just getting people registered to vote and having educational forums with the candidates. All candidates will be invited just to tell the people, "This is where I stand on these issues."

GABBY: And we're asking them to sign a pledge that they will not involve themselves with immigration enforcement and some other items about civil rights and how they're going to deal with those issues.

> LOUIS: *Where do you think the general population sits with this? Is it on their radar screen, or not until they see something in the papers?*

GABBY: I think it's definitely on the radar. I know when all the immigration marches happened, it usually takes something pretty bad to get people out in the streets chanting and protesting. There was a really overwhelming response. It goes both ways. Sometimes we're on the radio, and we have these nuts call and tell us that we're just helping the illegals and the terrorists and all this kind of stuff. Sometimes we'll be invited to a radio show, and we'll get several callers who say those kinds of things, but there's the other half who feel the opposite way; they don't go out there and show it. But when something really terrible happens, people go out and protest and speak up about it. And that was one of the things that happened with Operation Linebacker. The sheriff was telling me that when he started doing these sorts of things people were so angry. The church came out, and other social service organizations, and it was just one thing after another. And finally he had to stop using racial profiling.

BRIANA: But I think the other thing is that when you live here, it's not as if there's ever a day that goes by where it's not in the paper or on TV. I can't think of the day when there's not something about immigration enforcement or border enforcement stuff everywhere. And even people who wouldn't necessarily be in line with us on a lot of issues, I think some of them are so tired of hearing about it that they're just like, "Just stop," even if they don't have strong feelings. The *El Paso Times* did a poll recently, and even though they're pretty conservative and I don't trust their polling strategy—even that poll came out with the majority being anti–civil immigration enforcement by local law enforcement.

LOUIS: So with the violence against women, is that just a case-by-case thing, or do you all have a broader strategy for that?

GABBY: It's both. We get most of our clients from the shelters so we've developed partnerships with shelters in all the areas that we work in. It is also a case-by-case, because the clients that we help go out and tell their neighbors and their friends, and we work with churches and rural clinics—anybody who will listen to us and get the word out.

LOUIS: It's pretty amazing to think that you're so new, and you're the only ones doing this kind of work here.

BRIANA: Well, there was a void.

LOUIS: Do agencies and law enforcement folks kind of see you as having a contentious relationship? Do you think they wish you weren't here? Or do you think they say, "Well, you know, it's good to have somebody being our conscience."

BRIANA: I think it depends on the day and who the person is. Like just a few minutes ago the chief of police's office called us and invited us to a conference on law enforcement and immigration that's happening and wants us to be a part of it. So obviously they know that we're here and consider us a part of whoever the group is that should be discussing these issues. But, you know, as soon as their officer beats someone up, we're going to be in court again; the relationship totally changes. Same with city council. The other day we went there because they were passing a resolution on an issue that we had been working on, and it was all smiles and handshakes, but meanwhile we're writing mean comments back and forth on this other downtown issue in the papers and saying mean things about each other. And we'll sue them on another day on the exact issue that they just passed a resolution. As far as the sheriff's department goes, I think it's a more straightforward oppositional relationship.

LOUIS: Because they make deliberate decisions to be aggressive?

BRIANA: It's that, but also the culture of Texas sheriffs statewide is a real cavalier, cowboy mentality, and they have a lot of power under the constitution here in Texas. They really do have a different attitude than a more contemporary metropolitan police chief. They will generally be able to at least put on a facade of wanting to work these things out. But to be truthful, let's not forget that our current police chief is running for sheriff, so it behooves him to call us and invite us to these things and to ask us what we think.

LOUIS: Might it also behoove you to support him if he's going to take that policy over there?

BRIANA: Yeah. We can't support anyone, but we can support issues. What we're seeing a lot of now are politicians wanting to put our name on things so they can have the civil rights card.

LOUIS: It seems like a good thing in terms of influencing the discourse.

BRIANA: Yeah, it's a good sign. Whenever they're trying to co-opt you, you know you're doing something right or wrong, depending on whether you let them. We're not putting our names on people's stuff, but we're going to these conferences.

LOUIS: It must seem a little surreal at times. I was talking to Carlos Mar-entes over at the Farm Worker Center, and he was telling me about their relationship with the Border Patrol and about their being a safe haven.

BRIANA: Annunciation House is kind of like that. They're also a safe haven. But not long ago somebody was shot right outside by the Border Patrol, right in the street. So that's the kind of situation you get into.

LOUIS: Is there an agreement that specifies what it means to be a safe haven?

BRIANA: Well, sometimes Border Patrol will drop people off at Annunciation House, so there is some informal something. On the other hand, tomorrow they might shoot you right in the front.

LOUIS: Why would they shoot somebody?

BRIANA: In this particular situation, there's some disagreement. There were a bunch of more experienced officers surrounding him, trying to get it under control, and this new officer just showed up, didn't ask questions, and shot him. That's a perfect example of the need for training.

LOUIS: If people run from the Border Patrol at the border, can the agents shoot them?

BRIANA: I don't know if you heard about these two Border Patrol agents who got in trouble for covering up a shooting. Lou Dobbs has gotten a hold of this . . . that's here locally. The only reason those people went to jail was because they tried to cover it up, not because they shot them. The reality is that law enforcement can shoot people and get away with it pretty easily in Texas, or any state in this appellate court, because they have immunity under the law.

That case is really interesting, because even though he was just a kid, he wasn't armed. The jury no-billed [found insufficient evidence to prosecute] on that shooting in front of Annunciation House, even though our communities are made up of people who are immigrants or who have immigrant family members. And a lot of them have had these interactions with law enforcement. They are famous for no-billing.

LOUIS: Do you think it's the persuasiveness of the defense?

BRIANA: I think we have a real deference for law enforcement, and after 9/11 it's even worse. That's my spin. I think it's dangerous to have such a deference for law enforcement, and I see it played out in cases in our communities a lot. We have to turn away cases where horrible violence occurs because I know that the officer will get immunity. The law has developed to the point where you can shoot someone who's not armed in the back, and the court can find that you were reasonable in doing so. Therefore you have these ridiculous opinions where the court will say, "Yes, the officer violated your civil rights, but he wasn't patently unreasonable, or he didn't show a callous disregard for your civil rights; therefore, immunity." It's really two separate questions: whether your rights were violated and whether we're going to do anything about it. I'm pretty sure that's not the way the Bill of Rights was originally intended.

LOUIS: How long have you been out of law school?

BRIANA: A year and a half. This is my first job out of law school.

LOUIS: That's amazing. This seems like a very intense environment for this kind of work.

BRIANA: Every week there's an emergency, whether a raid happens, and there's an emergency action in Mexico and we're driving to Chaparral in the middle of the night going trailer to trailer, interviewing people, going to Juárez trying to track down people who have been wrongfully deported, trying to find people who have fled to Dallas because of the raids. There's always something.

GABBY: These people's lives are being torn apart. I can't be like, "It's five o'clock. I'm clocking out, Briana. Good luck with that guy who's just been beaten." There's such a need. You can't go home and not think about it.

LOUIS: Can you sleep better because you've done your job?

PAULINA: Or you can't sleep [laughter].

BRIANA: I feel satisfaction that we're doing the best that we can. I don't feel satisfaction that things are changing enough. We just keep having the same problems. Jim [Harrington]'s been doing this, for example, since the late '70s, and we're still talking about the same things that he was talking about when he started.

> LOUIS: Isn't that why you need to do it? It's one thing to say this is progress; it's another thing to say our role is to prevent things from getting worse.

BRIANA: That's what we always say, just put our pinkie in the dam every day [laughter]. Just keep showing up. That's the best we can do. I think that we've done really well. I don't think that anyone expected that after only a year and a half that we would be called to comment on resolution language and be a part of the committees on the city council that are addressing disability issues or be called by the chief of police or even the Border Network. They're famous for not wanting anything to do with litigation or with other organizations because of what's happened to them in the past. I think we've made a lot of progress and real change that matters to people on a daily basis.

I think it matters that people have somewhere to call. I think that it matters that people know that somebody's watching. For the longest time, problems that El Paso and communities like it have had is that nobody's watching, so this mafia-style culture of retaliation and intimidation and consolidated power can exist with no oversight. It's shocking to people that we're here and that we know that stuff is going on. They don't know how we find out. Well, people call us.

> LOUIS: What is the ideal outcome in terms of immigration here?

BRIANA: I think the reality is that whatever happens nationwide, El Paso and places like it are going to bear the brunt of it. If it's a good healthy reform package, or major change of mind, then it will be an important, productive change for communities like El Paso. If it's not, then it's going to be a horrific, violent situation for El Paso and everyone here. We live these realities every day. El Paso is a poor community in comparison to other places, so whenever you have poverty, marginalization, and violence and police power and government proposals that aren't actually informed by reality, bad things happen to poor people, especially poor people of color, immigrants. It's like the canary in the coal mine thing. El Paso and places like it are going to show whether these policies are going to work. That said, I would like for El Paso and our community to show that we can still be human and still uphold the values that we're supposed to believe in. We need to get realistic about what national security means and what the threat really is, and about equality of enforcement. A lot of it goes back to how we understand race and class, and it's so hard to disentangle all of that stuff. But if we don't, it's never going to work, and it's going to be a disaster.

Part of it is that people who are making these policies don't know what it's like here. I wish that people could come here and experience it to understand what they're talking about, what border enforcement means and what it looks like and how it impacts families, what some of the vigilante activities are about down here, how law enforcement acts like vigilantes and how that impacts people. Much of it doesn't even begin to touch the violence. It's a scary world out here for our clients. It's really, really scary.

> LOUIS: *Gabby, what do you think?*

GABBY: I'm very cynical about the whole thing. Whatever they decide nationally is going to impact El Paso, but I'm not very optimistic. I think it's going to be some sort of compromise that really isn't going to fix the problem.

> LOUIS: *Is going to law school your way of preparing yourself to be a part of the battle?*

GABBY: I'm going to be a part of the battle. All we can do.

> LOUIS: *That's not complete cynicism, because at least you're not giving up, you know. You're preparing yourself to have the tools to fight back.*

PAULINA: I've lived here all my life, and I've seen how things have changed. I don't know if it's because I also work doing this, but I also feel that it's been getting worse and worse. I don't see a very bright future either, sad to say.

VALERIE: I feel torn. I am young, and I want things to change. I just go back to, is it going to be change from the top? If so, we need to elect leaders who understand what's going on at the bottom. But the people who tend to be at the top aren't the type who sees what's really going on. I met this man who was doing a documentary on the border, and he was saying that if the Catholic Church really took on this immigration issue and started talking about that in their parishes to create consciousness, then that would be big.

BRIANA: I think we have a long history of the law upholding the civil rights struggle. Segregation was the law forever. It was apartheid, and it was enforced by law enforcement and by the courts, and I hope that most of us have gotten to the point where we would agree that that was a bad thing, but you can see it as the civil rights struggle of our times. Unfortunately it doesn't have the mass movement behind it right now. I guess we're all pessimistic, unfortunately. I would like to have a message of hope, but really we're just all trying to get out alive. [Laughter]

> LOUIS: *Do you imagine yourself continuing this kind of work, or do you imagine this is a stepping-stone towards something else?*

BRIANA: I see myself continuing to do this kind of work. I ultimately probably will leave El Paso because my family's elsewhere, but I don't see that happening anytime soon. Certainly haven't taken my first chance to get out . . . [laughter]. But I'm also torn about that 'cause I feel convinced that this is where the battle is right now. I'm convinced that so many of my friends who are in New York and San Francisco don't even know—they have it so easy [slight laughter]. I'm really, really committed to doing this work in communities like this and other smaller communities around the state. So, yes, I see myself doing this kind of work, which scares me to death 'cause it's hard. It's hard to live in a world that looks the way it looks when you do this work. It's hard to carry the burden of trying to give people solutions in a world that's basically built to deny them their rights as far as they can tell and to disempower them. It's hard to be a part of a system that disempowers them. I'm really conflicted about being an attorney. When I went to law school I felt that way, but the more I know, the more I feel like, "Am I really doing what I should be doing? Is this really a part of the answer, a part of the solution, or am I really just a part of the system?" I don't know. I'm committed to keep doing it, but I feel a lot of conflict about it every day in different ways.

> LOUIS: *You don't want to be too comfortable. What do you think, Gabby? You're going off to law school next year?*

GABBY: I couldn't do anything else. Even when I was an undergrad I still felt this was a losing battle, but it was something you have to do anyway. You do it because it's what's right, even though that sounds cheesy. I see myself doing this whatever happens. I know that we're in dark times, and they're going to get uglier.

PAULINA: I couldn't imagine doing anything else. It's a love-hate relationship. [Laughter] We work in a very sad environment every day, and it affects you. But it is very important what we do, and I really take pride in the work that we do, because I feel I'm *doing* something.

MÓNICA HERNÁNDEZ

Mónica Hernández of Casa Familiar in San Ysidro, California, is a University of California, Berkeley, Ethnic Studies graduate who grew up in Tijuana and went to school in San Ysidro. She has decided not to apply for citizenship, even though she has a permanent work visa and could be eligible. She is soft-spoken but powerful in word and deed as she contributes to bettering her community from the ground up through this powerful agency. The group's website explains its mission as follows: "Casa Familiar allows the dignity, power, and worth within individuals and families to flourish, by enhancing the quality of life through education, advocacy, service programming, housing and community economic development."[7] When Brent Beltran and I arrived at Casa Familiar's office, Andrea Scopica, the executive director, was about to leave but stopped and talked with us for a few minutes.

LOUIS: *Can you share your perspective on how life on the border has been impacted by the debates on immigration?*

ANDREA: Well, it has really changed. When I was growing up there was no fence; there was like three pieces of barbed wire. My grandma used to send our dog, Mongo, to my aunt's house in Tijuana with a note. He was gone for *un poco tiempo* [a little while], and then he would come back with the answer. It was a very different type of border. It wasn't until they criminalized the people who were coming that things changed. Before, everybody understood why they were coming and was okay with it, as long as there was enough work for them.

LOUIS: *What year would you say they started militarizing the border?*

ANDREA: Probably in the early '60s. At first they tried to say that immi-

Mónica Hernández at her desk in Casa Familiar in San Ysidro, California. Photo by Louis Mendoza.

grants were taking jobs, but the people knew that the jobs they were taking, nobody wanted those jobs, so it didn't work here in California. Then they started saying everyone was a burro bringing drugs. And that stuck. Then they also said they were coming over here to take advantage of all the services. Finally, after repeating it and repeating it and repeating it, I think it finally found some ears. I remember when Lou Dobbs was a financial guy. Now he has become the idiot of the century. It happened to our former mayor also, Roger Hedgecock. I knew Roger when he was the guru of putting people together. He was the first one who appointed Latinos to boards and commissions. But when he left, he had to find a gig.[8]

> LOUIS: *In your opinion, is it on a trajectory of getting worse, or is it part of a cycle?*

ANDREA: Well, if you look at it historically, it is part of a cycle. The country has always had xenophobia, and we went through this once in the '20s. But if you look at it just in your lifetime, it is getting worse and worse, and also the environment that sustains it has gotten worse and worse because of 9/11. They are exploiting that to the max. It is not going to ever go back to like it was before. I really do believe they are going to change the Constitution. It's scary. That is the way I see it, and I tell people, "If you are not a citizen, if for no other reason than securing your own place in society, you should become a citizen. Because first thing they are going to do is say anyone born to undocumented people here is not going to be a citizen anymore." There is a lot of support for that. After that they are going to start shutting down more and more employment opportunities. People are just willing to give up their rights.

> LOUIS: *You don't think there is any way to interrupt the debates in a constructive way?*

ANDREA: I think it is inevitable. I think we need to have some dialogue about it. Martin Luther King was able to get as far as he got because he had the SNCC [Student Nonviolent Coordinating Committee] people. And he could say to people, "You want to listen to these idiots, or do you want to listen to me?" He sounded logical in comparison to black radicals.

> LOUIS: *That is where your point is even more poignant, though. The Democrats aren't always willing to stand up and are pushed further and further to the right.*

ANDREA: That's right. You never swing all the way back. In fact, when Prop. 187 came up, I was against it, but I was really very happy that it happened. All of the Latinos and *mexicanos* and Chicanos and all of these people that had been passing for all these years, people were coming up to them saying, "What do you think about this?" And if you were an engineer, you would say, "Why are you asking me?" It was a good reminder for them to know that in the eyes of the world, if you are this color, then that is what you are going to be judged on first. Not your professional credentials or where you went to school. None of those things are important when you are in a racist situation. [Andrea leaves room.]

MÓNICA: I was born in Tijuana; my family is from both sides of the border. Andrea always brings up the citizenship debate because I am not a citizen. It is a decision I made. I was a permanent U.S. resident for a while, with a temporary permanent U.S. residence. I was deported at one point because I was caught in this technicality where my green card had not come in. Since I had status as a temporary permanent resident, I could get it extended. The way you go about it is, you go into Tijuana, but you have to come back and go into secondary to get that extension.[9] I actually asked them on this side before I went. I was like, "Is it going to be okay? Is everything going to be fine?" And they said, "Yeah, that is what you have to do." But when I did that, when I actually got into their system or whatnot, they had already mailed my green card. So since it was in the mail, I could not receive the extension, and therefore I was now an illegal alien and I was deported.

LOUIS: *How did that feel?*

MÓNICA: It was degrading, but what could I do about it? If anything, I was thinking, "Here I just graduated from Berkeley; I do a lot of work with migrant issues and whatnot, and to think it could happen to someone like me." Imagine what it's like if you don't speak English or don't understand—how much worse it is for them. So it was a very humbling and horrible experience. They fingerprint you, and they drive me to where the station is, only to drive me right back. It was ridiculous because they were within a mile of each other. So then you get to the border, and you have to get off. They escort you in to make sure that you go into Tijuana. I grew up in Tijuana. I have family there, I have family here, a lot of cousins and whatnot, and I have lived pretty much all my life in San Ysidro, with the exception of like five years I was up in the Bay going to school.

LOUIS: *What did you study at Berkeley?*

MÓNICA: Ethnic Studies.

LOUIS: *When did you finish?*

MÓNICA: In 2004. Not too long ago. One of the greatest things that I tripped out on when I went to Berkeley was that I didn't realize just how militarized the border is. You don't really feel it until you leave San Ysidro. And then on top of that, the whole Minutemen phenomenon just added to the whole thing.

LOUIS: *Did it sharpen your awareness about the issues?*

MÓNICA: Most definitely. I realize that it is not normal to have such a military presence, so that became another thing that I wanted to do more work on, to understand how this affects the psyche of the community, not just as an individual, but as a community in general, how we feel criminalized. One of my friends and I were talking about this. We were just driving around. She has a little kid, like five years old, and we saw a police car, and all of a sudden, we are not doing anything wrong, no one is doing anything wrong, but it is like automatically we go into a different mode. We are more aware of our environment, and we noticed that with her daughter too; she stopped talking. We got into a discussion of how a little kid who is five years old is already picking up on this intimidation and how right away we know that this is the enemy in a sense.

A little bit about Casa. It has been around for about thirty-seven years or so. It originally started off as a health service agency. Now it is a comprehensive community resource center. I grew up here in the community, and even when I was a kid I remember coming to Casa. What I remember is their toy drive, so I would always go get the toys from them, and then Thanksgiving, we had a whole dinner. We give out dinners to nine hundred or so families. It definitely has made an impact on the community. Growing up here in the early '90s, prior to, let's say, Operation Gatekeeper, my parents had a business down on the boulevard, and I would kick it a lot down there, by Larson Field and places where it is called Smuggler's Canyon. That is where we used to hang out as kids, and we would see all kinds of stuff. We would see the Border Patrol very blatantly beating up on people, or oftentimes, because I coached Little League, we would have to stop the games because they would be chasing people in the middle of the field. My parents had a video store, so sometimes people were being chased, and we would hide them there. It was weird, but like I said, even as a little kid we knew our place. We knew that the Border Patrol was out to harm us or out to get us, and it was totally based on racial profiling; they didn't ask for documents. I didn't understand a lot of it, but I knew at some point or another, it was not right, so I think that had a lot to do with my own political development and trying to make sense of things.

LOUIS: *What kind of emotions did that generate for you?*

MÓNICA: A lot of anger. Ironically, my parents are citizens, and I am not. So every time we cross the border I would have knots in my stomach, but I knew I could get away with it because of the privilege of my lighter skin. It caused a lot of confusion; it caused a lot of anger. And I think that at the same time I could channel it into trying to figure things out, like why is the situation the way it is, and how can we improve it?

LOUIS: *So those experiences influenced your decision on what to study and what you were going to do with your education?*

MÓNICA: Most definitely. The epitome of it was in high school, which was right around the time of Prop. 187 and Operation Gatekeeper. I first started to learn about those things in a more educational way through high schools. There was one other program in particular that was called the Chicano Latino Youth Leadership Project. They sent me off to that, and that was like a big awakening. Actually that was the first time I left the community, because I went to Sacramento, and it was really interesting. I got to meet Sal Castro, lots of people from César Chávez's family. His granddaughter was one of my roommates. It made a big, big impact on me to learn that there is a whole world out there of people who are willing to teach us about our own history, which was something we weren't being taught in schools.

> *LOUIS: You went to school here in San Ysidro, and you came across the border every day? Or did you stay here during the week and go home on weekends?*

MÓNICA: By that time I was already here in San Ysidro. Prior to Gate-keeper, going to Tijuana was like going to the store. It was not a big thing. We would come and go in five minutes, and that completely changed, after 9/11. Then you had the five-or six-hour wait lines, especially immediately after it happened. So it has been interesting for me to see that kind of change in my lifetime.

> *LOUIS: As someone who has decided not to become a citizen, what do you say when people raise questions about the law, because so much of the debates are framed around the law? What is the best framework for healthy debate?*

MÓNICA: Andrea briefly touched on this, but her sense of history starts at the point where there is already a border, and she uses that as a point of departure. But our history goes back further than that. The reality of it is that the border has only been around for a very short amount of years in the greater context of history. Somehow I think that type of perspective needs to be more present in those immigration debates to be able to find a better solution to deal with all this.

ENRIQUE MORONES

Enrique Morones is the founder of Border Angels and the host of San Diego's Super K 1040 AM's talk show, *Morones por la Tarde*. Morones is no stranger to talking, and he is clear about his stance that a more humane and honest means of dealing with immigrants is necessary. He has debated with Lou Dobbs and Bill O'Reilly a number of times, adopting a confrontational style that has seemed to earn him their respect. The extreme dislike of him by anti-immigrant groups only strengthens his credibility in the eyes of many people. Brent Beltran and I sat down to talk with him outside a coffee shop across the street from the radio station.

ENRIQUE: Two weeks ago I organized a protest against Lou Dobbs. I've been on his show a few times, but he won't have me on anymore. I had like five hundred people. We're all protesting. He comes out and says, "Enrique, I'm not surprised to see you here." He goes to shake my, hand and I say, "I'm not shaking your hand." So then I started going at it with him about the leprosy thing, crime, and all the nonsense he makes up. And we were having a pretty good talk, but then people behind me started getting out of hand, so we couldn't finish. He's the worst. At least O'Reilly's on FOX News, so you already know their agenda.

I did this thing called Marcha Migrante, which was in February of 2006. And it was from San Diego to Washington, D.C., and back. It was ten thousand miles. But it was a caravan of cars. It was called Marcha because I went out and asked people to march. And I said, "Hey, we need you to take to the streets and protest H.R. 4437."[10] We went to forty different cities in twenty different states in twenty-seven days. And every place we went was different. In San Diego, it was the union workers that organized the rally. In

Enrique Morones, founder and executive director of Border Angels, San Diego, California. Photo by Louis Mendoza.

L.A., we met with Dolores Huerta [cofounder of the United Farm Workers Union] at Plazita Olvera. We stayed at the house of the people that ended up being some of the main organizers for the March 25th march.

LOUIS: Tell me about your motivations for getting this effort started.

ENRIQUE: We weren't called Border Angels when I first started back in 1986. I was born and raised here in San Diego. My family came here like most Mexican families, legally, and they've been here for over fifty years. There are five of us. My older brother and sister were born in Mexico. Myself and my younger brother and sister were born in San Diego. I was educated through the bilingual, bicultural Catholic schools all the way through graduate school—Our Lady of Angels, St. Augustine, University of San Diego.

What happened was that my professional degree is in international marketing. I used to be director of a hotel chain called Krystal Hotels of Mexico. A woman that worked there from El Salvador goes, "Hey, Enrique, you always go down to Tijuana, and you bring blankets and food. Why don't you do that for the migrants that live here in San Diego?" And I thought, "Well, you're referring to where I live, in Golden Hills, the neighborhood I grew up in. There's all sorts of migrants." She says, "Oh, no, no, where I live, Carlsbad. There's migrants too." And I'm thinking, "Carlsbad, those are the rich areas, right?" She goes, "No, but in the canyons. There's people that live in the canyons." I couldn't believe it. So I started going up there on Saturdays. This is back in the mid-'80s. I was shocked to see entire communities living in the canyons. Immediately I started going there every Saturday and bringing food and water and ministry to them, and bringing more and more people along. You got to be very careful about who you bring along because you don't want them exposed. We had to be very careful about what we did, because, in 1986, there was amnesty at that time. The climate was bad then, but it was nothing like it is now.

I moved up to Los Angeles. We had done really good with Krystal Hotels and their marketing, and the hotel chain came down and made me the director of a group called Stouffer Presidente Hotels. The freeway shootings were taking place at that time. There was the Rodney King riots. It was 1993. There were a lot of things going on. We did a big event in L.A. called Reencuentro, which was an event that was put together by a guy named Armando Charles and myself and a woman named Marga Rojas. It was to bring the communities together, especially the multicultural communities—Korean, the Anglo, the African American, the Latino. It was a big success.

After that, we participated a very tiny bit in the renaming of Brooklyn Avenue to César Chávez Avenue. As a result of that, they invited us to sit in this special section of this renaming ceremony at East L.A. College. They sat me next to a woman, and everybody came by to say hello to her saying, "It's an honor to see you." She asked me, "What is it that you do?" I told her, "I go to the canyons and put water out and bring food to migrants." She said, "I've never heard of that." I said, "Well, in my upbringing as a Catholic and a Christian, why should people know about it? I just do the right thing. That's all." She goes, "Enrique, you've got to let people know about it. You're going to create a lot of enemies, even within your own community. But people need to know what's going on because most people are good and they'll want to help." I thought, well, coming from a source like her, I'm going to follow her advice. The woman was Ethel Kennedy. I'm a big fan of the Kennedys. So we got to know each other a little bit, and I followed her advice.

The very next year I moved back down to San Diego—1994, the year of NAFTA. It was the year of Subcomandante Marcos in Chiapas. It was when Proposition 187 was hot and heavy. And 1994 was when they started building the wall. So here I am, becoming more active in a visible way. I started making a lot of noise about this, especially about [Prop.] 187 and the wall. Sure enough, we started getting more and more exposure. We said, "Don't build the wall. If you build the wall, people will start dying. You know, there's one person dying every month right now crossing the two-thousand-mile border. If you build the wall, we fear that people will start crossing out in the desert." And unfortunately, we were right and they were wrong. The government built the wall, and since Operation Gatekeeper began in October 1994, we estimate that there's been ten thousand people that have died. Ten thousand. The next year, I was very vocal. Prop. 187 had passed. The wall was being built, and I said, "We need to do something about this." I was trying to be proactive and not always be reactive.

I used to play a little bit of baseball. I never played professional or anything, but I sent a letter to the teams in baseball about diversity. I wanted to promote Mexico and Latinos in a positive way. I wrote a letter to all the teams, and the team that responded happened to be the Padres and I'm a San Diegan. It was two guys that had just bought the team, Larry Lucchino and John Moores. So Larry Lucchino, who was the president, said, "Enrique, I've seen you in the news, and I like your letter. You know, I like your idea. Why don't you come and join us and we'll create the Department of Hispanic Marketing." I started doing that, and instead of just going out to the canyons and stuff—which I still did on Saturdays—we started going out to the desert. We started putting water out there about 1996. It wasn't structured the way that it is now. But the deaths had started. Operation Gatekeeper started in October of 1994. The first full year had just barely terminated, and there were about a hundred deaths that first year. From twenty deaths to a hundred deaths, so it was a dramatic increase but not as dramatic as it became later on.

We started putting gallons of water out there on the side of the road in the Imperial Valley and also in the East County of San Diego. In 1996 we started formalizing it. I was with the Padres; even players would come out with me sometimes and put water out there. That's how Border Angels went from being in the canyons to being out in the desert. We did a little bit of both. And then what happened was the deaths along the border got even worse. So we started being more organized. I was invited to be on a show with Don Francisco of *Sábado Gigante*. He labeled me, "El ángel de la frontera." And I thought—the border angel—that's too much for any one person to wear that title, but I like the name for the group. So we officially became Border Angels.

By this time it was two hundred deaths a year. So the death total kept on climbing up. And these deaths along the border are real people. It's not just a number. The reason we think it's 10,000 and not 4,500 like what the

Border Patrol says since October of 1994 is because of people like Lucrecia Domínguez. Lucrecia Domínguez was a woman that crossed the border with two of her three children, Jesús, a fifteen-year-old little boy, and Nora, a seven-year-old little girl. She crossed in a typical way that a lot of people cross, with a smuggler and a group of migrants. And as she crossed the desert, she started slowing down the group because she had these two children with her. So the smuggler, the unethical smuggler, said, you know, "Lucrecia, you're slowing us down. We're going to leave you behind. You gotta cross with your kids. You're going to get caught. We're all going to get caught." So they left her behind with two of her three children. She had an infant baby that stayed back at home, thank God. So what happened is that she literally dies in the arms of Jesús, her son, Jesús. I cannot imagine my mom dying in my arms, much less a fifteen-year-old little boy in the middle of the desert. So they laid her down in the desert. And here's these two little children in the middle of nowhere, by themselves. They go wandering around. Thank God, the Border Patrol found them. Otherwise they would have died. They get sent back to Mexico. They're from Zacatecas. Their grandfather is a man named Cesario.

Cesario contacts a group like mine but in Arizona where this death took place. I think it was Isabel García from Derechos Humanos. She talks to them and to No More Deaths, and they say, "It's very difficult to find someone when they're dead, but we'll help you." So he goes out there, and the day that he goes out there, he goes out there with a friend of mine named Rich Marosi with the local *L.A. Times* here in San Diego. He finds a body, but it's not Lucrecia. And then he finds another woman's body and then another woman's body. Bodies scattered. Women's bodies. They were not Lucrecia Domínguez. The fourth body he finds is the body of his daughter. And the only way he was able to recognize her was because of the skeletal remains, the ring she had on her finger. She was crossing for the number two reason that people cross—family reunification. Her husband was already in the United States. She died. And if Cesario could find three other bodies, how many bodies are out there? We estimate that there's about ten thousand bodies from what we have seen and the many people we've talked to.

I go down to Mexico all the time. I go to these places like Michoacán and Sinaloa and Guanajuato, where a lot of people are coming from. At first I would say, "How many of you know somebody that's died crossing the border?" And you'd see a lot of hands up. "How many of you know somebody that's missing?" They'd say, "I know five people that are missing." There's a lot of missing people out there that we don't know if they've died or not.

So that's why we think it's about ten thousand deaths since October of '94. And then we have the fact that it's not only men and women that are dying but also children. Like Marco Antonio Villaseñor. Marco Antonio Villaseñor was a five-year-old little boy, and he crossed with his dad for the number one reason people cross. Ninety percent of the people cross for economic reasons. The other 10 percent is family reunification. So he crossed with his dad, and the same thing. He needs water. He asks his dad for some water. But his dad didn't answer him. So he asks the next man and the next man and the next man. He asked them all, "Hey, I need some water. I need some water. I'm scared." They didn't answer him. Eighteen men, including his dad, didn't answer him because they were all dead. They had all died. Marco Antonio Villaseñor also died in the back of a semi truck in Victoria, Texas, in May of 2003. A lot of these deaths are just increasing, and more women and children now since 9/11 happened because it's more difficult to cross. We shifted our focus from being in the canyons to being in the desert and going out to put water.

My career with the Padres ended at the end of the 2001 season. I was doing all this activism stuff. I was being a lot more vocal, like Mrs. Kennedy asked me to. What happened was the owner was not a big fan of it. Larry Lucchino and John Moores got in a big fight. And then Larry goes to Boston. So he goes, "Hey, Enrique, I want you to come to Boston with me." I said, "Larry, you know, my work's on the border. When I first joined the organization, I told you that my activism comes first." Larry tells me, "Enrique, John's going to eliminate your position." Sure enough, John tells me soon afterwards, "Enrique, you've done such a good job, we don't need Latino marketing anymore." They eliminated it. This is the same guy that's one of Arnold Schwarzenegger's biggest supporters. He supports Roger Hedgecock, Ward Connerly [founder of the American Civil Rights Institute, a nonprofit established to oppose race- and gender-based preferences]. Of course, I was devastated. I was making really good money, but more important, I was helping the community.

It was a blessing because it gave me time to dedicate to Border Angels and to really establish it. That's when I formed a 501c3 [nonprofit], and it became a big organization. I go to schools and talk to kids all the time. I'll say, "You know, each one of us can make a big difference." Other times, they'll say, "Do you think you make a difference with what you did with the Padres and what you're doing with Border." I'll say, "Well, I don't know, but I'll tell you one thing. One day I'm out in the desert, and all of a sudden, we see these two guys walking in the Imperial Valley desert. One guy's carrying the other guy like out of the Bible. We pull over and go running over to where they are. We helped them, we put them under a tree, we gave them water. I was going to take them to the hospital, and they go, "Please don't," and I thought, "I'm going to give them a few minutes. If I don't see them start recuperating right away, I don't care, I'm taking them to the hospital. I don't want them to die." They start recuperating. We stayed with them for several hours, gave them water and food and shelter, and so on. Usually you don't run into people 'cause they usually cross at night, but this time we did.

Two weeks later, I'm at the stadium, and I get a message from a little boy and he goes, "Hi, Sir, you don't know me, but my name is Francisco. Two weeks ago my dad told me you saved his life in the Imperial Valley." And I was thinking, "Holy cow, this is the son of one of those two men." And I said, "Where you at?" And he said, "Los Angeles. We live in L.A. My dad was coming back to join us." And I'm thinking, "Oh, wow, this is fantastic. God bless you," and all this. So I go, "What about the other guy?" The other guy's name was Pedro. He said, "Well, we really didn't know Pedro that well. They met along the way." Pedro was the guy that was really ill. A month later after the incident, I get a call from Chicago, and it was Pedro's son. Same thing. So when people ask me, "Enrique, does what you do make a differ-ence?" I always go, "It sure made a difference to Francisco and Pedro." That was very inspirational because rarely do you run into people. You don't run into them drinking the water where we have our stations set up or anything like that. It was really a powerful moment.

I started concentrating my time on Border Angels almost exclusively. My savings ran out. We're an all-volunteer group. And what happened was that Jaime Bonilla—he's got a radio station—was so mad about the Padres elimi-nating the Latino Marketing that he doesn't want anything to do with them anymore. He says to me, "Enrique, I want to offer you a radio show." And that's why I have a radio show called *Morones por la Tarde*. I also had one in English, so we could counter all the right-wing Republican stuff. Right now I have just one in Spanish. It's from three to four o'clock every day.

I started this radio show, and the Border Angels continued to grow. And the deaths had risen to about four hundred a year. In December of 2005 the anti-immigrant rhetoric is really peaking. In April of that year, the Minute-men arrive in Arizona. The Minutemen—it's not a new group, but it has a name and it's the new KKK. I call up the Arizona Human Rights people, and I go, "Hey, listen, I see what's going on out there. We were out there last year and we talked to the governor-elect back then, Janet Napolitano, and we talked to them about the Barnett brothers." They were the guys that started the whole thing. The Barnett brothers and a guy named Spencer. I said, "These guys are really dangerous. Here's some information that we have on the Barnett brothers." I shared it with the attorney general, Terry Goodard, and Janet Napolitano, and I said, "You're going to need to take action." She did. She arrested one of the Barnett brothers for hate crimes and stuff.

But in April of 2005, Jim Gilchrist and Chris Simcox formed the Minutemen movement. Media's all over it. There was going to be a thousand Minutemen and all this. There was no thousand Minutemen. There was a thousand media, but there was only about 150 Minutemen. So I called Isabel García, and I say, "Hey, Isabel, I can bring a lot of people out there to join you and your protest against the Minutemen." She says, "That sounds good." So we went out there.

Then I hear they're coming to California. I thought, "Now they're coming to my neck of the woods. We're going to step it up a little bit." I formed something called Gente Unida [People United]. First it was just me, and then there was this other guy. He goes, "I like the idea," so there was two of us. And before you know it we had sixty human rights organizations. We formed this group called Gente Unida. We had one thing in common: We didn't all agree on every single thing, but we all agreed on we didn't like the Minutemen. We needed to shut them down. And the reason I thought it was important to form this was I knew some of the people were a little radical and I didn't want them to have physical clashes because the people that were going to pay the consequences were the migrants. So we formed this Gente Unida Coalition, which was very successful. The Minutemen arrived in Campbell, California, on July 16, which was a Saturday. We arrived on the same location, right where they were going to camp, on July 15. That morning the *Today Show* calls me—and I had been on the *Today Show* when I was in Arizona the first time the Minutemen showed up. It's Lester Holtz, and he has me on his show. He's got Jim Chase, the true founder of the San Diego Minutemen and the California Minutemen, and myself. So we're on the show, and Lester goes, "Hey, Enrique, in Arizona you said these guys were racist." I said, "That's right." And he goes, "Well, Jim says they're not racist." And I go, "It's not his call. It's not up to him. It's up to the community that's affected to determine if they're racist or not." And I go, "I'm a Mexican. He's racist." So we start going at it. He says, "I can't be a racist. I have relatives named Herrera that live in Tijuana." And I said, "What does that have to do with anything? There can be Mexican racists. Adolf Hitler had Jewish relatives, so does that mean he wasn't racist?" He doesn't know what to do. I say, "Lester, look at their website right now." He looks up their website, and it says, "Bring baseball bats, bring machetes. Stop the disease from crossing the border." Lester Holtz says, "As an African American, I know a little bit about racism—that's racism." So Jim storms off. He's furious. We were in different locations. We've run into each other many, many times. That night they changed their website to say, "If you see migrants, say buenas noches." As if that was gonna change the context of their spirit. So I look at this, and I go, "Okay, good."

So that night we're sitting there camping. You know, we have five hundred people. They have eighty. They were going to have eight hundred. So they're camping there with their guns and everything, and they're on patrol. So we get a little group and go 'round them with blow horns and megaphones and spotlights. It's pitch black. BOOM! About one o'clock we yell, "BUENAS NOCHES!" These guys are startled. We say, "BUENAS NOCHES!" And these Minutemen aren't very smart: "Who are you?" "We're migrants. We saw your website!" So these guys think about it a while. They realized it was us. They go, "Naw, you guys better get out of here." And we go, "We brought you some music. Would you like to hear some music?" So they say, "Get your mother—"—you know what—"outta here!" So we say, "We don't have that song. How about another request?" They're pissed. They get their guns and start chasing us in their trucks. We get back in our trucks and start racing back to the camp. All of this is caught on film. The next day, on Sunday the 17th, it's all over the news—CNN, even FOX covered it. They were exposed right away. The Minutemen have this thing where they call me Public Enemy Number One. Gente Unida is still very active.

In December of that year, Congress passes House Resolution 4437, and the Border Patrol kills that young man named Guillermo Martínez Rodríguez who was crossing for the number one reason, economic opportunity. I say, "That's enough." I announce, "We gotta go and get people to stand up and protest." That's when I decided to do this Marcha Migrante. On February 2nd we went from San Diego to Washington, D.C. We had a total of 111 cars. The most we ever had at one time was 35 cars or something. And we'd go to different cities and say, "We gotta take to the streets and protest what's going on." Wherever we'd go, they'd put us up. They would give us food. We would do different actions. Sometimes it was a prayer vigil. Sometimes it was a march. It was to talk to them about doing some massive demonstration later. When we're in Chicago a woman came and brought us a bunch of tamales. People would always bring us food. And this woman was a young lady named Elvira Arellano. We met with all the Chicago people, and then they were so fired up, they go, "We want to have a massive march at the beginning of March." We decided to do it on March 10th. We announce it while we're there. "March 10th!" We come back after going to all these different cities, and then March 1st, Carla Mahoney's office contacts us and says, "We're going to say no to 4437." On March 2nd, I get called by the people that we work with in L.A., and they go, "We're going to announce our march." So we do a press conference and announce the marches: On March 10th, the Chicago march; March 24th, Phoenix; March 25th, L.A.; April 9th, here. A hundred thousand people. It was a huge success. Three and a half million people marched. I know it wasn't just because of Border Angels and Gente Unida, but it happened, and we stopped 4437. These actions inspire us. We're very confident that we are going to see immigration reform; there's no doubt about it. Change takes time. Nobody expected that as soon as the marches were over, there was going to be immigration reform immediately. As a result of the *marchas*, now I go all over the country and give lectures on how we can all play a pivotal role.

> LOUIS: *How do we interrupt people like Lou Dobbs' ability to get to people? It's clear that he's influenced people who used to be in the middle, and now he's made them hate people. How do we sway public opinion and foster compassion?*

ENRIQUE: It's a challenge. Dobbs is, to me, the biggest enemy among those media pundits because he's on CNN.[11] Every month, I'm on Bill O'Reilly. O'Reilly, to me, is not a racist. I don't agree with him, but I don't think he's a racist. Lou Dobbs is a racist. What's so upsetting is that he started off with *Moneyline*. But then he started doing *Exporting America*, and he started saying things about Chinese and Indian people. And I thought, "Hey, this guy's a racist." Then when he started *Broken Borders*, I remember his first comments were real racist comments about Mexicans.

Lou Dobbs, who's Lou Dobbs? Nobody knew who Lou Dobbs was. After about a year, everybody knew who he was. He had me on the show several times. I've talked to Jonathan Klein, the president of CNN, asking him, "What are you guys doing? People have spoken out against him." I've worked closely with the Southern Poverty Law Center; Bernard Shaw, former CNN; María Hinojosa, former CNN. They said, "The guy's a racist. This unfortunately sells. You know what we can do? Boycott and be organized." And I know we're going to be able to do it. Lately, he's been getting a lot of pressure. He was on *60 Minutes* because of the leprosy thing. Leslie Stahl let him have it. Unfortunately, there's no watchdog. I think most of the people that he's talking to are people that already have their minds made up, and he's just feeding into that racism.

I really believe that the people of this country, like in countries around the world, are good people. If they know the truth they'll do the right thing, but they need to know the facts. We're 5 percent of the world's population. We consume 20 percent of the world's natural resources. Five percent of the world's population, we consume a third of the world's illegal drugs. We're responsible for a third of the world's environmental damage. Yet they like to blame Mexico for all these things. There's not one case of a terrorist crossing the Mexican border. I'm confident that we are going to have humane and comprehensive immigration reform. It's going to take time. We're going to have to do pieces at a time, but it'll go through.

SIX

INTERNAL MIGRATION

THE CHALLENGE OF SOCIAL JUSTICE IS TO EVOKE A SENSE OF
COMMUNITY THAT WE NEED TO MAKE OUR NATION A BETTER PLACE,
JUST AS WE MAKE IT A SAFER PLACE. *Marian Wright Edelman*

The Latino diaspora within the United States is a multilayered phenomenon
that does not adhere to many people's preconceived notions of immigration.
For example, a common misperception is that Puerto Ricans on the U.S.
mainland are international migrants. Furthermore, as was made clear by
Andrea Scopia's brief comments in the previous chapter, the racialization
of the Chicano community that has accompanied the ongoing immigration
debates has made every Latino vulnerable to the "charge" of being a new
immigrant. The persistence of the view of Latinos as perpetual outsiders in
the U.S. imaginary is played out in the lives of internal migrants. The genuine population surge of foreign-born Latin Americans notwithstanding,
many within the U.S. population fail to understand that this is in large part
a result of this population being much younger as a whole. The population's
youthfulness and the fact that they have a significantly higher birthrate than
whites in this country account for most of the population increase over
time. Yet because so much media attention is devoted to undocumented
immigration as the cause of demographic change, when Latinos migrate
internally to regions of the U.S. that heretofore have had few Latinos, they
are often perceived as international rather than internal migrants.

To fully comprehend the ongoing Latinoization of the U.S., especially
in areas where a Latino and/or Mexican population did not exist previously or was few in number, one must consider the cultural, economic, and
social implications of relocation. While it is true that the motivations for
international migration are usually stronger than those for internal migra-

tion, I have found that economic opportunity and necessity are the primary reasons for the latter. But a close second was the desire for a fresh start. Numerous times I heard accounts of families moving their children from an inner-city environment that was deemed threatening to a small rural community where the environment was perceived to be safer and less hostile, free from inner-city threats such as gang activity, drugs, and crime.

The three interviews presented in this chapter cut across generations, educational levels, and professions. All three of these interview subjects are originally from South Texas, which speaks to the perceived limits to opportunity for success in this region, especially for the Marinez and Fuentes families, who followed the migrant farmworker trails in the early and mid-twentieth century. What they also have in common is pride in their cultural and linguistic heritage—one that they have deliberately sought to maintain. Likewise, in their individual ways, each seeks to represent his or her community in deeds, action, or words and cares very much about the well-being of his or her community, whether "community" is defined narrowly or broadly.

HUMBERTO FUENTES

Humberto Fuentes was identified as a potential contact for me by a coworker who knew of his involvement with the Idaho Migrant Council. Humberto has two older brothers in Texas. Four of his siblings were born in Mexico. His father had a passport and moved from Matamoros to Portland before migrating to Caldwell, Idaho, in 1952, where he and his family lived in a labor camp and worked the sugar beet and fruit crops. At a Mexican restaurant in downtown Nampa, Humberto told me about his more than forty years of activism and advocacy and the changes he has witnessed in Latino activism.

HUMBERTO: I was the founder of Idaho Migrant Council, back in '69–'70. I was executive director for thirty-two years. I'm the national chair for Farmworker Justice in D.C. and on the Mexican Consulate Advisory Group. I'm still very much involved in the Latino community. For all practical purposes I should be retired. I spent thirty-two years with the *concilio,* and then we ran into a problem; *todo el tiempo* . . . there was a little group that wanted me out. Some thought I was too political and aggressive. So they got rid of me. We had a big battle. They are no longer an advocacy organization. They changed their name. We were known all over the place as the Migrant Council, and they changed to Community Council. It is terrible when you spend so much of your life to build an advocacy group and then you see something like that happen. But I guess we're not unique; in many, many places around the country that has happened.

We wouldn't have made all the gains if it wasn't for the walkouts and demonstrations of the '60s and '70s. This is a very conservative state. I developed the council from two people to an agency with about four hundred employees and a budget of $10 million. Politically we were very strong. We developed it into a membership organization. At one time we had five thousand paying members, similar to a union. César Chávez helped me develop it. He was one of my mentors. We structured the organization similar to a union, but we couldn't be a union because Idaho is a right-to-work state.

> LOUIS: *I'd like to hear your family story. So many people think immigration has only occurred in the past twenty years.*

HUMBERTO: The only thing we are not being blamed for right now is the Iraq War, and they may come up with some angle to blame us for that too. In the '70s *también* there were people trying to divide the community, so it's nothing new. I think the problem is that the conservative media has really done a number on us. Even good, decent, Anglo middle-of-the-road

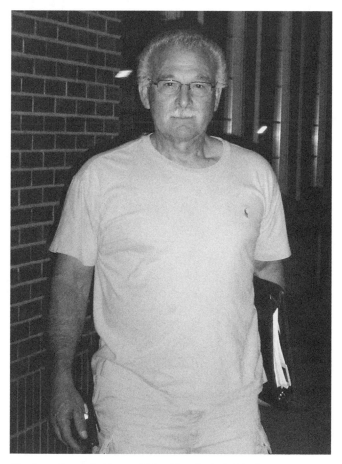

Humberto Fuentes in Nampa Idaho. Photo by Louis Mendoza.

citizens are convinced that it's really bad for the economy and the community. Unfortunately, they've convinced the majority of citizens that it is a bad thing. The ones with strong positions who are making lots of noise are the Minutemen types.

My family experience is not a lot different. In the '40s, '50s, there was a lot of opportunity to work in the fields, and my two oldest brothers were born in Tejas, and four of us were born in Mexico. In that time it was not hard to get a passport—it was maybe $15 or $20 and documentation and you were on this side. My father had contacts in El Valle,[1] so he decided to move there from Matamoros, Mexico. He had some *compadres* and one *compadre* was a *troquero* [truck driver].

In those days the *trocas* [trucks] were like buses; the families rode in the back. We came with six or eight families that migrated to Caldwell, Idaho— that was my first experience. The labor camp is still there. We came in and worked the fields—sugar beets, onion, fruits, apples, cherries—and then we followed the crops around—eastern Idaho for potatoes and then strawberries in Oregon. We moved around and ended up in West Texas usually around October or November. We went back and forth. I was about eight or nine years old, and I had two brothers, and we'd all work in the fields, until I got drafted. I was twenty-two or twenty-three. I served two years. That was when Vietnam was just beginning to get rough. I think I had four months left when things got really bad. I was stationed at Fort Sam Houston in San Antonio. They sent me home actually.

During my final two years in the military I joined the boxing teams. My older brother bought some gloves in Reynosa. He would beat the hell out of me until I started getting competitive in the military. I came out, and I could really play around. I considered going professional at one time. The thing that turned me around was in San Antonio—it's a boxing town—one time the gym at the base was closed for renovation, and we went to train with the professionals in the West Side of San Antonio. I saw some things there that I thought, "Is this what I want to do the rest of my life?" I still like the sport but decided it was not what I wanted to do.

I got out in April and got married in October. I met my wife in Bend, Oregon, but she was a Chicana del Valle—Alamo. I met her at a dance, and then I had to go to the army. She waited for me to get out. I started working construction for a while. I decided to go to school, so I went to Treasure Valley Community College. I wanted to be a pilot. And at the time *todos los mexicanos* you would be a welder or electronics. This was 1966–1967. I took the next most challenging trade, industrial electronics. They had a migrant program there. They gave me a job as a counselor. I think I had 120 Latinos at the junior college. At that time most of the grants the federal government gave were through the churches or colleges. We had an advisory group, and we were dissatisfied with the way things were going at the *colegio*. The *colegio* decided to fire me and two others. The farmers started complaining because we were organizing—going around to the labor camps.

César Chávez was very active and the civil rights movement was in full swing, and so that's how the Idaho Migrant Council got started. They fired us, but we'd already gone around to the Colorado Migrant Council, the Utah Migrant Council. Lalo Delgado, a poet and good friend of mine from El Paso, helped us, and OEO [Office of Economic Opportunity] was the funding source for the *colegio*. We filed a suit, and MALDEF helped us. We took it to federal court against the *colegio*. They were not properly utilizing the participants because they were supposed to have a policymaking power and the college wouldn't give that power to the community. We challenged them, and we won. When we won they no longer wanted us. They kicked us out. But we still had three or four months left on the grant, and they hired me as director to run the program for the last three months.

LOUIS: *So what did your parents think of all this?*

HUMBERTO: Both of my parents didn't know English. They were farm-workers. People were scaring them, saying there was a contract out for me, that I was too militant. They would just say, "Cuídate" [Be careful]. They were concerned about my safety, but they understood. They had suffered. They knew there were a lot of injustices, *discriminación*. You can imagine in those years. When we first organized the Migrant Council one of those things we did was to fight those signs saying "No Dogs or Mexicans Are Allowed." We were used to those signs in West Texas. We saw a lot on the migrant route. *Híjole*, I remember when we were on the road and we stopped to buy hamburgers and these signs would say to go around the back. It was not out of the ordinary. In the late '60s and early '70s *con el* Chicano movement and civil rights we started taking a stand. We hooked up with the Catholic church here. We made a lot of noise, and we were able to defeat that here.

LOUIS: *So most of your mentors were from elsewhere?*

HUMBERTO: Yeah. I was in Santa Fe when La Raza Unida had its first convention. There were sparks in that room because Corky [Gonzáles] didn't get along with José Ángel [Gutiérrez], but they were exciting times. You probably heard of [Colegio] Lincoln Juárez in Austin. I was the chair at the time. I was the national chair for the Farm Workers Organizations. The Colegio was going very strong. And then those two guys got into a fight, estando todo, and they pulled the grant. Things were going terrible. So they called us at the national office. I went there and I became the chairman and tried to put it back together, but it was so far gone. We had to let that thing go. We had a building there and we had attorneys trying to help us and we spent dos años. The concept was good. And then the other one was the Colegio César Chávez in Oregon in the mid-'70s, early '80s. They took over a Catholic training school in Mount Angel and ran it for a while. There were a lot of attempts to get *colegios* going. Some of them never made it.

We built the organization to do great stuff. I feel proud that a lot of the *movimiento*, of what happened in Oregon, I had my hand in it. Where the Migrant Council is there is a *mercado*—we built that. I started working on it in '81–'82 and completed it in '84. I was able to get some funds and some local banks to finance it. We had a very strong housing program. We built programs around the state for Migrant Head Start, mental health, a strong housing program. We had funding from foundations, federal government, however we could fund it. That's how I got involved with the Northwest Council because they funded us for three or four years. In Twin Falls there is a labor camp there that was really torn down. There was a guy who managed the camp with a gun, and at ten o'clock he'd lock it down and wouldn't let any of the workers in or out. It was terrible. We demonstrated, and we were able to correct that, but we had so many problems that the farmers were ready to tear it down and so I came in and negotiated with them. And I bought it from them—forty acres. We got city block grants. We got some federal grants to renovate some of the units. It's a good asset.

LOUIS: *It turned into a housing complex?*

HUMBERTO: Yeah. It's called El Milagro. Now it is inside the city, but before it was on the edge. All the labor camps were outside—outta sight, outta mind.

LOUIS: *You've been forty years now in the struggle; do you feel that we are finally claiming our place in society?*

HUMBERTO: We had a lot to do with paving the way for a lot of the Latino professionals. They had a lot of opportunity. The only regret that I have now is that I think a lot of young Latinos have not taken the time to learn about and prepare to take over *el movimiento*. In the 1980s and early 2000s we went through a change to the "Me Generation," and some of us fought for that to happen so the young people would have better opportunities than we did. Unfortunately, somewhere along the line a lot of the commitment to the community was lost. Now you see some changes. Now you get some of the college students saying that they want to do something. But saying that and actually doing it are different. In the '60s and '70s there was total commitment. We were committed to *el movimiento,* and whatever it took we did it. And now I don't think we have that same commitment from the young people.

> LOUIS: *Is it a paradox that they have had it easier so there is no fire in the belly?*

HUMBERTO: In fact, you will run across a lot of young Latinos who say, "I've never been discriminated against." A lot of the undocumented immigrants have not experienced the long-term racism, and they come here to work. They are mistreated; there is no question about it. But to them it is not like us; we had no place to go. I mean we were here, we were discriminated against, and we wanted to do something about it, and so we organized to do it. I get a sense that there is a lack of organization. In those years you had Corky Gonzáles, very radical, very ideological. You had José Ángel Gutiérrez. More political. And you had Reies López Tijerina fighting the land issues [in northern New Mexico]. César Chávez, very humble, talking about farmworker rights. Together you kind of hit all the parts, but now where do you turn? I am sure you have some good *movimiento*—the immigration movement, it's one thing. Some of us who have been here for a long time still support the immigration issue, but it's not the same thing. We used to have a really strong coalition here; unfortunately, in the last five years it has crumbled a little bit. There seems to be a lack of strong leadership. Times have changed. Now we don't have one national leader. It's up to everyone to get things done. It's complicated. You work hard to get others prepared to have a better life, but you still want them to keep that fire in the belly. In Idaho, we were lucky that we were able to keep it together for a long time. We had a lot of power. I think the Republicans resented that. The Democrats backed away. The Democrats here in this state are so weak because they are almost like Republicans now. I read Paulo Freire's *Pedagogy of the Oppressed* a long time ago, and it stuck in my mind that it is so easy for you to become the oppressor.

I often think that what we really need now, Louis, is a Latino think tank. Taking the old and the new and the not so new. We don't have enough research. We have bits and pieces. If 9/11 hadn't happened, who knows? But the vast majority of folks want to see *mexicanos* as a threat to national security now.

Juan Marinez introduced me to his parents, Efrain and Francisca Marinez, at their home in East Lansing, Michigan. Originally from South Texas, they came to the upper Midwest in the late 1920s as migrant workers. As one of the oldest Latino families in the region, the Marinezes had been instrumental in making change in the area as they stood up for their rights to own a home and have fair working conditions.

FRANCISCA: Nacimos en México, pero nos criamos en Tejas. [We were born in Mexico, but we grew up in Texas.]

LOUIS: *¿En qué parte de México? [In what part of Mexico?]*

FRANCISCA: Piedras Negras yo nací y él nació en Cuatro Cienegas, Coahuila. [I was born in Piedras Negras, and he was born in Cuatro Cienegas, Coahuila.]

JUAN: How old were you when you came?

FRANCISCA: Cuando yo vine aquí, tenía como cuatro años. [When I came here I was four years old.]

LOUIS: *Did your parents ever tell you why they decided to come?*

FRANCISCA: Well no, porque mi papá agarró trabajo aquí, so se trajo a mi mamá para acá. [Well no, because my dad got work here, so he brought my mom.]

EFRAIN: At that time the border was open. Then they started putting a lot of stuff, a lot of red tape, and made it impossible. In the '30s, the immigration department was worse than it is today. There was a lot of people deported, people in bunches, a lot of people born here that were deported.

LOUIS: When did you first come to Michigan?

EFRAIN: I came here very, very young. We come here in the twenties, and I was probably five years old. Those years, those years don't count. [Laughter] My father brought us here from Texas. He was a young guy. He liked it here. We all worked in the beets when I was seven or eight years old. They didn't let the *gabachos* [white kids] work in the fields; they force them to go to school. But us? Shoot, in those days they got the kids like me out of school to go and work on the sugar beets. Sometimes I think back and I say, "Golly, it was worse than the Germans." They just did whatever they wanted to us. My dad was very liberal; he didn't ever let people push him around. We had our own car. It was an advantage, so he didn't have to depend on the sugar beet company.

Efrain and Francisca Marinez in their home in East Lansing, Michigan. Photo by Louis Mendoza.

LOUIS: You all went back and forth to Texas?

EFRAIN: Yes, to Crystal City. Some years we didn't go back every year. We stayed here because we had no money to go back, and a lot of people, they would do the same thing. When I was a kid, I used to know a lot of people born in St. Paul, Minnesota. I used to work not too far from St. Paul in a small town called Buffalo Lake. It was very lonely. The people who worked there were very nice, but not all the people was like that.

LOUIS: So when you stayed in the winter, what kind of work would your dad do?

EFRAIN: Nothing. Whatever little money we made was for food. We had to freeze. We lived in the company trailers. We had one of those heaters in the middle, and me and my brother, we used to go and pick up coal around the railroad to heat the trailer. It was hard. A lot of people came from Mexico on the train and stayed because they didn't know English, and they didn't know when the train went back.

LOUIS: When did you get married?

FRANCISCA: In 1944, but we knew each other since we were little.

EFRAIN: We didn't have it so bad, but there were a lot of people that had it really bad, and my dad always liked to help people.

LOUIS: Since you would go back and forth to Texas, did you think of Texas as home? Or did you think of yourself as having two homes?

FRANCISCA: He still wants to go back.

EFRAIN: Once the kids started to come, I and Francis have to do something. I knew what was here in Lansing; there was very good schools. And we knew in Texas there were bad schools. They'll say there was no discrimination here, not like in the South, but it was worse here because you don't know who discriminated against you. In Texas you knew. There was no job for us. The door was open, but you never qualified for the job. You gotta go to the fields . . . the fields. The first place here in Lansing that started giving a job to the *mexicanos* was the Motor Wheel. Then they tried to get them out of there, but Motor Wheel backed them up because they were good workers. Then they started working in the steel mills and then other places. People didn't start getting jobs until the war because then they needed us; then they were begging us to go to work. That's when I got a job in the factory. It was very good pay. I made about $200 a week. In those days that was really good. So we bought a house. Francis, she's a very good administrator. I gave her the money. I kid her now, I said, "Francis, I think I've got to sue you, because I never cashed a check." We never suffered. We were lucky.

LOUIS: *What did you think about leaving Texas?*

FRANCISCA: I didn't have any family. My mother died, and then my father died, and then I got married, so this was my family.

LOUIS: *Do you still think of yourself as being Tejano?*

FRANCISCA: Yes, I do. Some people ask me, "What are you?" I said, "I'm Mexican." "Oh, I thought you were Italian or Greek." "No, I'm Mexican."

EFRAIN: I'm a *mexicano* 100 percent. I think the kids got that from us, and their grandkids, they're proud to be *mexicano.*

LOUIS: *Was it hard to raise your kids to be proud of who they were?*

FRANCISCA: No, they heard us talking about it, so they knew. We never forced them. The only thing we told them is to get married with Mexicans and they didn't . . . [Laughter] Just Juan.

EFRAIN: We made great sacrifices for the kids. We buy a house in East Lansing, and they don't want *mexicanos*, but I just happen to know this lawyer that got us a house. He had a brother who was a real estate lawyer. That's how we bought our house in East Lansing.

JUAN: The lawyers, they were Arab Lebanese. They knew what discrimination was.

EFRAIN: He used to tell me, "You remind me of my dad because you always fight for what you believe in. My dad was the same way, and he didn't speak English."

LOUIS: *Where does that come from, the spirit to fight for what you believe is right?*

EFRAIN: My dad was like that. A lot of people complain that the gringo had everything—the money and the land. But my dad used to tell me when I was a kid, "Hey, you know, gringos are not smarter than you. You are as smart as any gringo." I believed it. I said I can do anything better than the gringos, and I've proven it many times. I had a good job in Texas before I came here. I was the foreman on a farm. I was the only *mexicano* that had that job. They hired me because they knew I didn't let anybody push me around. It was hard. After a while they respected me.

I still have the *respeto de* [respect for] Texas. Texas to me is the same one I saw in my mind. When I go there, I'm disappointed. Everything has changed. The *gabachos* there discriminated against you, but they tell you, "I don't really like you. As a matter of fact, I don't like Mexicans." They're just that way right in your face! And especially in my hometown area. So you say I don't like the gringos, we're in the same boat. So you knew these guys didn't like you. In a small town Mexican people don't let the gringos push them around. In Cristal, there were only ten thousand in population; I remember *mexicanos* made a riot there, because of the way they treated us.

LOUIS: *When you moved here, there weren't many* mexicanos?

FRANCISCA: No, not really. We felt isolated. The neighbors, they don't even say hi.

EFRAIN: I was thinking for my kids. It was not easy. I had to pay double down here in East Lansing. They do it because they didn't want any people to come and pay the rent or buy a house. So I bought my house, and it's all paid off. When I got the house through this guy who helped me to with all the house papers, he said, "I'm going to tell you something, Frank, to make you feel good. You're the only one in the whole area that owns his house. All these people, they don't own the house." I found out the *gabachos*, when you're like them, they can't believe it. He kind of thinks, "Mexican can't be on my level."

LOUIS: *Did you feel isolated growing up?*

JUAN: Isolated in multiple ways. When I first played baseball at my elementary school, Saint Thomas Aquinas, I was the only Mexican kid. It was all-white, and a lot of kids came from Haslett, Okemos, farm kids, and suburb kids and city kids. They gave me a hard time, but at the same time it was very confusing. I remember in the fifth grade when I was playing baseball 'cause the cheerleaders were cheering, it will always stay vivid in my mind, "Hit it like you used to hit in Mexico." That was really strange because I'd never been to Mexico. I had an image of Texas but not of Mexico. In my mind I was from here, but in their minds I was always an outsider. What made me participate in and out of those circles was sports. I was in the first teams in baseball, and in football. It was interesting to me, especially in football; it was like a license to hit gringos. The harder you hit them, the more you knocked them out of the game, the more you got complimented. I made it a goal to wipe out a player at each game.

EFRAIN: I remember when Juan was playing, I was watching, and this guy, he was the owner of the plant that I was working at, and he had four or five kids. One of them was in the school there, so he called the coach and said, "Get that Mexican out of there and put my kids in there." And I turn around and gave it to him. "I pay the same taxes you do, and I pay the school like you." The coach didn't say anything. The guy kind of embarrassed himself. That's the way I was. I was never afraid to talk.

LOUIS: *You went to parochial school?*

JUAN: Yeah, all the way through high school. When I went to high school there was only one other Mexican kid. He was a González, but the majority of Latinos were Cuban refugee kids. They were brought in to our school as a big group. A lot of Cubans that I went to school with, I got to know them well. I was asked to translate for them by the school principal. That's also when I became knowledgeable that they spoke a different dialect, because I didn't understand everything they were saying.

LOUIS: *Were they treated differently?*

JUAN: Oh, very much. Their tuition was paid for, they were given apartments, and they were given stipends. Immediately their parents were given jobs, if not the mother, the father.

EFRAIN: Good jobs, in the offices. They never worked in the fields. The Cubans were very grateful to the *mexicanos* that were here that helped them settle in. But the breakup was in the '60s when we had the grape boycotts. The *mexicanos* took on the issues of the civil rights battles. That's where the *mexicanos* and the Cubans started to separate, because I think that they were afraid. This is what they saw in Cuba—people standing up, a revolution. They didn't want any kind of politics; they had it good. That's when you saw the distancing. We still know families, we say hello, but not that closeness because we were associated with the civil rights movement.

I've been in several marches. I marched with Chávez. He impressed me a lot. He earned people's respect. At my work, the *gabachos* didn't talk to us, and I didn't care. I told them this all the time. I told the foreman one time, "I don't want these guys to like me; I want these guys to respect me for what I am." That's what I wanted. Mr. Lupe Orta, who also was a fighter, he didn't take any guff from anybody. Mr. Elleno Medrano, he too was a fighter. The rest of *mexicanos* at the plant were just chickens. They were afraid to lose their job. They would come to me and say, "Aren't you afraid to lose your job? You've got a family." I would say, "That's a chance I have to take."

LOUIS: *Do you think things have changed for the better?*

EFRAIN: Yes, I think in that plant I made a lot of change. They didn't do it when I was there, but when I got out of there, they started making a lot of changes. They didn't want you to know they made the changes. I had a big fight in the church, and they made a lot of changes too but only after a long time. They didn't want to admit that they were wrong. I told the bishop one time, "You're not my bishop. I don't respect you." And he asked me, "Why?" "Because you don't stand up for the civil rights of the *mexicanos*." The church didn't support the *mexicanos* during the marches. They just closed their eyes. I got mad with a priest once. Juan used to have a girlfriend, and he [the priest] would go and he would tell the girl's family to watch their girl 'cause she was dating a Mexican. I gave it to him, and he said, "I am sorry. I don't know what I was thinking."

> LOUIS: *What do you think about the issue of immigration? What do we still need to learn?*

EFRAIN: I think that *mexicanos* should be more conscious. We don't support the movement the way we should.

DINA MONTES

Dina Montes and I spoke at her apartment in Spanish Harlem. I knew Dina when she was an undergraduate student at St. Mary's University in San Antonio, Texas, in the late 1990s. Originally from the Rio Grande Valley of Texas, she went to Syracuse to get an M.A. in journalism and had moved to New York to work as a journalist. At the time we met, she was working for the U.S. Fund for UNICEF and was on maternity leave awaiting the birth of her first child.

> LOUIS: *When I began this trip I thought I was going to talk to mostly recent immigrants, but so much of the story has also been the experience of Latinos throughout the generations who have relocated and contributed to the new geography.*

DINA: That's one thing that freaked me out when I first came to New York. I expected to find Mexicans here, like every other group, but not at such a high volume. What also surprised me was just how indigenous they were. One thing people ask me here is, "Oh, what are you?" I tell them, "Mexican," and they're like, "Oh, you don't look Mexican." They tell me that because they expect me to be something more exotic. This one cabbie asked me if I'm Egyptian, and I'm like, "No," and he's like, "Italian?" I said, "I'm Latino," and he's like, "Oh, what kind?" and I say, "Mexican." He says, "Mexican women are short and fat." He told me he goes to the Copa Cabana, and all the Mexican women there are short and fat. It's people's perception, but it is also that this indigenous population has come.

In Staten Island there's a lot of construction. It's more suburban there, so they have day laborers standing on the corners being picked up for work. For the most part, even though Staten Island is very Republican, people are still pretty respectful. There hasn't been a lot of hate crime, but one story I

Dina Montes in her apartment in Spanish Harlem, New York.
Photo by Louis Mendoza.

was doing was inspired by a study in California. Two UCLA professors had done a study on L.A. and New York, and one thing they had noticed is that a lot of day laborers here in New York are homeless. I went out to report the story, and I met this guy from Mexico City who was camping out in an abandoned trailer in the North Shore. He had $500 on him, but he was like, "I need $100 more because my family's building a house back in Mexico so I'm going to wire it to them and then I'll think about getting a home." I met a lot of those guys, and most of them were single and really, really young. A lot of them shack up eight to a one-bedroom apartment. A lot of these laborers were getting cheated. I mean, they were being told, "We'll pay you at the end of the week," and then they wouldn't pay them. There was definitely a lot of resentment. This other reporter did a story on contractors. A lot of contractors were pissed off because rival businesses would hire undocumented workers and provide a lot of services, and they were being undermined business-wise.

LOUIS: *What started this recent wave of Mexican immigration?*

DINA: That's the first thing I asked this one kid in Queens when I first arrived. I asked him, "Why do you guys come over here when Texas, California, are so much closer, and you know you could be closer to communities out there?" He said, "Well, my brother came here, and he liked it, and then I came here." And that's pretty much what I got from everybody else. It's so expensive, but they have this tight community. There's also a lot of Colombians here. I was doing a story on this Latino soccer league in Staten Island. This Colombian started a Latino soccer league, but when the Mexicans started coming, instead of just integrating with them, they made their own league. He complained about it, because he thought Latinos should be more united, regardless of nationality.

> LOUIS: *With New York being such a cosmopolitan city, where do issues around immigration come into the conversation?*

DINA: I think a lot of people are getting on the bandwagon of this anti-immigration thing. To me it all seems very scapegoatish, because we have a war going on. It's a distraction. I definitely see it a lot on TV. New York is different. The immigration rallies that happened here included everybody, people from Africa, a lot of Asians. Even the Republican mayor, Bloomberg, is very vocal about supporting immigration. He definitely wants to protect immigrant rights, and there are laws here that protect immigrants. That's one thing that cops always want to tell people—if there's a crime, report it; we have nothing to do with INS. If a New York City mayoral candidate were to say he was anti-immigrant he would lose. I feel like New York is different from other cities because it has many different ethnic groups.

In Staten Island, there was a problem between the black and brown communities because a lot of black youths were starting to rob Mexicans, knowing that they had a lot of money on them because they don't have checking accounts. These are men that don't belong to gangs and definitely don't tend to be criminally oriented, but some of them were getting pissed. I remember talking to some of them and they were like, "We just come here to work, and this isn't right. I have nothing against black people, but they're really mean." You were starting to get those kinds of tensions. There were some young kids wanting to beat up people for kicks and money. I haven't seen that here in Spanish Harlem.

> LOUIS: *Having been raised in Texas and being here now, has your identity changed?*

DINA: I don't really question how it's changed my sense of identity. It has opened me up to a lot more different people. A lot of my close friends now tend to be Asian or white, and that has opened me up to knowing different people from different ethnic backgrounds but also realizing how much we have in common. For example, this Thai girl I'm really close to, her mom sounds just like my mom. They have the same traditional values that children are supposed to support their parents and they're not supposed to

225

leave the house until they get married. That tells me we need much more awareness of how a lot of immigrants have the same values even if they might be from different religions or different continents. Out here there are a lot of Ecuadorians, Peruvians, and there's also a lot of people from Guatemala, Central America, Honduras, and Panama.

LOUIS: *Do you feel equally connected with them?*

DINA: Yeah, I do. Recently I went to go get a haircut, and there was this girl from Ecuador. She was an indigenous girl, and she was asking for help. She wanted to take bilingual classes. She had just gotten here nine months ago, and so I'm telling her, do this, do that. There's a lot of classes that are free, but she thought she needed money. She just got here and she's a shampoo girl at this small salon, so I'm just pretty much telling her where to go. The language barrier is horrible. Once they hear you talking Spanish they're so relieved because usually they speak very little English. At work there are Puerto Rican coworkers, and sometimes we do start talking in Spanish, especially if they're trying to tell me something a little bit on the DL [down low]. But it's a different history for them given that it's a commonwealth and they don't have this whole immigration issue like we do, so sometimes you hear them making these snarky comments.

LOUIS: *Do you think they get their ideas from the media, or do they get cultivated among themselves as a way to get a leg up on another group?*

DINA: I definitely think a lot of people get their information from FOX News. A lot of times when you start talking that's one of the things they immediately say, "I saw this on the Chris Matthews or Lou Dobbs show." I hear a lot more from people just walking down the street. I once heard these two Puerto Rican guys discussing immigrants, and one of them was like, "You know, they're good people. They work hard." And the other one's like, "No, they're taking over the neighborhood."

LOUIS: *So you sense some tension within the Latino community?*

DINA: Yeah, but it hasn't gotten bad. One positive thing you definitely do see is delis being opened up by Mexicans. If you walk on 112th there's a little produce stand. It's Mexican. Within a three-blocks radius of this building there's probably five Mexican businesses. It's nice to see because they definitely tend to be a lot cleaner, and they sell a lot more produce, which is good for this neighborhood because it's really hard to find fresh tomatoes, lettuce, and fruits. The Puerto Rican community has been hit really hard with diabetes.

LOUIS: *I was surprised in Chicago to hear people talk about the Latino community and how well the communities get along. There the Puerto Ricans are very much defenders of immigrants. Elvira Arellano was holed up for a year in a church in Humboldt Park, a Puerto Rican neighborhood, and they rallied around her.*

DINA: I think Chicago has a longer history of Mexican immigration. It just started here in the '90s. I moved to New York City in 2000, and everybody said the Mexican immigration boom started in the last five years. The one thing that I'm really interested in seeing is, ten years from now, how things will be for this Chicano population springing up. You see the little Chicano kids now . . . they talk to me in English and Spanish. The oldest kids might be like ten or twelve, and they definitely have that strong work ethic. In Brooklyn, the first year I lived in Park Slope, there was this guy who used to sell mangos with chili powder, and the guy asked me, "What are you?" and I told him, "Oh, I'm from Texas. My parents are Mexican." He's like, "What do you do for a living?" I told him I was a reporter, and he turns to his son and he's like, "See, you can totally accomplish something for yourself." The little boy's looking at me like, "Yeah," and I was just like so humbled by this. They are trying to tell their kids to stay in school and do this, and the little boy was awesome, because I think most kids would be embarrassed of having to sell fruit at a fruit stand in Brooklyn and this little kid's telling people in English, "Hey, man, do you want some fruit? $1.25."

LOUIS: *Tell me a bit about your family history.*

DINA: We're first-generation American. My family came from Michoacán, which is a central Pacific coastal state. My grandfather jumped ship from the Mexican army, so he had to escape because he was AWOL. He found a job in the Rio Grande Valley. My grandma came with him, and she tells us that she hated that area because it was very different from her state, which is cool and lush, with steep hills. The valley is just flat and hot and dry. It was part of the Bracero Program because he worked close to Anzalduas Park for a big rancher out there, and that's one of the reasons why my grandma gets Social Security. But she never wanted to move to the U.S. She still lives in Mexico. She's a diehard. My mom and aunts settled here because of work.

LOUIS: *What do they think of you living up here?*

DINA: They don't like it. I've definitely settled into like the New York lifestyle. There's a lot of things that I would miss about New York if I were to leave. At the same time, it's so expensive to raise a family here. Ideally, I would like to stay in one of the boroughs, like South Brooklyn or even East Queens. I like the fact that one-third of the population is immigrant, and that's something you won't find in any other city. It's extremely diverse. You definitely get the idea that the world is shrinking here, and I think it is something that people here are very aware of. Being here has opened me up to different people and different experiences.

> LOUIS: *What are your aspirations for your daughter in this world with respect to a sense of identity and belonging?*

DINA: Her name will be Vida. I definitely want to teach her Spanish. I already bought bilingual books for her. I want her to retain that language and have a sense of other people's rights and dignity and take this holistic approach to life that, okay, we have differences, but you know when it comes down to it, we all have the same rights. I definitely want her to be proud of who she is. Both races. He's Welsh, Irish, and English. Language is important for me. Out here I don't really get to practice my Spanish as much as I would like. But unlike back home where most of the time I'd use Chicano slang, out here it has to be clean. It's nice to keep practicing because I'd find that when I go to the valley and talk to my grandma a lot of the words have escaped me. My grandma speaks purely Spanish. I hope my daughter can retain that language. I know it's going to be difficult. The great-grandchildren of my grandma still talk to her, but I think generationally people tend to lose the language. You'll find second-generation Chicanos that don't speak as fluent or any Spanish. I hope not to have that be the case with my kid. That's one of the reasons why being here in New York is hard. I'm so far removed.

SEVEN

LIVING IN THE
BORDERLANDS MEANS . . .

LIVING IN THE BORDERLANDS MEANS . . .

. . . YOU ARE THE BATTLEGROUND

WHERE THE ENEMIES ARE KIN TO EACH OTHER;

YOU ARE AT HOME, A STRANGER,

THE BORDER DISPUTES HAVE BEEN SETTLED

THE VOLLEY OF SHOTS HAVE SHATTERED THE TRUCE

YOU ARE WOUNDED, LOST IN ACTION

DEAD, FIGHTING BACK . . .

TO SURVIVE THE BORDERLANDS

YOU MUST LIVE *SIN FRONTERAS*

BE A CROSSROADS.   *Gloria Anzaldúa*

The fluid, multifaceted, contradictory, and rich experience of living in the
U.S.-Mexico borderlands so eloquently articulated and popularized by Gloria Anzaldúa in the mid-1980s is a useful starting point for gaining insight
into this unique space that at once evokes the future and the past.[1] In this
place that often makes one feel outside of the U.S., the issue of Latinoization might seem moot, as the population in most cities along the border
is overwhelmingly composed of people of Mexican descent. Newspapers,
radio, and television, as well as billboards, are bilingual or primarily in
Spanish, as is the chatter of people on the streets, in the *mercados*, and in
stores and restaurants.

But life along the border has changed drastically in the past few decades
and especially since September 11, 2001. While it would be a stretch to make
generalizations about the two-thousand-mile international boundary, all the
people I spoke with in Texas, Arizona, and California mentioned the intensi-

fied militarization of the border following 9/11. This phenomenon is seen as a spiritual breach of the cultural ethos that has reigned on the border since it has existed, where linguistic, cultural and even human fluidity have been the norm. What was once a consensual and mutually beneficial partnership is now being regulated and hyper-scrutinized as part of the ever-increasing scrutiny of an increasingly militarized state. The convergence of the prison-industrial complex with the military-industrial complex and immigration and customs enforcement under the rubric of national security strives to pervert, congeal, and control that which was once much more fluid. This is not to say that it has succeeded, but this is exactly what has many people horrified as the mainstream attitudes of the U.S. heartland are played out on the nation's margins.

This final chapter of interviews presents five conversations, one of which is with relatives in El Paso I had never met before. Everyday life on the border continues to be a palimpsest of old and new, north and south. While neglect or ignorance of border life is nothing new, attention from politicians and pundits is. Any number of other conversations could have been placed in this chapter, but I've chosen these because of the controversies and contradictions to which they speak. Discourses on the law and belonging permeate these conversations. The insights offered here reflect the ongoing dilemma of immigration: as both an integral part of border life and U.S. labor and economic history and as fierce under- and overdevelopment that continually marginalizes Mexican culture and people. They offer glimpses of life on both sides of the border and the efforts to obliterate the cultural history and contributions of the working class. They speak with historical awareness about intensified violence and generational cultural wars, even as they eloquently represent how the dialectics of border culture are unique and empowering.

Lupe and Jesse Vega are third cousins on my father's side whom I had not met prior to visiting with them on this trip. They spent part of a Saturday sharing family history and their views on how El Paso has changed since they moved there from Houston in 1946.

> LOUIS: *I'm glad I've had a chance to meet you. I haven't met too many relatives outside of Houston. When I was young, we visited relatives on my mom's side in Mexico once. We don't know too much about our family history before coming here. But I always keep in mind that we're immigrants too, and it wasn't that long ago.*

JESSE: Those stories account for everybody in this country except the Indians.

> LOUIS: *I think people forget that, and they forget that a lot of this land was once Mexico. The border's there and it's enforced, but at the same time culturally and linguistically there's a connectedness between people.*

JESSE: People like my mom that came to this country, and this applies to people here in El Paso the same way—they crossed to Mexico at will, and they came back at will. They didn't have to go beyond downtown El Paso. When I was growing up in Magnolia, when I went to school, we didn't know English. Teachers had to learn Spanish. Some of us were Mexican Americans, some were illegal, and some were Mexican citizens.

> LOUIS: *Did it make a difference to you?*

JESSE: Nah, we were friends. We played together.

> LOUIS: *Were you given a hard time for speaking Spanish?*

JESSE: Here in El Paso . . . yes.

LOUIS: Isn't that strange?

JESSE: The thing is that you know going back everything was up there in the Second Ward. They had grammar schools, they had parochial schools, they had churches, they had high schools, La Bowie. Everybody talks about La Bowie High School. A lot of success from people in the Segundo Barrio. We came here from Houston when I was fourteen and my brother was fifteen. The next day we went to see my dad where he used to work, and the secretary says, "You guys going to school?" I say, "Yeah, we going to school," and she said, "You guys are Mexican, you have to go to Bowie . . . all Mexicans go to Bowie." Bowie was way up in Second Ward. The next day we caught a bus, and we went as far as we could on the bus, and we got off, and we walked like two miles to get to Bowie and went into the registrar. My brother says, "We'd like to enroll for school." So they gave us a piece a paper, we filled it out, and this lady says, "Oh, you have to go Austin. You people belong in the Austin area." And Austin was right here, walking distance, but we were uninformed. So the next day we went to Austin. Boy, what a big surprise from Houston, where everybody was *mexicano*, to a completely different cultural school, *puro gringo* [all white]. I think in the whole school there was something like three thousand students there, and there was like twenty *mexicanos*.

LUPE: We just mixed. We didn't care if you were Mexican, black, or Puerto Ricans, Orientals. We didn't care. We got along just fine. Grammar school was hard because I didn't know English when I went to school, and then if we talked Spanish we were punished.

LOUIS: How were you punished?

LUPE: They'd say, "Get in the corner," or they'd hit your hand.

JESSE: Horrible times.

LUPE: So you get to the point where what do you do? You can't speak English that well, and you're not allowed to speak Spanish. So what do you do?

LOUIS: Be quiet? [laughter]

LUPE: Yeah, and that's what you did! The whites had more doors open to them because they were always taught more.

JESSE: They were better prepared, their parents. My mom never went to the PTA; my dad didn't. All they did was send us to school, so we went to school. We weren't prepared. When my kids went to school, my wife and I prepared them. We taught them to be leaders. We taught them to sit in the front. When I went to school, we used to hide in the back or in the corner. My kids, they were prepared. They weren't told that they were Mexican. I remember my kid came in one day crying. I said, "What's the matter?" He said, "David called me a damn Mexican." He was about seven years old. I said, "Come here, boy, we're gonna talk." And my boy didn't look Mexican. He's light-skinned, green eyes. But that kid learned it from somebody, and the only other place he could've learned it is at home. My next door neighbor—Baptist, God-fearing people—always ready to help you. But then I wondered, what did they teach this kid about "damn Mexicans"?

LOUIS: *So what did you tell your son?*

JESSE: I told my kid that there were different kinds of people in this world. And we just happen to be Mexicans, a proud race, you know? Our kids were all prepared. We made sure that they did their homework. And when there was a question asked in the class, they were the first to raise up their hand and say, "I have the answer." My kids, when they had a holiday, they used to get mad because they wanted to be in class. When they were sick, they didn't stay home; they wanted to go to school. They were afraid they'd miss something. Entirely different atmosphere. By that time they had Mexican American teachers. In my senior year in Austin High School we got the first Mexican American teacher. His name was Pérez. And before I graduated we talked. He called me and told me about going on to higher education and trying to get ahead and trying to help Mexican people to stay in school.

LOUIS: *Did you go to college?*

JESSE: I went to school under the G.I. Bill. And my kids, all my kids, went to UTEP. When we went to school that was the only college in Texas . . . we figured . . . hey, there's no way we can go to another school outside of El Paso.

LOUIS: *Did you go to college?*

LUPE: Yes, I went to college after twenty-five years.

LOUIS: *And what did you get your degree in?*

LUPE: In management. I went at night for four years, and I had to work full-time. It really helped me a lot. I had a good-paying job with benefits. But I had to quit my job to take care of Mom. I was already sixty-two, but I wanted to go to sixty-five. But I couldn't. I didn't regret it.

LOUIS: Do you have kids?

LUPE: I have one daughter, from my first marriage. She lives in Norfolk, Virginia.

LOUIS: Is she in the military?

LUPE: *Was* in the military. She retired two years ago in December, after twenty-one years. She thought I was going to hold her back when she told me. She was going to college here at the community college, and she couldn't find a job. By that time I was by myself and working. And one day when I came home she said, "Mom, I want to talk to you. Sit down." [Slight laughter] "Why sit down, *mi'ja*? Whether it's good or bad, I can take it." "Well, I'd like to go into the navy. What you think?" I told her the truth. "*Mi'ja*, I can't keep you with me all the time, and you can't depend on me either. You need to go to the outside world and find out how it is. It might be easy; it might be bad. There's all kinds of people, nice people and mean people. I only want you to do two things for me. Continue your college education and don't get into drugs." So I gave her my blessing. But I was very bitter for about a year and a half [slight laughter]. Very bitter at the navy, because they took my baby away. At that time they used to come home and pick them up, and I felt that the navy had taken her away from me. But then after a year and a half she told me that she liked it and that she wanted to make it a career. I said, "OK, *mi'ja*, if that's what you want, I stand by you."

LOUIS: How does she like living in Virginia?

LUPE: It's too cold, and the cost of living is high. There I have a grandson, and he's in school over there. She's waiting for him to get out of school to see where they're going to move. She wants to move to either Dallas or Austin. Back to Texas. She's doing good, but she says it's hard. I said, "*Mi'ja*, I did it too!" Working full-time and going to college at night. There were many times in the wintertime that I wanted to give up, especially in the wintertime. Class at ten o'clock. [Shivering] I look out, it's cold, bundle my jacket like this, and run to the car. I would say, "Oh, God. Help me, help me continue." It was hard, but I did it.

LOUIS: Is her husband white?

LUPE: Well, she had a white baby . . . and my *mi'jo* he's white. But he's changing to a little bit of both. [Slight laughter] I made the mistake of not teaching him Spanish when he was with me. He stayed with me and my husband for four years when my daughter went in deployment overseas.

With *mi'jo* I made the mistake of not teaching him Spanish. I really, really regret it now. But my husband is Anglo, and we always spoke English. I feel bad that I didn't push him to speak Spanish.

JESSE: There's an advantage to speaking Spanish. My son-in-law used to speak Spanish. In fact, his whole family—he came from a big family of twelve. I imposed it on my kids when they were little, "When you grow up we want all of you to get married . . . and you should marry within your race and your religion." There was no if, and, or buts about it, that's the way they were raised.

Well, here comes one of my daughters with this Anglo guy. And he talks to me and says they want to get married. My daughter was there, and I say, "What happened to your race and your religion?" And the guy says, "Well, I'm Catholic and I know Spanish and my mother was born in Mexico. Six of my brothers are married to Mexican girls." [Laughter] His mother was born in Mexico. Her dad was a dentist in Gómez Palacio. He had a contract with the American government to go down there and provide services. She stayed there, she went to school there, and she speaks Spanish better than we do. My feeling is that all of these Anglo people that learn Spanish . . . most of them are learning as a plus to make money. Finally, they're looking at the Spanish market.

LOUIS: *That doesn't seem to be part of the equation when they talk about immigration.*

JESSE: That's because we have so many racist people in this country. You talk about Tancredo, this guy from Colorado. In Arizona they authorized the police to pick up "illegals." They even had a semi, you seen it on the news? A big semi, *"For illegals, call this number."* And you know what? People called that number. So they're looking for an illegal, you look like an illegal, they'll call. Immigration is going to be an issue in this coming election.

LOUIS: *How has that affected El Paso?*

JESSE: Years ago you couldn't find a Mexican American in the Border Patrol. A long time ago, to get into many government jobs, you had to pass an exam, the Federal Service Entrance Examination. It was geared towards the upbringing of the Anglo people. It was hard to pass. I took it like five times. When I took it the last time, I didn't need it. I had already graduated from college, and I had a good job, getting promotions at work. I was on the way up. Finally, the courts decided that it was illegal.

LOUIS: *Because it was culturally biased?*

JESSE: Yes. That's when the minorities started going into the Border Patrol, the Customs. So consequently now there's a whole bunch of minority people in the Border Patrol.

LOUIS: *What do you think about that?*

JESSE: I find they can do just as good a job as anybody else. I find that there's a few crooked ones here and there. You read about it in the papers. You also have those in the Anglo population.

LOUIS: *What do you think should be done about the immigration issue?*

JESSE: Well, you're in this country, and you're in a nation of laws. And I think the laws should be enforced. There's no question about it. Since we are a nation of laws. If there is an immigration reform law, enforce it. There was an article in the paper here not so long ago, this guy, this G.I., this soldier that got killed in Iraq. Before he got killed he had written a letter to his family. And they got to talking about brave people, and he wrote in there, he said, "I think the bravest people in the world are the illegal aliens that had to cross the desert to get to this country." This was a white guy writing this.

LOUIS: *What do you think?*

LUPE: I feel the same way. Have it enforced. Have these illegal people coming pay their taxes. We, senior citizens, pay for their schools. That's the only way that will stop them. They want to come over here, enforce the laws and make them pay the same that we do.

LOUIS: *Do you think that they don't pay taxes at all?*

LUPE: I think some do.

JESSE: Most of them pay taxes. They pay taxes when they buy stuff.

LUPE: I'm referring to property tax, school tax. We are paying for them to be educated.

LOUIS: *But if they own property, don't they have to pay property tax?*

LUPE: Yeah, they do, but most of them don't.

JESSE: There was an article in the paper about one particular family. This guy was an illegal alien. He wanted to live in this country, and he got a number from the IRS, an ID number instead of a Social Security number. He worked, he paid taxes, he sent his kids to school here, and there was a picture in the paper. The immigration had left him alone; they hadn't bothered him. I don't know why. He's illegal, but he's got a number and he's paying taxes.

There's a bunch of people that bring their kids from Juárez, send them to school here. They live in Juárez; they use a local address. When the kids get out of school they go either to their aunt's house or grandma's house. Then their parents come over and pick them up later. They spend the whole week over here. On weekends they take them back to Juárez. That's illegal. How you going to stop that?

> LOUIS: *A lot of people I talk to don't necessarily want to leave their home country, but they feel like they have no choice to make a living. A lot of times they leave the families behind, and the men come, or the mothers leave the children behind. They feel like they have no choice but to do something out of desperation.*

JESSE: You ever seen the show *Última hora* on Univision? There was a program last week, "Ni de aquí ni de allá" [Neither Here nor There]. They picked up people here, they were illegal here, there was a guy that had spent forty years over here, picked him up and deported him. And forty years he lived over here, raised a family here, finally caught up with him and sent him to Mexico. He went up there, he didn't know the customs, didn't have no job, didn't have no family, didn't have nothing. Is that humane?

> LOUIS: *That's the big question. Laws are really important in terms of trying to keep the social order, but the question becomes, are the laws always moral? This is not just a United States–Mexico problem. It's all over the world. Populations move. Most often it's from the poorer countries to the rich countries because they go where the resources are.*

JESSE: In Mexico, they have riches, they have oil, they have all their natural minerals, and so on. What have they done?

> LOUIS: *That's also a big question. What has to happen for people not to leave Mexico?*

JESSE: I keep telling my kids, I say, "When you guys grow up you need to give back to the community." And that's what my three grandkids from this interracial marriage do, a lot of community work. In fact, on Thanksgiving Day they were on the serving line at the Salvation Army.

> LOUIS: *Where does that come from? It comes from some beliefs you learned,* verdad?

JESSE: Yes, from what I saw, my experience as an adult.

LOUIS: Is that part of being a responsible citizen?

JESSE: Oh yes, and from school too. I used to coach Little League baseball. After that I joined an Optimist Club and belonged for about fifteen years, until my son-in-law died and I had to help my daughter and I didn't have time. I also belonged to the American Legion, and I belonged to the VFW. When I retired I let my membership at the American Legion go. But I stayed with the VFW because I think that people that serve in war zones are special people. In fact, six of my brothers here wore the uniform of this country.

LOUIS: During the Korean War?

JESSE: Yeah, Korean War. And my brother Juan was in Vietnam. My son was in the first Gulf War. His son was in the second Gulf War. So I feel that my family as a whole, we've done our share, we've done our part. You find a lot of people doing community work, many Hispanics and Mexican Americans. Very good people.

LOUIS: Do you go to Juárez much? [Collective "No."]

LUPE: I used to take my mother across the border to buy her medicines, but we stopped when she got a better medical insurance for her medicine. I think the last time your daddy and mom were here they went across the border for vacation.

ABUELITA: Hay ciertas medicinas si dejan pasar de Juárez para acá. Y hay unas, estas pastillitas que tomamos, nos dejan pasar, se las venden en Juárez pero con receta. Con refill, que tenga la botella, no, no le venden a uno esas pastillas. [There are certain medicines that they allow you to pass from Juárez to here. And there are other little pills that we take, they allow to pass. They'll sell it in Juárez but with a prescription. Even with a refill, even if you have the empty bottle, they won't sell you those pills.]

JESSE: The Dream Act, I thought that was gonna pass. The 2006 number one student in Princeton was an illegal. After they found out he was an illegal they took away that honor. And then a lot of people complained, and then they gave it to him. Immigration is going to be a big election issue.

Carlos Marentes is director of the Centro de los Trabajadores Agrícolas Fronterizos [Center for Border Agricultural Workers], a farmworkers' center and safe haven in Segundo Barrio near one of the bridges from the United States to Mexico and across the street from a Border Patrol office. I went to the center unannounced, and Carlos took some time to talk with me in one of the lounges. I was also able to view the permanent exhibit on braceros on display in the lobby of the Centro.

CARLOS: I did a presentation on international encounters of migration recently. I was explaining that immigration is a hot issue, but in reality society doesn't know what to do with immigration. In my presentation I was trying to explain to Europeans that we in America have a large segment of the society that is finally facing the dilemma. For many years immigrants were ignored by the majority. We knew that they were working in Mr. Bob Smith's farm or with Ms. Lucy taking care of the children, but this was not an issue until recently. The issue is now a debate in every home in every place. You have the two extremes: the one that is pro-immigration either because of beliefs or because we appreciate our immigrant origins or because many people have a sense of humanity and solidarity and for many people immigrants are all human beings. On the other extreme, you have the anti-immigrants, who are racist, who believe in the idea of supremacy but also who understand things need to be kept this way; this way a few can benefit at the expense of everybody. But between those two groups you have North American society, which does not know what to do, which listens to us and thinks what we say makes sense but also listens to the opposite side and thinks some things that they say makes sense. So what we have right now in the United States is a dilemma of conscience and morals, and peo-

Carlos Marentes in the lounge of the workers' center, El Paso, Texas.
Photo by Louis Mendoza.

ple are afraid to make a decision. Sometimes they are pro-immigrant; sometimes they are anti-immigrant. Here at the border immigration is a way of life. It's nothing that happened when Mr. Reagan came to power.

We live immigration every minute of the day and the night because we live on the border. Human rights violations, militarization, all these anti-immigration measures, the campaigns of deportation, the division of families, is nothing new; it's part of the life of the border. So pretty much we understand the implications of migration to our families, to our friends, to relatives, to people who are desperate because they are unable to survive in their homeland. We understand that reality. The farmworkers' center is located right across the street from the United States Immigration Service, and there's a purpose for that. We are here to support the farmworkers. In dealing with the issues affecting farmworkers every day, we have to deal with the immigration policies and the human aspect, the inequality, the hypocrisy, the contradictions of immigration policy. We have to take into account the reality of life. We cannot just come up with these beautiful theories or romantic views about immigration. Immigration to us is part of the life of America, especially part of the economic life of America. And it's been like this since this place was Mexico. This place where we are right now used to be the farm of Mr. Alvarado, who was a poor Mexi-

can campesino. Then somebody came from outside and took over his land
[LOUIS: By force?] Yeah, in Texas, land was taken through the combination
of law and law enforcement like the Texas Rangers. The farmworkers use
this facility for a safe haven. This is the recruitment site for farmworkers.

"Safe haven" means that they can stay here, that they can take a bath,
have a hot meal, rest for a couple hours before going back to the fields,
instead of staying in the streets. Here they are safe from harassment from
criminals, from the weather. The *migra* is across the street. We are like one
of those marriages that take place without love, only by convenience. We
hate each other, but we are together here. In fact a lot of farmworkers feel
safe as long as they are in this area inside or on the sidewalks right here.
They leave the area, and they are in trouble. ICE knows us, plus I imagine
they have much technology. I imagine maybe they are even listening while
we are talking. They know what is going on here, and they know that our
purpose is to serve migrant farmworkers. To us the immigrant status of a
person is not what matters. To us it is a condition of unfair laws and regula-
tions. The other thing is that we are in a city in which Mexicans or Mexican
Americans are close to 80 percent of the population. What else are they
going to do? This morning I was in a coffee shop, in a convenience store
buying a coffee. And this Border Patrol officer came to buy a coffee, and he
told the lady, "Oh, cóbrame también el periódico," in Spanish. [Grab me a
paper too.] "¿El Paso Times?" "Sí."

So this is our reality. Migration at the border includes the tragic aspects,
the suffering of people, the cases of aggression against the border population. However, September 11th made things worse for us at the border,
so now we live in an environment which is clearly anti-immigrant, anti-
Mexican, and anti-poor. Because if you, for example, review the latest activity against immigrants in this area, you'll see those activities have been in
poor communities like Chaparral. It's a very poor community; it's a totally
immigrant community. And recently the sheriff department with the Border Patrol did several raids and deported many people. You don't see the
Border Patrol activities near the fields. In New Mexico the chile industry is
the most important—most of the workers here go to the chile harvest—and
you hardly see any activity of the Border Patrol during the most intensive
months of agricultural activity. It only takes a phone call from one of the
largest growers in New Mexico to Washington, D.C., and the activity will
stop.

We have to suffer the consequences of immigration policy. We have
to put up with all these tragedies that are results of a distorted way of looking at the immigration issue. For example, many sectors of society are now

convinced that terrorism and immigration are connected or that drug smuggling and immigration are connected. We have never suffered a terrorist attack on the border. Drug smuggling? Well, I remember listening as a kid to all these *corridos* [folk songs] about smuggling in the border; it's a form of free trade. Immigration is another issue. Immigration has to do with the economic and social conditions. You can interview a lot of the people here. They are from farming communities that have been destroyed by free trade policies and bad foreign policies.

Who wants to leave their community? I bet you they would prefer to be with their families. But they have to be here to work; they have to find a means of survival. And all the workers here will tell you pretty much the same story. They are here for a reason, to sustain their families back home. That's their reality. We deal with our reality that is here. We oppose the anti-immigrant anti-actions and policies. We also are concerned about the anti-immigrant discourse in the media and from the TV, how this anti-immigrant rhetoric creates a situation where extremist groups think that they have to do something against immigrants. We see immigration as a matter that has been used by the North American government and the economy in many ways. These recent attempts to pass immigration reform, they included the issue of national security, you know, "Making our borders safe." Safe from what? We don't have any problems here. The only problem that we have is that people are risking their lives because of all of these activities. Most of the immigration legislation before Congress and Senate and House of Representatives that failed included strong measures to control the border, included a temporary guest worker program. So you have two contradictions . . . the more you think about it, maybe they are not contradictions, that what they want is the type of policies that have been working in this country for many years.

To me the immigration policies of this country resemble a case of domestic violence. The man beats the woman, does whatever he wants to do with the woman, and it's not because he wants the woman to leave. It's because he wants the woman to stay under his control. So this is where we have immigration policies that attempt to have an immigrant population under control. But we don't want them to leave; we want them to do the dirty jobs. In the case of agriculture, at least in this area, we have from 9,000–12,000 agricultural workers in this region, I'm talking El Paso County, southern New Mexico, and Ciudad Juárez, depending on the time of the year. We now have fewer workers because the chile harvest is almost over. We will start picking pecans soon. From July to October we have thousands of workers in this area, and the majority, at least one-third, are undocumented. So what happens in the fields? What happens in the fields is that they have a system that they call *acoplado*, which basically means they work together as a team and one of them gets paid for the work of both.

If the United States Department of Labor comes to check the payroll records, they will find that he's earning more than the minimum wage, that he has Social Security, the proper deductions. But in reality his records and salary belongs to two or three workers. So you go to a field, and there's sixty or seventy workers, picking chile in the fields. Then when you review the payroll lists of the labor contractor, there's only thirty persons there [slight laughter], and then thirty persons means $60 to $80 a day, but what happens is that salary belongs to more people. It's the same way that it used to be with the migrant workers from South Texas going to the north. Everybody would work, including the grandfather, but they would only issue one check for the head of household. And they worked very hard; they are the ones willing to work when they're soaked muddy, when there's cold weather. Guess what? Everybody's happy. All of us can go and buy red chile in the stores to make our tamales or enchiladas.

We've been organizing since 1980. The center has been open since 1995. So since 1996 we started the Bracero Project. It's an attempt to rebuild the history of farmworkers in the United States, and now we have hundreds of files of braceros. We have some interviews that we have done but mainly files and folders. And the idea is that at one point the Bracero Project will help us make society understand the purpose and the contribution of immigrants. We chose the Bracero Project because in 1996, following welfare reform under Clinton, many of the old farmworkers that were receiving Social Security benefits suddenly were disqualified because they were not United States citizens and they were not able to prove the required quotas to receive Social Security benefits. We decided to do something to help the farmworkers rebuild their history. We found that the majority of farmworkers here with us had been working jobs in agriculture in the United States since the 1950s.

LOUIS: How do you plan to share this information?

CARLOS: We are afraid of the academic institutions [laughs]. We attempted to make a collaborative project with UTEP, but we were unable to. I went one day to visit their Special Collections in the warehouse where they have a lot of their files. I was very disappointed. [A woman serves coffee to Louis and Carlos; Carlos asks for a *galletita* (cookie).]

Have you heard this story about this man that goes to visit his *compadre*? The *comadre* offers him a cup of coffee. "¿Compadre, no se toma un café?" [*Compadre,* would you like a cup of coffee?] And the *compadre* answers, "¿No me hará malo con el estómago vacío, comadre?" [Won't it make me sick on an empty stomach, *comadre*?] [Slight laughter] So the *comadre* had to bring him some food. [More laughter]

LOUIS: *Did you grow up here?*

CARLOS: I'm from Juárez. My father was from Aguascalientes, and my mother was from Zacatecas. I came here to live and stay here when I got married.

LOUIS: *It's important to me that people understand this story, so they will see immigrants as human beings who struggle.*

CARLOS: If one day they understand and realize that immigrants are part of the economic and social development of this nation, things will be different. In the minds of the regular Americans, immigrants are people who just crossed last night, swimming the river . . . running through the desert.

Verónica Carbajal, a former student during my one-year visiting professorship at Brown University, is now a lawyer with the Texas Rio Grande Legal Aid Office and chair of the local ACLU chapter. She hosted me in El Paso, taking time from her busy schedule to give me a tour and to set up meetings with people. Born in El Paso, Verónica grew up in Juárez and attended schools in El Paso. She has returned to her hometown to provide leadership and advocacy in several areas, including environmental justice and housing.

VERÓNICA: I was almost born on the bridge. My mom used to work in El Paso, and my grandpa used to work on Mill Street as a parking lot attendant. She would get a ride from him in the morning, and then she would stop at a church and wait for him. She would go and pray. She didn't tell her parents she was pregnant until she was seven months along, so she did a lot of praying, and waiting for him to get out of work. Then they would go back home to Juárez. My mom didn't have any prenatal care. My dad found a doctor, at the South El Paso clinic, and the doctor told her, "You know, you're really healthy, so I'll look at you." Thank God, she was healthy and didn't need any extensive prenatal care. I had a due date of August 8th. She went in for a checkup, and they said, "No, you're fine. Send her home." She kept working. On Saturday she went out shopping with her sisters in El Paso. They went out shopping all day, stopped by to get a hamburger, and Mom came home and started feeling a lot of back pain. They're already in Juárez, and her water broke . . . and so my grandfather told my aunt, "Es tú pendeja, la traistes todo el día en la calle, ahora tú llévala a El Paso." [You're an idiot. You bring her with you all day on the streets, and now you take her to El Paso.] It was a Saturday night, and there's always a lot of traffic on the bridge on Saturdays, 'cause people want to go out partying or they've been

Verónica Carbajal at a scenic overlook in El Paso, Texas. Photo provided by Verónica Carbajal.

visiting family in Juárez and going back to El Paso. My aunt honked her way through the line, which she couldn't do now 'cause there's so many concrete barriers, but back then it was a lot more flexible. She honked her way. She was screaming, "Pregnant lady in the car." They made it over near midnight, and I was born at 2:54 in the morning on August 15, 1976.

   LOUIS: Was it important to your mom that you be born on this side?

VERÓNICA: Yes, my mom was second generation and I was third generation, U.S. citizen. My grandmother was the only noncitizen in the household. My grandfather was born here, and their four daughters were, but my grandmother did not want to give up her Mexican citizenship. She was very proud of it. She was blond, green-eyed. My grandpa always worked outside, so he was the color of copper, took off his shirt and he was white; he was half copper, half white. It's ironic, but she never wanted to move here, and he always worked here. Their dollar stretched a lot farther in Juárez. They always lived really well.

LOUIS: *Would you not have had U.S. citizenship if you weren't born on this soil?*

VERÓNICA: I would've had derivative citizenship through her, but it's not automatic. So you have to prove certain things. One of my cousins, actually my mom's eldest sister, decided to have my cousin in Juárez, and his life was really a lot more complicated.

LOUIS: *Did you use an El Paso address?*

VERÓNICA: We did. Initially, my mom worked for a notary public, when she was pregnant with me. She was so healthy because she used to walk everywhere, had a pretty healthy lifestyle. She saved up a lot of money 'cause she lived with her parents. My dad was never around. I've never met him, no financial support at all. When I was born, the hospital told my mom, "You're a citizen, your baby's a citizen, we can get you into public housing, we'll get you food stamps, everything." I was born in '76; things were very different. My mom was offered a slew of public benefits, and she refused them. She told me, "I really thought about it, and I thought, my daughter is gonna grow up in the projects. I'm not gonna have immediate family around, and it will be really easy for her dad to come back, and we're never gonna get married, and I'm gonna have ten kids and it's not what I want. If I'm at home, I'll be safe. I don't have to worry about being a single woman living by myself and my baby. My mom and my dad will help me out."

LOUIS: *Did she face any stigma for being a single mom?*

VERÓNICA: Oh my God, she went through so much. She didn't tell her parents she was pregnant until she was seven months because of that. My grandpa found out. The first thing he said was, "Is it too late to have an abortion?" My grandmother flipped out, of course, and said, "We'll figure it out." Some of my uncles claim they didn't meet me until I was three years old. I think my mom was really brave. She put up with a lot of comments. I don't ever remember seeing her act ashamed or embarrassed because really the blame was on my dad if anyone. She didn't carry any shame.

LOUIS: *You grew up mostly in Juárez until you started school here?*

VERÓNICA: Yes. My mom didn't work for four years because she took care of me. My grandfather was the type that he never asked his kids to pay for the bills but you contribute to the house in any way, you just say, "No me des pero no me quites." [Don't give me anything, but don't take anything away.] So we were all very frugal about the bills. My mom was very savvy with money, and my grandmother helped out a lot. We never had public benefits, 'cause we were always living in Juárez. When I turned six, my mom was like, "You have to go to school now."

LOUIS: *It was always her plan that you would go to school here?*

VERÓNICA: My mom went to school in Juárez until the sixth grade, and then they came to an all-girl school, but in the past it was mostly students from Juárez. My mom never learned English fluently, and after that she went as far as the eighth grade. For her generation it was difficult to go into a training program or a vocational program. They all went to Durham College, and my mom was certified as a secretary.

Her goal was for me to be fluent in English, and for me to do that I had to go to school. I wasn't going to go to private school 'cause we couldn't afford it, and so I had to go to public school, and I had to use a family member's address. My mom had friends and a lot of family living in El Paso, so I think initially we used one of her friend's addresses. She was working at a garment factory at the time; I think it was Viola Jeans. Because she had to be at work at 7:00, we would get up at 5:00 and cross the bridge, which would take forever because it wasn't as organized and there was also commercial traffic with passenger traffic, so we were battling trailers, people carried guns, it was really the Wild West. It was very stressful for her, and we did that for two years. After that she decided to get an easier schedule, and so she started working for the school system, and she was in the cafeteria, and so we had the same hours, and she would actually get out of work early. I think she was done by two o'clock. When I was gonna start junior high I went from going to school in central El Paso with mostly immigrant kids—all first generation, we were all in bilingual classes together, we were all working-class kids—to middle school, where kids didn't speak Spanish, their names were like Sarah, Edrick, names I had never heard before. The quality of education was so vastly different. We weren't talked down to, we were really challenged, kids questioned the teachers.

LOUIS: *Did you have to hide the fact that you lived in Juárez? Did your mom tell you to say you lived here?*

VERÓNICA: She didn't have to 'cause I knew it was illegal. A couple times we got caught. One time was serious, so we went to the superintendant's office, spoke to him, he saw my school records, and he said, "You know, I believe in you. She's about to graduate. We're not pulling her out of school."

But I remember having panic attacks when I was seven or eight because we would get to school late at times, and I was scared that I was going to get caught, that people were gonna find out.

  LOUIS: Do you ever wonder why you didn't go to school in Juárez?

VERÓNICA: No, I knew. My mom was very good about communicating with me, and I was always privy to very adult conversations, so I knew exactly why we did what we did. It was definitely a very stressful way of earning my education. One time my mom was really upset—this was when she was still working at the factory—because the lane that we were on wasn't moving and she was already late, and she still had to drop me off at the daycare, and she was pissed off. My mom always taught me that, yeah, we were breaking the law by me going to school here, but we were citizens and no one could take that from us. So at the border she could do whatever she wanted, and if other people couldn't honk 'cause they were afraid of losing their green card, she wasn't gonna hold back 'cause she was pissed off. We got to the checkpoint, the inspector asked her if she was the one honking, and she said, "Yes." So he asked her to go into the special inspection lane. He then asked us to get out of the car. He handcuffed her, dumped her purse on the counter. She had to go through it. No one said a word to me, and we never talked about it. I learned to be quiet. In some ways that helped me because when stuff happened, I was seen as a good kid. I wasn't a troublemaker. I think growing up that way was exhausting more than anything. It was really tiring for both her and for me. I think back now, and I had a really cool childhood. I had a duality that other people don't have. Every night we went home to a really warm meal, always had family over, had a very strong sense of family. We never needed anything, not shelter, food, clothing, or anything. And we were middle class, like we lived in a really nice house in Juárez, and it was amazing that when we crossed over immediately we were poor, and immediately she was barely making ends meet.

  LOUIS: Did living in Juárez prevent you from participating in after-school activities?

VERÓNICA: No. My mom went out of her way for me to have a full education. I wasn't really into activities in junior high 'cause my grandmother was diagnosed with cancer when I was in the seventh grade. So for two years my mom quit her job and was her full-time caretaker. I was not interested in after-school activities. I still did really well in school, somehow, even though I didn't have any role models that had gone to college. I figured that middle school wasn't going to affect my future, and so I did really well, but I wasn't trying to get into an honors program or anything like that. When I was in high school, early on I started getting involved in a bunch of stuff, and my mom started working again, and my grandpa got sick. She quit her job again to take care of them. Some days my mom would make three or four trips across the border. I was a sports medicine trainer. And that was like my heaviest activity, so I had games almost every day of the week. She would drop me off in the mornings, stop by at four o'clock to give me dinner. She would buy me stuff or make me stuff, and she would pick me up after the games at eight or nine.

> LOUIS: *So the border was an inconvenience, but it really didn't slow her down?*

VERÓNICA: No, what slowed her down at times was her car breaking down, or stuff like that. She never once said, "We can't do this." Somehow we both intuitively knew that I had to go to college and I had to be well rounded. In high school, I didn't have friends in Juárez. All my friends were here, and my close friends knew that I lived there. Now I feel like I identify with both of them equally. I'm more comfortable identifying with Juárez than I was before. Maybe part of it was just shame and fear. I grew up in a different time. It wasn't cool to be Mexican; it wasn't cool to be Latino.

> LOUIS: *Was going to Brown University a big step socially and culturally?*

VERÓNICA: My life changed drastically, but no way I could say that being there helped me assimilate more or get in touch more with my American-ness. It did the opposite. It made me reject it a lot more, whereas I think I had tried to embrace it when I was younger.

> LOUIS: *Why is that?*

VERÓNICA: Because it was so eye-opening to me in terms of finding like-minded people. If you talk to people who knew me in high school they'll say, "Vero was very outspoken all the time, and if you wanted to get the pulse of the nation we would talk to her about abortion or whatever but not about race." We just never talked about it in school, even in our history classes where we talked about MLK [Martin Luther King]. We had a really cool history teacher that used to march in the South, and she never talked about César Chávez or any other Mexican American leaders.

> LOUIS: *Isn't that typical of the border experience—that a lot of Chicanos/mexicanos don't experience their minority status until they get away from the border?*

VERÓNICA: That's right. I felt very in touch with my Mexican roots. I spent a lot of time with my great-grandparents, especially my great-grandfather, interviewing him, talking to him, and both of my grandparents were very expressive about being Mexican and had a lot of negative things to say about this country, which is why they never moved back. In terms of my identity as a Mexican American, I didn't know how to express it, embrace it, or how to really understand it.

> LOUIS: I hear you say that you were very in touch with your Mexican-ness. There's a part of you in high school that understood it's cool to be American. Then it's like you became Mexican American or Chicana in higher education.

VERÓNICA: Yeah, it's like three identities. The one that I felt most comfort-able with and most at home with was the Mexican one, 'cause it was loving and accepting. It was my grandmother's cooking; it was love and devotion and taking care of each other.

> LOUIS: So does your mother look back and feel like she did the right thing?

VERÓNICA: She wouldn't have done things differently, I don't think. Our bilingual program at Hillside was very much about forgetting our Spanish, overcoming our Spanish handicap. It wasn't about making us bilingual. And if I retained my Spanish, well, I lost a lot of it during middle school and high school during the whole "It's not cool to be Latino" thing, and then my grandparents died and they're the ones I spoke Spanish with the most. But I wanted to retain as much as I could, and reconnected with it, because my grandmother was always like, "You can't forget that you're Mexican." But it wasn't even a cultural thing; for her it was a think-about-your-future thing. I remember her telling me that her dream was for me to be a pro-fessional secretary or a stewardess. Back then that was like, you know, she did not want me to be a housewife. She was like, "If you're bilingual you're gonna have many more job opportunities, especially on the border. Just don't lose your Spanish. Don't lose your Spanish." And she never once said, "Don't lose it 'cause you're going to lose me." 'Cause I would've lost her. And I remember having those moments when I was talking to my great-grandfather and even my grandparents, 'cause I had less time with him, so every conversation was precious, just having those stumbling blocks where I couldn't think of the word, where language wouldn't flow anymore in Span-ish. Now with my younger cousin, her Spanish is perfect and her English is perfect. In fact, she dates guys from Juárez; she doesn't date guys from El

Paso. I think for me, if I was going to be around white friends, it was best to minimize my Mexicanness, 'cause it was just easier. Once I was at Brown, I started to alienate myself from white friends, because it wasn't comfortable and I couldn't be myself, and I think the difference I see with my cousins is that they can be themselves; they can be Mexican wherever they are. And that's one of the great things about being in El Paso too, is that my racial identity can take a backseat. That was not the case in Austin, and certainly not at Brown, where I think my racial and ethnic identity defined me.

> LOUIS: *How does one talk about immigration issues in a border town that has such a long history of being a Mexican/Mexican American place?*

VERÓNICA: I'm very blessed to have been born in this country. When you meet someone who is not here legally, every move they make . . . involves a fear that they live with constantly. This affects them driving home from work, driving home from the kid's school, questioning what kind of investments to make in this country because they might be deported tomorrow. I've seen it with clients, with flood victims who lost their home, their ability to negotiate. Luckily for us we had people at the city who were not interested and who didn't want to know whether clients were here legally or not. Even when it comes to accessing public benefits or accessing our legal services, we can't provide services for people who are undocumented unless they're a victim of violence or trafficking or one of those special visas type of issues, or if it's a public benefit case, if the loss in the benefit will affect a child, for example, if it's a food stamp case . . . the mom is really the one receiving them and using them. Especially working now, I realize how important it is; it's so difficult to live with that stress.

When my great-grandfather immigrated here in 1918, he started working as a farmworker worker, then he left for a couple of months, and then someone said, "Hey, the railroad is hiring, and they'll help you get your papers." He got his papers. I don't think he became a citizen, but he was a resident, and once they moved back to Juárez with his family, he emigrated to the U.S. every day. Now, no employer of working-class people is going to help them get their papers. We've definitely taken a million steps back with regard to access to legalization.

> LOUIS: *How would you characterize the challenge being represented by the Segundo Barrio struggle?*

VERÓNICA: Cultural genocide. Culture is food, it's history, it's values, it's religion, part of it is ethnicity, part of it is class. I think of Segundo's history and what it is now, and I think the city council and their private partners want to obliterate it because they don't like what it is. They don't like the fact that there are a lot of Mexicans transitioning, there are a lot of Mexican Americans who live there, that they're old or poor, that they rely a lot on social services and public transportation. But in many ways they're pretty self-sustaining, and for someone to say, "We're going to knock this building down regardless of history," to me that is cultural obliteration; our history is devalued. When they talk about, well, we're going to relocate you to a nicer home, statements like that are so loaded, they're condescending, they're full of assumptions. When we talk to our clients they say, "My home is old, and it is deteriorated, but if someone helped me make it structurally better, it's not for lack of wanting, it's for lack of money. My home is safe. My home is where I raise my kids. My home is full of history and feeling, and it's my community and my neighbors." And they'll say, "This is one of the few neighborhoods where people know each other. If something goes wrong you can go knock on your neighbor's door and they are going to help you out. My clinic is down the street. My doctor is only a bus ride away. I can go shopping at the stores. I can afford what's there now. I can eat at the restaurants now, but if you're going to bring in high-end restaurants and stores, I can't visit them, I can't go shopping there. And if you raise my property taxes, I can't live here. If I'm a renter and I have to pay more rent, I can't live here anymore." So I think people don't understand that, or feel that what they're offering someone is better. If you've never been poor, and if you don't have a sense of family or roots, then of course you're not going to value Segundo. You're not gonna value the history that each person has there. If you don't appreciate that, then of course, a new home would be appealing.

> LOUIS: *Do you think the challenge with that is how to tell that story to a larger public?*

VERÓNICA: It definitely is. A friend of mine had a website, SegundoBarrio.com. He was getting hits on the website from all parts of the U.S. but also from random places—Australia, Spain, and Germany. I think it's the only part of El Paso that has that beauty, that history of having been a passage for so many people. You still find people who are on their way through Segundo. They're gonna use it as a stepping-stone to a better way of life, because it is so affordable, and there aren't many places in El Paso where you can do that. And then you're gonna find people that have been living there for a very long time, who can't and don't want to go anywhere else.

ERNESTO PORTILLO

Ernesto Portillo, *Arizona Daily Star* columnist and Tucson native, attended a small reception for me hosted by my friends Sandy Soto and Miranda Joseph. He offered to share his perspective on Mexican Tucson's history and social well-being. On the following Monday morning, we spent several hours driving around. We stopped to see Rebecca Tapia of the Yaqui Pascua community center.

ERNESTO: This was the mainstay of Barrio Viejo. Not to romanticize it, it was a viable barrio. They had businesses, professional offices of middle-class *mexicanos* and some blacks. And then urban renewal came. It was something that swept the country in the '60s; take out the old "blighted" inner city, put in a convention center. It tore the heart out of the barrio. There's still a lot of scars remaining from that. Right now there's a new development in downtown. They're trying to avoid the mistakes, but one thing that is happening obviously is the gentrification of the neighborhoods. You see some of the gentrification going on in El Hoyo. We're going to go up what we call "A" Mountain [Sentinel Peak]. We'll have a bird's-eye view of Tucson and talk a little history.

Mi *jefito*² came here from Juárez in 1954. He was about nineteen or twenty years old. He came as a Spanish-language announcer; he had gotten into radio in Juárez. He's from Chihuahua. His brother-in-law was in radio, and my father became a deejay too. Very early in his career, Tucson started up a full-time Spanish-language Mexican radio station, the first one. One of the main deejays went out looking for talent, and he'd heard of my father, and so they invited him to come. He came up on the bus one day, and the next day he goes into the studio, they give him a sound check, and he starts.

My mother was born here. My *abuelos* [grandparents] from my mom's side are from Sonora and Sinaloa. Her father was born in Sonora not far from the border here. At a young age he goes to Chihuahua, and most of his family came out of Chihuahua City, and he lives in El Paso-Juárez. About 1920, he came to Tucson, and he eventually begins fixing gas heaters, stoves, furnaces. He goes to Los Angeles. There's this traditional route from Tejas, El Paso, Tucson, Los Angeles. *Las familias* went back and forth and still do. In Los Angeles he meets my grandmother. My grandmother was born in Mazatlán. Her family leaves Mazatlán after the revolution in the late teens, and they set up in Los Angeles. Their house is now part of USC. My grandparents marry, come to Tucson, they start the family. My mother's born here in 1937 in Tucson, and she's part of that generation of *familias mexicanas*, where everyone knew everyone else. My father, through his work in radio, he was a celebrity. They're retired now, *pero* they're very active, and that's where I get my activism.

LOUIS: *What is the industry here?*

ERNESTO: Primarily it's tourism and military. Davis-Monthan Air Force Base has had a big impact on the community. The university is one of the larger employers in the city. Tucson's been trying to become like all other southwestern communities, trying to attract high-tech, but Tucson's not gonna do it. There are some high-techs, because of the university's reputation and research in optics. Retirees are an industry. Building has become an industry itself. The European Tucson starts right there with what they

Ernesto Portillo on "A" Mountain overlooking Tucson. Photo by Louis Mendoza.

call El Presidio. This area, the archaeologists and anthropologists say, is one of the oldest continually inhabited areas of the United States, and you wouldn't think of it because of the harshness of the *desierto*.

The first early people are the Hohokam, and they established along the *río*. There used to be water that would surface and submerge. So the Hohokam set up these little villages, and they created these pit houses along the base of Sentinel Peak, and they did rudimentary agriculture, were gatherers of beans, mesquite, and the cactus, nopal. Why they disappeared they're not really sure. Then the Pimas came and establish themselves; we know them as the Tohono O'odham. *O'odham* meaning "the people," and *Tohono* meaning "people of the desert," and there are other variations of O'odham, north along Phoenix along the river O'odham. So the O'odham established villages and communities here and down in San Xavier at the Mission, and all along the river, because the river is life. They also engaged in agriculture, but in the late seventeenth century the Europeans begin to arrive. The explorer Jesuit priest Eusebio Francisco Kino comes in the late 1700s. The *españoles* were already here. They established a presidio in Tubac, a beautiful area called the Santa Cruz River Valley. They decide they need a presidio a little further north, and so a small detachment comes up the river, it's led by a mercenary Irishman, Hugo O'Connor, who was fighting for the Spanish crown. He comes here, and he likes what he sees. There's water, there's wood, the bosques and mesquite; the village is here; Kino's mission is near here. It was a typical Spanish presidio. They build the earthworks, and the village starts from there. And they contend, just like all throughout the Southwest, with the difficulty of living in this kind of environment, and the Apaches, who are trying to chase them out. But the *mexicano* and *español,* they tried to coexist with the indigenous people here.

San Agustín is the first church. It's now the Cathedral. Originally there was a church there, and the patron saint of Tucson is San Agustín. So a little village develops and it's so isolated from Mexico City, it's isolated from Santa Fe, but from here the Spanish colonialists continue west. From here de Anza continues his exploration and goes to Yuma. He founds San Diego. He founds San Francisco. The two de Anza expeditions come out of Arizona.

LOUIS: Tucson was a gateway to the west for Spanish exploration?

ERNESTO: It was! No question. Because although they were sailing on the coast and they had gone into the bays, the actual establishment of the presidios was done through the explorations of the colonists here. I'm not going to romanticize the Spanish. They were who they were; they did what they did.

LOUIS: Was it through the mission that the process of mestizaje *[cultural and biological mixing] began?*

ERNESTO: That's where the process of European agriculture begins. Although the presidio established here in the early 1800s, they established the *convento* and built a two-story granary for storage. The Franciscans have gardens here, and they do some agriculture. Of course Tucson's history has always been that we destroy whatever we can, so all remnants of it are gone. They're now trying to do archaelogical digs because eventually they want to put some new housing and commercial development here. This barrio will eventually be squeezed out; this is *barrio sin nombre* [laughter]. This is the site of the Spanish church mission complex, and they're going to do some re-creation of the buildings. Mexico gains its independence; the *españoles* are kicked out; Arizonans basically became part of Mexico, but they really don't know it . . . word travels slow. Of course the *americanos* are already coming in. In 1849 the California gold rush begins to transform this area. This area pretty much escaped the Mexican War. Tucson remained a part of Mexico after the robbery of 1848, but the northern part of Arizona, which we now call Phoenix, is part of that land grab. But with the Gadsden Purchase of 1854 Tucson becomes part of *gringolandia.* Of course this is a Mexican town. There are very few gringos here in 1854, and those that do come, some are merchants, some are speculators, some are no-good type of men.

But some men marry *mexicanas* from Sonora. Then you're starting to see the *mestizaje* of the gringo and the *mexicanas.* We have schools and parks named after the *americanos,* early pioneers who married *mexicanas,* and they start creating these bilingual, bicultural families. By the 1880s, Tucson really goes under radical change. The railroad comes. That is when the transformation really begins with the gringo infusion and influx; up until then Tucson was oriented towards the south. The Gadsden Purchase is made because they needed a southerly all-weather route to California, because the mountains are *chingón.* Once again southern Arizona is this conduit, this villa for growth—not for here, but for California. By the 1880s, the gringos come en masse, and we no longer are a Mexican town. By 1900, the gringos are pretty much in control of the government. They have the land, and the *mexicano* is just put off to the side, with the exception of the elite families.

LOUIS: Is that by sheer numbers, by force of violence, or by intimidation?

ERNESTO: Manipulation of the law, by numbers, by money, you know . . .

gringos come in and offer the *familia* some money for their land. Not so much violence. Tucson wasn't a horribly violent town. Other than robbing the indigenous people of their lands through violence, but they took the land through extralegal means. Slowly it's taken away. By the 1900s, Tucson is already expanding south. El Hoyo is one of those many barrios that begin to establish, because the *mexicano* isn't allowed—the indigenous and *mexicano* aren't allowed—to live in or near the presidio. So they start establishing these poor barrio communities, Barrio Libre, Barrio Viejo, Barrio Sin Nombre, Anita Barrio on the West Side, and then Tucson starts slowly moving east.

Army Park is where the railroad comes in and the gringos build their midwestern homes. They forsake the Sonoran style of energy-efficient building, adobe. They bring in their wood, they bring in their brick, and so the community begins to expand, and prewar it's slowly growing. This is Menlo Park, what I consider my childhood neighborhood. Before 1900 these are *milpas*, fields. You see old maps, and these are subdivided, and *familias mexicanas*, most of them, own the land, and they're growing whatever, beans, squash, corn. Because there is still water channeling from the Santa Cruz, they learn how to build retention dams, save the water, and use it when it's dry. But right after the 1900s gringos come in and start buying up the properties. Menlo Park is now a *mexicano* neighborhood, but now through gentrification it's becoming a gringo neighborhood. It's very interesting, because *familias mexicanas* are selling out; taxes are getting too high because of the commercial growth.

Before the war, Tucson was just a sleepy town, this backwater, southwestern town. There's really nothing here, but little by little gringos are discovering it for health reasons. People escaping the East because of tuberculosis, primarily, and asthma and other respiratory diseases. Tucson [snapping fingers] is nirvana for them; it is their lifesaver, and then these dude ranches start establishing prewar, the Wild West. So tourism becomes a part of Tucson catering to the gringo. There's still this trade interaction with Sonora. Tucson is still very *sonorense*. You had the *familias* going back and forth, back and forth. You still have this southward-northward migration and interaction, and then you have this west-east access going. It's a crossroads.

Then the war comes, and again a major transformation. Davis-Monthan becomes a major air force base. Some early military aircraft companies established here on the South Side by the airport. They become bomber production for the war effort, like in many other areas in Tejas and San Diego. The train depot downtown becomes a transit point for soldiers going west to the Pacific, or going east home. But after the war, like many other southwestern cities, the gringo soldier discovers this beautiful community—warm, year-round sunshine, land, opportunity, speculation. There's this huge influx, an infusion of people, either connected through the war or the university. The university begins to boom because you have the G.I. Bill, and so you have not only *tucsonenses* coming back and going to school and re-creating their lives after the war. Those who came back could not go into the middle class in terms of going to the university, getting a white-collar job. They had to come back and help their families, so they'd go back to work where only they're allowed to work, the mines, the railroad, whatever land work is being done, construction work. And these blue-collar Chicano soldiers come back, and they think, "What the fuck did we fight for?" We're still having serious racial problems here. Segregation is serious here in Tucson. *Mexicanos* are relegated to this side of town, West Side; South Side of town, *los negros peor* [the blacks worse]—they have it even worse 'cause they're so few. Tucson had segregated schools, and it wasn't until right before *Brown v. Board of Education* that Tucson desegregated its black school. All that meant was that they put the *mexicanos* in with the *negros*.

After the war Tucson begins to explode. People are coming here for work and to find second homes from the Midwest and New York. Throughout the '50s Tucson just continues to grow. The *gabachos* who brought midwestern-style homes, midwestern trees, midwestern lawns, also brought pollen! They brought the mulberry trees. Tucson then becomes a horrible place for respiratory conditions because they brought the non-native trees and the grasses. Tucson expands.

The regional population is now at a million. Tucson proper itself is a little more than half a million. It still continues to grow. Of course twenty years ago you would have seen very few homes inching up on the sides of the Catalinas; now it's just *casas y casas*, and those are big houses, those are rich houses. Tucson has allowed sprawl to occur. Developers still rule here, car dealers, real estate, they're the powerful forces here. The military still has a lot of say in what goes on . . . quietly. When I left here and went to San Diego, I was surprised that there were very few *mexicanos* in decision-making positions because I came out of Tucson. Our postmaster was a Chicano, at one time the University of Arizona president was a Chicano, a school superintendant was a Chicano, the bishop was Chicano.

Still, it's a struggle. Immigration has never stopped here. We've always had people that have come through here or have stayed here, but most of them are people from Mexico going through here. They go to Phoenix, they go to Los Ángeles, they go to the Northwest to pick, and the Midwest. But the immigration debate has really transformed any kind of civil discourse. Now the *mexicano* here has to contend with the negative backlash *contra el inmigrante* [against the immigrant], and say, "Wait a minute, but I've been here for generations, why are you stopping me Mr. Policeman, do I look illegal to you?" And now we're all suspect of being anti-American. All of a sudden we're all cliquish again. All of a sudden we don't learn English, and unfortunately a lot of *mexicanos* here of second and third generation, even first generation, they too have become anti-*inmigrante*, they too say things like, "Oh, we're not like them, we're not like them, they're poor, they're dark, they don't even speak good Spanish. Not that we speak good Spanish. But we've been here for generations. My father came with the first presidio." "Sí Chuy, toma." [Laughter]

> LOUIS: *What is Tucson's identity with its Spanish Mexican past? Do they embrace the* mestizaje *here, or is it Mexican American?*

ERNESTO: It's Mexican American. There are pockets in town where it's, "We're *mexicanos*." You know, recent immigrants. But in the larger picture people see themselves as Mexican Americans, that their families came from Mexico, they may not speak Spanish, they may not have been to Mexico for many years if at all, but they are Mexican American, and there are a lot of Anglos who know that their grandfather or grandmother came from Sonora. One of the biggest names in Tucson is Ronstadt. Linda Ronstadt's family comes from Federico Ronstadt, a German immigrant who goes to Sonora in the early 1800s. He's an engineer, like a lot of Europeans who come to Mexico, they're engineers and do other professional jobs, and August Ronstadt establishes his family in Sonora. His son is Federico José María Ronstadt, who then comes to Tucson as a young man in the 1880s, about the time the railroads come in. He learns the arts and crafts of wagon making and wagon repair. He establishes a small shop; the railroads come in; he makes the transformation into hardware selling farm ranching imple- ments and establishes a hardware store; his sons become major *tucsonenses*, and they become Anglicized. Yeah, we come from Mexico, but we're very *americano*.

You have changes going on, but you still have the struggle of identity. You still have the struggle of economic independence, and dependence. Our education is still lagging behind. I don't know why. I don't understand it, Louis. We have so many wonderful *maestros* and *maestras* [male and female teachers], and they're in a system that still doesn't allow them to teach the young people how to cope, how to learn, in this very inflexible world. We still have a lot of issues of poverty, of underemployment, of lack of employment opportunities. The university still remains an institution that has major walls to the community. Even though the university admirably has done a lot of outreach to the barrios, it's still very difficult for *raza* to get in and to stay in the university. It is culturally so far removed.

LOUIS: *Was there a civil rights movement here?*

ERNESTO: Yeah, there was one. The movement really doesn't begin until the mid- to late '60s. It corresponds with the Chicano movement, throughout the Southwest. It corresponds with the antiwar movement. In the late '60s, you had a major walkout in Tucson High School. At the same time, you have the community becoming braver and bolder and demanding the city government to create more parks, more recreational facilities, sidewalks, lights, pave the streets goddammit [laughter]. Bring the tax money back into the neighborhoods. And one of the many young leaders is now a *congresista* [congressman], Raúl Grijalva. He comes out of the South Side, Sunnyside High School; he goes to the university. Late '60s, he becomes a MEChista,[3] and he and others begin to agitate and demand for opening the university to *raza*, and he eventually goes on the school board, goes on to the Pima County Supervisors, and now is in Congress. But he's one of very few who was able to do that. During the civil rights movement there's an explosion of young people who've become increasingly demanding and angry, and rightfully so. That peters out, as you see in other movements. I think they fizzle out for different reasons—lack of continuation of energy, individuals go their own way, or there's clashes within the movement, personality, egos, agendas. But then within the institutions you have changes, because of that movement. Now within the school districts like Tucson Unified you begin to see that, 'cause some of these people are now students or are now teachers.

The fight's still occurring within institutions, within government, within the media. I've been in the media now for some twenty-five years, and we still have fights. The institutions are locked; they have their rules; they have their little boys, now, their little girls club. And so it's still a struggle. But now, something I've been writing about, the mass student protests of last year and this year, a new cadre of young leaders are emerging. They're undocumented, but they know their rights, they know what's at stake, and they're no longer gonna be silenced, and they're organizing and gaining political skill.

LOUIS: *I've seen that all over the country. I guess it just tells you that some of our young students who are citizens got comfortable.*

ERNESTO: I admit, I got comfortable. But when I see these young people, undocumented young people, so eloquent, so strong, they're inspiring. I said, "Oh my gosh, if they're going to put themselves on the line, then I have to also." So this is the beautiful Tucson. It's still a beautiful place to be. Tucson has roots going back past 1775; because of the indigenous roots, it's a strong place.

> LOUIS: *So what is its relationship with its indigenous roots? Are they marginalized, and it's like, "Oh, okay, we claim them for tourism purposes but not really"?*

ERNESTO: No, not even for tourism purposes. I don't even think we do that. We have two major indigenous communities. We have the O'odham, and then we have the Yaquis, who came out of Mexico fleeing the persecution—talk about ethnocentric persecution in Mexico. They established communities here in Marana and in Phoenix, and we have an old one, called Pascua. It was created officially on an Easter Sunday. So you have these communities that at a certain level have intermixed with the Chicano community, and they've blended in, and it's seamless, but then there are some very distinct boundaries. The O'odham are still very much marginalized, even within the *mexicano*/Chicano community. The *indígena* is very much on the outs. Their education rates are even worse than ours. They don't use indigenous for tourism purposes, though you might see some indigenous-looking arts and crafts in the boutiques.

The history of the *mexicano* worker everywhere he goes is that it's alright that you're there working, toiling, sweating, building, but just shut up, don't speak out. As soon as a *mexicano* speaks up, *a la madre*. And in some ways—and I don't want to equate myself with a heroic immigrant who really has struggled—but in some ways they apply that same principle to me: how dare I as a Chicano write from a Chicano perspective? I'm un-American.

> LOUIS: *Has your paper been supportive?*

ERNESTO: They haven't fired me yet. [Laughter]

> LOUIS: *Were you raised bilingual?*

ERNESTO: Yeah, I was, though I followed a traditional route. I refused to speak in Spanish, *a la chingada* [fuck it]. I wasn't going to speak Spanish. I'm in *gringolandia*, man. I'm going to school; if I speak Spanish, I'm going to be ridiculed even though there's a lot of mexicano students, but they didn't speak Spanish. But I had to speak Spanish to my *abuela* and my *tías.* My father would try to drive home the point: "You're going to speak Spanish!" And so we fought about it. But finally I saw the light. I realized I needed to learn Spanish if I'm going to meet some darling *mexicanas,* no? ¡Pues sí! [Well yes!] I went to Guadalajara, and I saw these beautiful women, and I said, "Oh my gosh, I better learn Spanish."

So right here to the left is El Río Golf Course. It's city-owned. It's been around since pre–World War II. There's great irony in El Río Golf Course. It was created to provide a golf outlet for Jews, who were not allowed in the exclusive Tucson golf courses. Early on, the Tucson Open was held in El Río. This golf course is a beautiful oasis within the poor barrio, and basically the golfers that are here are gringos, with the exception of a few middle-class *mexicanos,* like my grandfather. It's the young boys in the barrio who are shagging balls; they're the caddies. Your Lee Treviño–type story, but it still was a closed facility, and golf ain't a Chicano sport [laughter]. In the late '60s some of the Chicano students and other activists, older people too, began saying, "Wait a minute, we have nothing here!" There's only a small Menlo Park on the West Side attached to a school. They held demonstrations here. My father was then reactionary conservative, *muy mexicano.* It was improper for people to be doing this, much less for *mexicanos* to be doing this. How dare they? I remember one day he brought me out because he was doing reporting. He wanted me to see what was going on, because he also knew this was his community that listens to his radio station. He just didn't understand the concept of Chicanismo, of taking it to the streets. One day he came out here, there was a protest. It was pretty peaceful, and I had heard on the TV, probably through the television news, "Burn, baby, burn." And so I remember saying it: "Burn, baby, burn." I'm in middle school, and he *me regañó* [scolded me], "You do not talk like that, that is not the proper thing, we're not here to burn things." "Well, but they're right."

What came out of the protest here was the El Río Neighborhood Center. The people wanted to convert the golf course into a park. The city wasn't going to do that. They just weren't going to give up the golf course. So they built the center here. We now have GED classes, a full-fledged neighborhood center. Just on the other side, a mile away from here, El Río Neighborhood Health Center was born—health facilities, health programs for the community. That is also a result of the movement.

A lot of these streets during the '60s were still dirt. The only way you could get them paved, you have to access the home owners, no? *Raza* didn't have money. So through the '60s Model Cities and the federal government, through the War on Poverty program, money starts coming into Tucson. A lot of it gets lost through administration and *chingaderas* [bullshit], but some money does come in, and sidewalks are built, some low-cost home improvement loans are available now to the community, and over the years you've seen a resurgence of people rebuilding homes or improving their homes, although the community still has problems of poverty and educational facilities. It's a proud community.

LOUIS: *You said your father was very conservative?*

ERNESTO: He changed. He's quite liberal now. It's really interesting to see his transformation. The Vietnam War politicized him; the crass GOP policies. There was a time that my *jefito* started talking about, I'm coming of age, of draft age, I'm in high school again, the war's still going on. He's actively talking about hauling my ass to Mexico. He got dual citizenship for me and my siblings. He still had this nostalgic longing to go back to Mexico, and he saw the war, and he didn't want to see me go to war. He's becoming radicalized in his own way.

Here's something that's really important that hit the community hard, the freeway. Interstate 10. In the late '50s, early '60s, I-10 was created. It split the barrio. It split the community. Psychologically, it put the West Side barrios apart from downtown Tucson. Still to this day there's a psychological barrier here. This is Barrio Anita, another one of the old barrios, a *mezcla* of *raza, negros,* and *chinos* [a mixture of Latinos, blacks, and Asians] for many, many years. It's still a very Chicano neighborhood.

LOUIS: *Were you a writer when you were young?*

ERNESTO: Nope. My growth in Chicano awareness was in the '70s. I go to a West Side school, and I become part of MEChA. In college one summer they sent me to Torreón, in Coahuila, to study Spanish. It was after my freshman year, that's where I learned I'm a Chicano. I'm walking down the street, I'm living with a *chino/mexicano* family, and I'm going to the American School of Torreón to learn Spanish. One day I'm walking down the street, and this *morrito* [little guy] from the neighborhood, I don't know who he is, but he knows who I am. He knows that I'm this guy living with a family down the street, he passes by me, and I kid you not, Louis, he looks up to me *y me dice* [and he says], "Gringo." And I was startled, I was awakened . . . it was an epiphany. I thought, the little shit is right. I am gringo *en los ojos de los mexicanos* [in the eyes of Mexicans]. Up until then I had taken on my father's *mexicano* identity, *yo soy mexicano* [I am Mexican]. I grew up, Louis, listening to ranchera music, *música mexicana.* I didn't listen to the Beatles, I didn't listen to rock 'n' roll. I listened to Antonio Aguilar, Flor Silvestre, Lucha Villa, Pedro Vargas. 'Cause my father was in radio, he listened to classic, beautiful Mexican music, which I adored. I saw myself as, I'm not gringo. I'm not *americano*, I'm not Mexican American, I am *mexicano*. And so I went to Mexico, and my cousins were baffled—"what do you mean you don't listen to the Beatles! [Laughter] What do you mean you listen to Antonio Aguilar?" They ain't going to listen to that. So one day this *morrito* says to me, "Gringo!" He's right. I then discovered I'm Chicano; it all made sense to me. Because in the eyes of the gringo, I'm Mexican; in the eyes of the *mexicano*, I'm gringo. ¡Pues qué la chingada! [Well, what the fuck!] Then what am I? I'm something else, I'm Chicano. So I began to realize what the Chicano movement was all about. I go to the university, and I discover I'm more than Chicano, *mexicano*. I'm pan-Latino. While I'm in the university the Central American movement was growing. Reagan is president, he's conducting his illicit war, I join in with a small group of activists on Central American issues, and I become aware of my pan-Latino roots. So I grow from that.

We're going to drive through downtown Tucson. I'll point out to you some of the neighborhoods from the early first part of the presidio. We'll pass by the Dunbar School, the segregated schools for blacks. It's now closed. There's a dream of renovating it into a black history cultural center. So we're entering an area where the original presidio was constructed. There's no remnants of it anymore. This is where Tucson's Anglo elites built their mansions. They call it Snob Hollow, and this is some cheap recreation of a presidio wall. Tucson never valued its history. It just destroyed it. I'm not just going to blame the gringo 'cause the gringo has no regard for Latino, Chicano, *mexicano* history, but even the *mexicano* himself unfortunately was taught that his history, her history, was not worth keeping, and so we have very little of it left.

Some of the apartments here are new immigrant families, and as we go farther south into the South Side of town, that's where more of the undocumented families live. We're going to pass through a small community. It's a separate municipality called South Tucson. This community was created because it felt neglected. This was a traditional low-, low-income *mexicano*-Yaqui-O'odham community, very poor. It felt neglected, and so it petitioned and it became incorporated. It's one square mile. It's still a low-income community. Over time South Tucson is trying to maintain some kind of identity; it only lives off sales taxes. There are many good things about South Tucson—some of the best *mexicano* restaurants are here. They have their own political problems. There's a couple of families that think they're the caciques. I prefer the South Side 'cause it's more rootsy, a lot of history, a lot of good *familias* are here. As I told you, some of the older *mexi-*

cano families are resentful of the new *mexicano* families. Eventually the new *familias mexicanas* will be the older *familias mexicanas*, and they will resent another group that follows them. Hell, for all I know they'll probably be *guatemaltecos* [Guatemalans].

LOUIS: *It's sad to think about these cycles.*

ERNESTO: It is one of the themes that I try to write about in my stories about immigration. We've been down this road before. This is not new to America. The Irish got their assess kicked, the Jews got their assess kicked, the *italianos*, all the previous groups, but unfortunately they have forgotten their immigrant history. This whole thing, Louis, I don't understand the fixation that people have with legal status.

LOUIS: *That's how the debate has been framed—around "We're a nation of laws"—as if that somehow is necessarily moral or just.*

ERNESTO: We're a nation of lawbreakers. We have a president that invades a country under no law. But I can't, Louis, I can't articulate the best argument to use against people who say, "It's law, it's legal." What I come down to is, "Fuck the law!"

LOUIS: *I have tried to approach it by making a distinction between what's legal and what's right, because they are not necessarily the same thing. In my mind morality supersedes the law if you have any kind of notion of morality and how we're connected as human beings.*

ERNESTO: And that argument works for some people who understand the language, but when you're talking to John Q. Public you can't use those arguments because it goes over their heads. They don't understand it, and they maintain, "Well, it's the law." Then I try to tell them, "Well, you know your grandparents are from Europe," because as you know the myth is, all European immigrants came from Ellis Island. Well, no, they came through Canada, they came through Cuba, and yes they came through New York, but they weren't all legal. They hunker down, and they stay anchored on this, and they won't move, and it's hard to argue with them because they're just, "No, it's the law." It's hard.

Manuel Vélez met me at his office at San Diego Mesa College shortly before his morning Chicano Literature class. He had recently moved from El Paso to take this position, but he's not a newcomer to California, having grown up in Salinas. Manuel eloquently shared his perspective on life in the geographic, cultural, and political borderlands.

MANUEL: I moved to El Paso from Salinas when I was fifteen. There were a number of reasons. My parents, my dad, had just inherited some land in El Paso, and over in Salinas, me and my brothers were already into gangs and stuff like that. It was a way to disconnect us from it.

LOUIS: *And how many generations back do you go in the United States?*

MANUEL: We are the first. My father was born in Durango. My mom was born in Aguascalientes. They met in Juárez. My dad has been here for a while. He is a musician, so he used to travel all over the southwestern United States with his band. My dad has been in and out of the United States since I would say like '60, '62; 1966 is when they both moved to the United States. They got married in Juárez, and they went to Salinas for their honeymoon and liked it so much that they stayed there. My dad was a musician, but you can't make a lot of money off of that, so he had odd jobs—construction, laborer. I think for a while he was plating bumpers and stuff like that. My mom is *campesina* all the way. She has always worked in the fields.

LOUIS: *Did moving to El Paso keep you out of trouble?*

MANUEL: Yeah. If we stayed in Salinas, we probably would be dead, in jail, or something like that, so moving actually did work. The gang life in Salinas was prevalent. I used to say if you were Chicano, you were going to be a *cholo*

Manuel Vélez in his office at San Diego Mesa College. Photo by Louis Mendoza.

[defiant working-class youth]. That was it. It was that pervasive. If you were Mexican that was going to be a part of your life. In El Paso, there are so many Mexicans that it's just a small part of the experience. In El Paso, the overall majority of the population rejects gangs, so it was a completely different thing for me coming from a place where just simply being a Chicano meant you were part of that lifestyle.

LOUIS: *That is an interesting way to think about it. What school did you attend?*

MANUEL: Coronado. Coronado had the reputation of being the uppity school. It was the school where all the rich kids went. That made it twice as hard. When we moved to El Paso, we were still *chavalitos* [young kids], all *cholo*'d out. My mom had heard all the stories about Coronado High School, and she said, "Oh, you are going to go to a high school where all the rich kids go. They are going to make fun of you. They are going to laugh at you." Which gave us all the more reason to stay dressed as *cholos*. I was already in Honors English from the stuff I had been doing in California, but they didn't trust me to be in Honors. So instead of putting me in Honors, they just moved me to the next level. No one believed that I was supposed to be there because of the way I dressed and stuff. I remember that was when I realized how different it was going to be between Salinas and El Paso.

LOUIS: *What did you do after high school?*

MANUEL: Went right to El Paso Community College. I think that was when the whole school thing kicked in for me. I started to focus more on my classes. And then I went to U of I [University of Illinois] in Chicago.

LOUIS: *Did you come of age along the border?*

MANUEL: Definitely. My identity is completely a border identity.

LOUIS: *What does that mean to you?*

MANUEL: That means that in my everyday life there is neither anything that is purely Mexican or purely American; everything is a kind of conglomeration of the two. I tell my students, my first language is not Spanish or English, and when I go to speak only English there is a concerted effort to speak only English, even though English is the dominant language for me. We all talk about the border as its own culture; it is not just the line itself. I think being from the border is that balance. It is understanding that you are of two cultures and those two cultures make one, but you are still struggling with larger society's negative portrayal of one of those cultures and this prevailing idea that you need to accept the American culture to be successful. Being on the border is this constant conflict, just like the border itself, within ourselves.

LOUIS: *I hear you talking about being comfortable with a certain kind of fluidity, but at the same time that fluidity bounces up against the walls.*

MANUEL: Yeah, it is being comfortable with yourself, but the perception of what you are comfortable with is not accepted, so you are asking, who am I? I am talking about this with my students right now. I am having them write an essay, but instead of analyzing something else, they are going to analyze themselves. I ask them, "Who are you?" I get the blankest looks. They have no idea how to answer that question. I think we have become so afraid of discussing identity or even identity politics that we have lost touch with the self. We have no idea what the self is anymore. My students don't understand how community, how ethos, how all these things play a role in their own development as a people, as an individual, as a self. It is always shocking to me when I ask them that and some of them react defensively. For the Mexican family, it is kind of compounded even more, because we, as border children if you will, are very much enamored with the American culture and because our parents are part of that older culture, say the Mexican culture, there is that clear delineation between us and our parents that we begin to conflict with them over.

LOUIS: *So the typical adolescent rebellion takes on a Mexican American dimension?*

MANUEL: Exactly. For instance, my daughter loves the American flag, and she will say it is prettier than the Mexican flag. Why? I was reading an essay with my students today about a Chinese student who writes about that same idea. She says, "My mom speaks the Chinese language, it is rough, it is ugly, it doesn't sound as beautiful and flowery as when my American teacher speaks English." It's a cultural clash. It is something that we have to deal with, and we see it in our own family. We are taught as children not to speak Spanish. But language is such an important part of identity that when we are told not to speak our language, what we are being told is not to accept our identity. And then when we see that identity in our parents, we rebel against it in a very clear and very harsh way.

LOUIS: *You grew up bilingual then?*

MANUEL: Spanish was the only language that was spoken inside the home. It creates those interesting dynamics where when we are at school we speak Spanish and we are having trouble with the language at school, they call our parents and say, "You need to speak English more with your son. Make sure that when your son is at home, he speaks more English."

LOUIS: *Public versus private forms of language, as Richard Rodriguez would say?*

MANUEL: Exactly. Of course, I didn't respond in the way Richard Rodriguez did. We would go home, and my parents would be upset and my dad would say, "Habla inglés." So there we are trying to speak to my dad in English, and he can only take it for like fifteen minutes before he begins speaking in Spanish. For me, moving to El Paso, the language issue was even crazier, because in Salinas Spanish was my first language. By the third grade, we have lost everything, whereas closer to the border more Chicanos retain that language, that linguistic connection. When we moved to El Paso, I could understand Spanish, but I couldn't speak a lick of it. For the first time, I was actually being made fun of by people my age for not speaking Spanish, whereas before it was the parents would chastise you for not speaking enough English. It was a kind of pressure. I have to learn this language, I have to reconnect with Spanish.

LOUIS: *What has life been like living on the border for you as an adult with respect to a sense of belonging?*

MANUEL: I lived outside of the border for the first fifteen years of my life and saw the way the Chicano community interacts from that perspective. Even though Salinas has a strong *mexicano* population, it is still miles away from the border; even the Mexicans and Chicanos separate. For some reason, it gave me the ability to look at the Chicano community in El Paso from a more political and sociological perspective. I was able to see it from the outside as well as experience it from the inside. I think El Paso is such an interesting town because there are so many Chicanos there that they don't really understand the dynamics of race in society. In El Paso, you can't scream racism because the mayor was a Chicano, the principal of the school is a Chicano, the superintendent is a Chicano. And not to say anything bad about El Paso, but most communities don't understand the whole process of neocolonialism.

And that creates that interesting dynamic where politically El Paso is to the left. They always were Democrat, the opposite of the rest of Texas. But in terms of social issues, El Paso is to the right. They are more prone to the death penalty. They are more prone to English Only laws, so in this kind of weird way, while they are to the left politically, socially they are still to the right. El Paso struggles with its own kind of identity complex, as I think the whole border does.

All of the negative perceptions of being a *mexicano* are amplified in the border area. I tell my students when the immigration protests started happening against H.R. 4437, the people who experienced the backlash most against those immigration marches were not the immigrants themselves but the Chicanos that were already living here, who probably had never even thought of attending one of those marches. That guy in Houston got beat up because he was a Chicano by his classmates. Here in Temecula they burned down a Mexican restaurant following an immigration protest, and more than likely those people aren't immigrants. Maybe they didn't even support the immigrant protest.

LOUIS: *Do white folks have a border identity or not? Or do they live here and not get it?*

MANUEL: That is a great question. To reflect on that, I would say the white individual on the border will either completely accept the border culture or will completely reject it. I don't think I have ever met a white person who is right in the middle. Unfortunately, a good amount of people in El Paso who say, "I hate the city, I can't stand the city, I don't want to be in the city," and I think what they are struggling with is not necessarily the city but the culture, the cultural synthesis that is happening in El Paso.

LOUIS: Any thoughts on the current debates on immigration in terms of what the future holds for our society?

MANUEL: The biggest observation that I would make is that the immigration debate is at the center of everything that is happening in our community right now. All the issues that are impacting our community have been either redirected because of immigration or their immigration foundation has become more prominent. The question of immigration fuels the negative perceptions of Chicanos. We are the ones that take the first impact from that debate. So the question of immigration is the main fuel that is going to push our community forward. At the same time, it is creating conflicts that our community has to deal with. In the last two years, we saw all these students marching out of their high schools in droves, hundreds of thousands. We hadn't seen that since like '68. That same issue is beginning to fuel the fire in our younger kids, who are beginning to pick up the banners and protest. There are a lot of parallels between what happened in the sixties and what is happening now. The interesting thing is now we have that experience from the sixties. I have been saying this since all the marches and walkouts in the high schools started happening. In the sixties the students walked out. They were creating the blueprint for protest at that point. They had no idea what they were doing. They felt compelled, and they moved, and they did an excellent job with what they did, and many of those students who walked out had no idea why they walked out. Many may have walked out simply because their friends were doing it, because it was a day off from school. But participating in those walkouts did something to them. They were the ones who picked up the banner later on. This time, we have the exact same thing happening, where the students themselves are the catalyst; they didn't wait for us to tell them. They got out on their own, and they started marching. The only difference is now we have this body of older *veteranos* who can then guide these students into something more positive. And I think that is where we see the struggle now when all the students were protesting. You had two clear organizations that were trying to sway the students. You had one that was more pro-American, so they would tell the students march with the American flags and don't say too many negative things. And then you had the ones that were more radical who were saying use the Mexican flag. We are at a real interesting point right now where I think as a community we can benefit from the past politicization of our community in order to compel us forward.

Conversations Across Our America is and is not my story, just as it is and is not your story, wherever you position yourself within the debates on immigration. "Latinoization" refers to the ongoing process of cultural, social change occurring in the United States as a result of the profound demographic shifts of the past forty years. Latinoization is not a phenomenon that occurs with the United States as a passive actor; rather it is a consequence of the interconnectedness of imperialism and globalization, processes in which the U.S. plays a central role and of which it is a primary beneficiary. Immigration policy is at the nexus of domestic and foreign policy. As I prepared for my research trip in spring 2007 the nation was in the midst of a heated debate about immigration reform. These debates went to the core of who "we" are as an immigrant nation, the cultural, philosophical, and political qualities that define who "belongs" in the U.S. Between the calls for amnesty, guest worker programs, border walls, and the repeal of birthright citizenship, a rampant xenophobia tinges and informs the debate as many people expressed their fears that Spanish would supplant English as the national language, that a vast conspiracy was at work in which Mexico was planning to retake the southwestern states, that new immigrants were "dumbing down" the nation or stealing jobs, social services, and education without paying taxes—to name but a few of the more salient issues.

The anxiety of the mainstream population and social conservatives regarding demographic change has been primarily projected onto the undocumented population of Latinos in the U.S.; this is true, despite the fact that these trends would hold true even if entry into the United States by undocumented migrants was to be stopped completely. Inflammatory rhetoric notwithstanding, the facts of how undocumented immigrants contribute to the U.S. economy are often overlooked or misrepresented.

According to the U.S. Social Security Administration, undocumented workers contribute $8.5 billion to Social Security and Medicare annually—a contribution that supports maintaining the viability of these programs that they will never benefit from. Researchers have verified that at the federal level undocumented workers pay more in taxes than they receive in public benefits and proportionately use less state and local benefits than do other populations.[1] A 2007 report from the President's Council of Economic Advisers notes that "wage gains from immigration are between thirty and eighty billion per year."[2] Recent reports assessing the impact of immigration on local economies, such as the Wilder Foundation's *A New Age of Immigrants: Making Immigration Work for Minnesota*, argue that concerns about the competition for jobs between U.S. citizens and undocumented migrants reveals that though it is true that there is likely a negative impact for those workers in direct competition for jobs and those in smaller communities, employers report great difficulty finding native-born applicants for many jobs in agriculture, meatpacking, poultry processing, and manufacturing. This is particularly true in rural areas across the country.[3] This, of course, has to be considered in relation to the settlement patterns of contemporary immigrants from Latin America into the U.S. Their settlement in regions of the United States that heretofore had little permanent presence of Latinos has changed the cultural geography of the country. Many of the interviews in this collection exemplify what Victor Zúniga and Rúben Hernández-León highlight in their important anthology, *New Destinations*, which focuses on the "novel geography of diverse receiving contexts," where each context "has its own racial hierarchy, history of interethnic relations, and ways of incorporating immigrant workers and their families."[4]

As a result of failed efforts to pass comprehensive federal immigration reform in summer 2007, the issue emerged as a heated topic in the then still nascent 2008 presidential elections. This debate was not divided along traditional partisan lines, as it was spurred, in part, by tensions between a normally conservative business sector that benefits from immigrant labor in the manufacturing, agricultural, and construction industries and social conservatives who decried the threat to the fabric of American culture by insurmountable linguistic and cultural differences that were incongruous with American values. Not insignificantly, these concerns have been sparked by the still recent emergence of Latinos as the nation's largest ethnic minority and the rapid demographic change in regions that heretofore had been relatively culturally homogeneous, for example, the Midwest, some parts of the Northeast, and the South, which had historically understood social relations through the lens of a traditional black-white paradigm. Perceptions of intense workforce competition also emerged as social conservatives strove to argue that there was a one-to-one correspondence between unemployment among "legal" citizens and the presence of "illegal" workers.

Two phenomena further fanned the fires of the national debate after the December 2005 passage of H.R. 4437, the Border Protection, Anti-Terrorism, and Illegal Immigration Control Act, by the U.S. House of Representatives. This controversial bill raised the stakes of the debate by requiring the construction of a border fence, modifying the status of "unlawful presence" to a felony, and, among other harsh provisions, authorizing state and local law enforcement agencies to enforce federal immigration laws. Though this bill stalled in the Senate, it was followed by the 2006 passage of the Illegal Immigration Relief Act, a local ordinance in Hazelton, Pennsylvania, that declared English its official language, fined employers for employing undocumented workers, made it illegal to rent housing to those without documentation of citizenship, and served as a model for more than one hundred municipalities around the country. Faced with an increasingly hostile national and local climate, immigrants rights activists organized two massive multiethnic marches in spring 2006 in cities and towns across the country. The purpose of these campaigns was to make visible the large number of workers, families, and broad-based support that existed for immigrants as workers and family and community members.

As we consider the still emergent economic and political clout wielded by Latinos, whose population will double in a few short decades and who will continue to be the largest ethnic minority as the nation inevitably becomes majority-minority in less than three decades, it is also important to remember three important facts about our presence so that we are not conceived solely as a new immigrant population: (1) our complex, albeit controversial, "indigenous" relationship to the land precedes the establishment of the U.S. as a nation-state; (2) our presence in the U.S. is the result of our absorption by imperial conquest; and (3) large segments of the Latino population have entered the U.S. by legal means. This last point, in particular, deserves elaboration as immigration policy has historically played a crucial gatekeeping role in determining the cultural and ethnic composition of the United States.

There is no question that Latinos played a pivotal role in determining the outcome of the 2008 election, as approximately 67 percent voted for Barack Obama. Such political clout in the face of their increasing numbers of eligible voters also informs the immigration debate and has been shaped by previous immigration reform efforts. The contemporary trend toward increasing the diversity of this country has its roots in the 1965 Hart-Celler

Immigration Act. As was noted in a recent *Boston Globe* article, the impact of this legislation "arguably rivals the Voting Rights Act, the creation of Medicare, or other legislative landmarks of the era. It transformed a nation 85 percent white in 1965 into one that's one-third minority today, and on track for a nonwhite majority by 2042."[5] In the four decades since 1968, when this law went into effect, the vast majority of new immigrants coming into this country have been from Asia and Latin America. The demise of the national origins quota system under the Hart-Celler Act favoring European immigrants has profoundly altered (for better or worse) our national sense of identity and commitment to the application of civil rights laws designed to promote equitable opportunities and protection under the law. Advocates of the Hart-Celler Act assured opponents that their intention was to eradicate bias in immigration laws as part of a larger civil rights platform to diminish systemic inequities; no one foresaw the dramatic impact this reform would have on the nation's demographics four decades later.

INFORMATION TRUMPS IGNORANCE: HOPE FOR THE FUTURE?

Originally from Texas, I have learned several things from my experience in Minnesota—most fundamentally, that experience and information trump ignorance almost all the time. Just as this is true for those whose preconceptions have led them to believe that Latinos represent a threat to their way of life, safety, or standard of living, I, too, have learned that the only constant in culture and society is change and adaptation. As I traveled through small towns in West Texas, where being stopped for being brown (or being "meskin") was all the probable cause needed in the 1960s, I was impressed and surprised at how much things have changed in these communities and how relationships have become more complex and layered. In these small communities where Friday night high school football is king and civil rights movements were once sparked by resistance to exclusion on the cheerleading squad, the local newspapers report on teams now comprising a majority of Latinos. These newspaper stories reflecting profound everyday changes in the composition of local communities resonated with a story I heard about a basketball team in Melrose, Minnesota, that refused to continue a game when an opposing player spat out a racial slur against their Latino teammate before an apology was made. This anecdote contrasts sharply with one shared by Rogelio Núñez in South Texas where local basketball fans taunted opponents by threatening to call *la migra*.

I returned from my research trip with an abundance of emotionally charged stories and insights and renewed by the positive possibilities for the future, even as I remained cautious about the current dilemma we face, a dilemma best articulated by Carlos Marentes:

> [Immigration] is now a debate in every home in every place. [We] have the two extremes. On the one hand, some are pro-immigrant either because of beliefs or because we appreciate our own immigrant origins or because many people have a sense of humanity and solidarity, . . . immigrants, after all, are human beings. On the other extreme, you have the anti-immigrants who are racist, who believe in the idea of supremacy but also who understand things need to stay the same; this way a few can benefit at the expense of everybody. But within those two groups you have most of North American society, which doesn't know what to do. . . . So what we have right now in the United States is a moral dilemma and people are afraid to make a decision.

Carlos Marentes poignantly speaks to the many challenges to a comprehensive, meaningful, and just immigration reform. Perhaps because of the controversial nature of the House proposal and the ensuing public debate, and despite several proposed compromise solutions, the last effort to pass a Senate bill, including a pathway for citizenship for undocumented immigrants, was defeated on June 28, 2007, just a few days before I departed on my trip. A month later, Hazleton's anti-immigrant ordinance was declared unconstitutional. And while many other such ordinances ended similarly, a number have been upheld. Unfortunately, this does not mean that anti-Latino rhetoric has lessened or that meaningful, just, and comprehensive immigration reform is within reach, even under an Obama presidency. A week after Obama's presidential victory, even as his supporters were at their peak in believing that he would lead the way to comprehensive immigration reform legislation, national news was marred by the group killing of Marcello Lucero in Long Island. According to a November 13, 2008, *Orlando Sentinel* article on Lucero's murder, FBI statistics reveal that "there were 595 incidents of anti-Hispanic bias in 2007, with 830 victims reported by law enforcement agencies. That's a 40 percent rise from 2003, when there were 426 incidents involving 595 victims." These crimes have not lessened, as the economic crisis has only intensified anti-immigrant sentiment. As we enter the third year of Obama's presidency, we are witnessing an increase of incidents of hate crimes against Latinos, rampant enforcement of immigration laws, intensification of border security, and zero action on immigration reform.

As we can discern from the interviews included in this book, from the debates raging in small-town America, and from the range of responses by residents and leaders alike, local leadership makes all the difference in whether a community develops a reputation for being inclusive or exclusive. Many communities have been defined by how they choose to respond to new arrivals. Across the country I have seen the dramatic difference between embracing diversity and acknowledging that it has always been a part of our social fabric or resisting it and cultivating an illusion of cultural homogeneity. However much accommodating difference and change is hard work, communities that embrace newcomers have found that they are made stronger. Finally, communities that strive to be inclusive by respecting and embracing diversity have adopted a moral and ethical framework that views others as whole human beings with distinct histories, values, and qualities that complement their own and enrich their lives—not threaten it. Evidence of this way of viewing new immigrants is manifest in numerous ways, not the least of which are indicators revealing that people get along quite well. For example, Latinos have the second highest intermarriage rate in the country, as noted by Rogelio Saenz.[6]

At the national level, leadership is needed more than ever. The ongoing economic crisis has ensured that immigration remains a controversial political issue. The election of Barack Obama and a Democratic majority in Congress in 2008 were unable to utilize their power or gather the courage needed to pass comprehensive immigration reform (notwithstanding the Obama administration's challenge of S.B. 1070 in Arizona), but the continuing emergence of Latinos as a political force to be reckoned with provides some basis for hope. The Sunday following the presidential election in fall 2008, Senator Mel Martinez (R-FL) made this statement on *Meet the Press*: "The very divisive rhetoric of the immigration debate set a very bad tone for . . . Republicans. The fact is that Hispanics are going to be a more vibrant part of the electorate and the Republican Party had better figure out how to talk to them."[7] Martinez's words hold hope that in the crucible of political and economic necessity, Latino immigrants and thus all Latinos will be treated with greater respect. This hope, however, has to be tempered by the harsh reality of the persistence of anti-Latino, especially anti-Mexican, sentiment that drives hate crimes, the desire to create copycat local and state laws aimed at driving away new immigrants, and the persistent denial that the U.S. economy is dependent on immigrant labor and thus that the well-being of this country is intertwined with the well-being of those who are too easily dismissed as dispensable outsiders.

Senate Bill 1070 may well be the catalyst for ensuring that immigration reform is dealt with on the national level. Leaders must lead, and though one may understand why President Obama has been unable to tackle immigration reform in the face of a sustained and devastating financial crisis, unemployment, two wars, and so on, the extreme hateful rhetoric that emerges as a result of legislative efforts like S.B. 1070 may finally compel us to act as once again the world sees us forget our own history and the fascist rhetoric of anti-immigrants assumes a prominent place on the world stage and places us in company with nations we purport to be better than. Though the immigration debate is ostensibly about immigrants and the law, anyone who has experienced social marginalization knows that it is about much more. Notions of the law, legal status, and belonging are intimately intertwined with and often pitted against one another. This is why this book is about the Latinoization of the country and not just about immigration. Latinos' pursuit of social justice and equity does not start and stop at the border. While it is not necessarily the case that if people just knew the interrelated history and facts about the economic interdependency of the United States and Latin America, the immigration dilemma would be resolved, any honest assessment of why we have such difficulty with expanding our sense of who belongs has to begin with the identification of why so many fear demographic and cultural change. The rise in numbers as well as the new geography of Latino demographic change mandate different conversations about inclusion and exclusion.

Conversations Across Our America provides only a glimpse into the dynamics associated with an enormously complex and contentious issue— one that, if it is to be resolved, will require a diligent and protracted effort to lead us to a place where we gain new insight not only into our common ground, but our mutual destiny with the occupants of both the United States and the Americas. We sit at yet another important crossroads in U.S. history. We once again are confronted with the choice between being the very best we can imagine being and continuing to be a nation willfully blind to its past and its future. Can our compassion for others be greater than our fear that "we" will change? Need we strive to maintain a fantasy that "we" are a monocultural nation incapable of changes that we ourselves have wrought on the world? Are we once again confronting our inability to grasp that "they" *are* "us"?

NOTES

INTRODUCTION

1. "Lengua Americano, Corazón Chicano," in *Telling Tongues: A Latin@ Anthology on Language Experience*, ed. Louis Mendoza and Toni Nelson Herrera (National City and Austin: Calaca Press and Red Salmon Press, 2006).

CHAPTER ONE

1. The year the Immigration Reform and Control Act (IRCA) was passed. IRCA included an amnesty option if applicants could demonstrate residency and employment.

2. See the glossary for the significance of *México profundo*.

CHAPTER TWO

1. The Intergovernmental Personnel Act (IPA) mobility program allows temporary assignment of employees between federal agencies and state, local, and Indian tribal governments, institutions of higher education, and other eligible organizations.

2. Federation for American Immigration Reform.

3. The Border Protection, Antiterrorism, and Illegal Immigration Control Act of 2005 (H.R. 4437) was a bill in the 109th U.S. Congress. It was passed by the House of Representatives on December 16, 2005, by a vote of 239 to 182 (with 92 percent of Republicans supporting, 82 percent of Democrats opposing) but did not pass the Senate. It was also known as the "Sensenbrenner bill," for its sponsor in the House of Representatives, Wisconsin Republican Jim Sensenbrenner. The bill was the catalyst for the 2006 U.S. immigration reform protests (Wikipedia, retrieved January 7, 2009).

4. Oregon Law 181.575: No law enforcement agency . . . may collect or maintain information about the political, religious or social views, associations or activities of any individual, group, association, organization, corporation, business or partnership unless such information directly relates to an investigation of criminal activities . . . 181.850: No law enforcement agency of the State of Oregon . . . shall use agency moneys, equipment or personnel for the purpose of detecting or apprehending persons whose only violation of law is that they are persons of foreign citizenship residing in the United States in violation of federal immigration laws. Retrieved March 9, 2011, from online archive of ACLU Oregon, http://archive.acluor.org/news/2002fall/2002Fa llNews181protection.htm.

CHAPTER THREE

1. Judith V. Jordan, "The Meaning of Mutuality," Working Paper Series Work in Progress (1986), Paper No. 23, Jean Baker Miller Training Institute at the Wellesley Centers for Women. Retrieved February 12, 2011, from http://74.6.238.254/search/srpcache?ei=UTF-8&p=The+Meaning+of+Mutuality%2C+judith+jordan&fr=yfp-t-701&u=http://cc.bingj.com/cache.aspx?q=The+Meaning+of+Mutuality%2c+judith+jordan&d=4617029951096690&mkt=en-US&setlang=en-US&w=799d060b,5ecbdb9d&icp=1&.intl=us&sig=cYO34FrfaxBsFzZqGtGGmw—. Also published in Judith V. Jordan, Alexandra G. Kaplan, Jean Baker Miller, Irene P. Stiver, and Janet L. Surrey, *Women's Growth in Connection: Writings from the Stone Center* (New York: Guilford Publications, 1991).

CHAPTER FOUR

1. Unlike the other interviews in which the translation of Spanish words or phrases is provided in brackets, in this interview Spanish is not italicized and translations are not provided to preserve the integrity of this regional dialect. Rogelio's use of code switching between Spanish and English is common parlance among familiars in South Texas, a style of speech often referred to as Tex-Mex.

2. The University of Texas–Pan American and the University of Texas–Brownsville respectively.

3. In the San Diego-San Ysidro area, Brent Beltran was instrumental in introducing me to Cecilia Brennan and numerous others who are present in this book. At times his presence and contributions to the conversations are included.

4. Proposition 187 was a 1994 ballot initiative in California whose goal was to establish a screening system that would prohibit undocumented immigrants from using health care, public education, and other social services. It was passed but found unconstitutional by the federal courts in 1999. Proposition 209 was a 1996 California initiative approved by voters that prohibited the consideration of race, ethnicity, or sex as factors for admission into public institutions of higher education.

CHAPTER FIVE

1. José Ramón Sánchez, *Boricua Power: A Political History of Puerto Ricans in the United States* (New York: New York University Press, 2007).

2. Frantz Fanon, a descendant of slaves, grew up in Martinique and became a renowned revolutionary thinker and philosopher who had profound influence on 1960s radical movements in the United States and Europe. Fanon's writings, *Black Skin, White Masks* (1952) and *The Wretched of the Earth* (1961), were foundational books that inspired civil rights, anticolonial, and black consciousness movements around the world.

3. H-2A visas permit foreign workers entry into the United States for temporary or seasonal agricultural work when employers anticipate a shortage of domestic workers. More than thirty thousand H-2A visas are authorized each year.

4. Baldemar Velásquez, cofounder and president of the Farm Labor Organizing Committee.

5. Oscar Romero was a Catholic archbishop in San Salvador, El Salvador, who was assassinated on March 24, 1980, while saying mass one day after he appealed to Salvadoran soldiers as Christians to stop carrying out the government's repression and violations of basic human rights.

6. The Violence Against Women Act provides immigration status to the abused spouse and child of a U.S. citizen or lawful permanent resident. See www.immspec .com/green-card-through-vawa.htm.

7. www.casafamiliar.org/index1.html.

8. After being forced to leave office because of a campaign finance scandal, Roger Hedgecock became a radio talk show host. Once a moderate Republican, he has cultivated a reputation as an ultraconservative taking hard-line stances on social issues such as immigration.

9. "Secondary" refers to an inspection procedure at ports of entry in which the authorities conduct additional inquiries into an individual's background or confirm information the individual has provided.

10. H.R. 4437, the Border Protection, Antiterrorism, and Illegal Immigration Control Act of 2005, was passed by the U.S. House of Representatives on December 16, 2005. It was also known as the Sensenbrenner bill, for its sponsor, Wisconsin Republican Jim Sensenbrenner. The bill is seen by many as the catalyst for the 2006 U.S. immigration reform protests. Among the many controversial provisions it mandated: 700 miles of a border wall to be built, the federal government to take custody of illegal aliens detained by local authorities, employers to verify workers' legal status through electronic means, and helping an illegal person remain in the United States to be a federal crime. The bill was never passed by the Senate.

11. As others included in this book have noted, Lou Dobbs' coverage of immigration in his "Broken Borders" series on CNN earned him a reputation as an anti-Latino racist. Not only was his coverage perceived as sensationalized and biased, it was seen as promoting inaccurate information and fomenting social and political division by consistently giving anti-immigrant groups a national media platform to espouse their views. One of the more notorious anti-immigrant stories that galvanized Latino sentiment and initiated a long campaign against Dobbs' continued employment at CNN was an April 2005 segment in which he erroneously reported an explosion of seven thousand cases of leprosy in the United States in the past three years and blamed Latino immigrants for this perceived increase. Following an intense campaign by Latinos against CNN, Dobbs resigned his position in mid-November 2009. Both he and CNN claimed that the anti-Dobbs campaign had nothing to do with his decision to leave. In an October 2010 article, the *Nation* ran a story indicating that despite his rants against employers of "illegal aliens" Dobbs himself employed numerous undocumented workers on his multimillion-dollar estates ("Lou Dobbs, American Hypocrite," retrieved July 16, 2011, from www.thenation.com/article/155209/lou-dobbs-american-hypocrite).

CHAPTER SIX

1. The Rio Grande Valley of Texas.

CHAPTER SEVEN

1. Gloria Anzaldúa, "To Live in the Borderlands Means You . . . ," in *Borderlands/La Frontera: The New Mestiza* (San Francisco: Aunt Lute Books, 1987).

2. *Jefe* literally means "boss"; here the endearment *jefito* refers to Ernesto's father.

3. A member of MEChA, Movimiento Estudiantil Chicano de Aztlán (Chicano Student Movement of Aztlán), an activist student organization that emerged from the 1960s Chicana and Chicano civil rights movement. Though a national organization, it operates as a loose network of over four hundred "chapters" throughout the country with no central organizing body, leader, or required common set of activities, actions, or positions other than a presumed shared allegiance to the founding philosophy articulated in "El Plan Espiritual de Aztlán," which advocates the promotion of Chicana/o unity and empowerment through political action.

CONCLUSION

1. See Greg Owen, Jessica Meyerson, and Christa Otteson, *A New Age of Immigrants: Making Immigration Work for Minnesota*, Report for Wilder Foundation, St. Paul, MN, August 2010, 15–18.

2. Executive Office of the President, Immigration's Economic Impact (Washington, D.C.: Council of Economic Advisers, June 2007. Retrieved January 5, 2011, from http://isites.harvard.edu/fs/docs/icb.topic803549.files/Week%205–October%206 /council_immigration.pdf.

3. Owen, Meyerson, and Otteson, *A New Age of Immigrants*, 22–28.

4. Víctor Zúñiga and Rubén Hernández-León, eds., *New Destinations: Mexican Immigration in the United States* (New York: Russell Sage, 2005), xxvi.

5. Peter S. Canellos, "Obama Victory Took Root in Kennedy-Inspired Immigration Act" [electronic version]. *Boston Globe*, November 11, 2008. Retrieved January 5, 2011, from www.boston.com/news/politics/2008/articles/2008/11/11 /obama_victory_took_root_in_kennedy_inspired_immigration_act/.

6. Rogelio Saenz, "The Demography of Latino Immigration: Trends and Implications for the Future," PowerPoint presentation, ASA Congressional Briefing on Immigration, April 19, 2004. Retrieved January 5, 2011, from www2.asanet.org/public /saenz_brief.ppt.

7. Michael Scherer, "The GOP's Big Hispanic Problem," *Time Magazine*, November 10, 2008. Retrieved January 5, 2011, from Swampland: A blog about politics and policy, http://swampland.blogs.time.com/2008/11/10/the-gops-big-hispanic-problem/.

a la madre: watch out; all hell's about to break loose; literally, "to the mother"

a la chingada: as used in the context of the text, fuck it, the hell with it, forget it

mezcla of raza, negros, and chinos: a mixture of Mexicans, blacks, and Chinese

abuelos: grandparents

acordeón: accordion

ambiente: ambience

americanos: Americans

amimiados: a colloquial Spanish term used in mining communities to refer to hard rock miners whose lung and digestive tissues have deteriorated due to their unhealthy working conditions

arroz con pollo: chicken with rice

bodega: a small convenience store sometimes combined with a wine shop that typically stocks many ethnic products purchased by residents of its immediate neighborhood; term used especially among ethnic Puerto Ricans and other Caribbean Latinos; a mom-and-pop store akin to *tienditas*, a term U.S. Mexicans use for such stores in their own communities

barrio sin nombre: barrio without a name

bosques: forests

botana: a restaurant that serves Mexican and Latino food

bracero: literally, "one who works with his arms"; a term used for temporary legal and mostly agricultural Mexican workers allowed to work in the U.S. The United States and Mexico initiated the Bracero Program in 1942 to allow temporary contract workers to enter the U.S. to ameliorate labor shortages resulting from World War II. The program officially concluded in 1964, but the continued reliance of the U.S. on guest workers in the agricultural industry has led many to believe that it continues to exist in practice.

buenas noches: good evening

carnicería: butcher shop

campesino, campesina: male and female farmworker, respectively

casas y casas: houses upon houses

chavalitos: youngsters; youth

chilango: Slang for person residing in or from Mexico City. While it is sometimes used as a pejorative term by Mexican nationals living outside of Mexico City, it has come to be embraced with pride by many residents of the capital city to connote their difference from outsiders.

cholo: in the U.S. context, the term refers to working-class Mexican and Latino youth who have adopted a lifestyle where a specific dress, speech, and behavior are in effect. This aesthetic and the social stance accompanying it are often deemed rebellious or antisocial. However, as with the pachuco generation (cholos are often seen as the contemporary manifestation), their self-perception and social attitudes are complex and deeply rooted in social and class circumstances. At worst, being a cholo is associated negatively with being a gang member and in conflict with legal authorities generally.

colegio: college

comadre: godmother or close female friend; a term of fictive kinship; the equivalent term for men is *compadre*.

compañeros: male friends or companions; fem. *compañeras*

compatriotas: compatriots

concilio: council

con el: with

chingaderas: bullshit; as used here, a damn waste of otherwise good money and the unspecified events that led to it

chingón: as used here, huge, impassable

congresista: member of the U.S. Congress

convento: convent

contra el inmigrante: against the immigrant

corridos: ballads

cuando pasamos: when we passed

cuídate: take care of yourself; be careful

del Valle: literally, from the Valley; in Texas, it means to be from the Rio Grande Valley, which properly speaking includes only four counties: Cameron, Hidalgo, Starr, and Willacy (a geography most outsiders often misunderstand).

derechos: rights

desierto: desert

desmadre: disaster, a chaotic situation

discriminación: discrimination

dos años: two years

escuela del aventón, la: as used here, the school of hard knocks.

españoles: Spaniards; sing. *español*

estando todo: everything being

gabacho: colloquial U.S. Spanish for Anglo, white; sometimes also used to refer to a Yankee; pl. *gabachos*

galletita: endearing term for cookie (*galleta*)

gente: people

gringo en los ojos de los mexicanos: gringo in the eyes of the Mexicans

ha habido: there has been

Habla inglés: Speak English.

Híjole: Mexican interjection, akin to Wow! Good grief! Jeez! An expression of surprise, exasperation, or annoyance, depending on the context.

indigenismo: indigenism

familias: families; sing. *familia*

gringolandia: land of the gringos, i.e., the United States

jóvenes: young people, the youth

licorerías: liquor stores

lucha, la: the struggle

madrina: godmother

maestros: teachers; fem. *maestras*
marchas: marches
maquilas: manufacturing plants in Mexico that produce for the export market, especially those located along the U.S.-Mexico border; known to pay outrageously low
wages to their primarily female workforces.
mariachi: a genre of Mexican music; an ensemble of musicians who play this music
mercado: market; a single store or a series of stores
mestizaje: miscegenation
mexicanos: Mexicans; fem. *mexicanas*
México profundo: Literally, "deep Mexico" or "profound Mexico"; refers to Mexico's
identity and future. The Mexican anthropolgoist Guillermo Bonfil Batalla's book,
México Profundo: Reclaiming a Civilization (published in English by the University
of Texas Press [1966], trans. Philip A. Dennis), argues that Mesoamerican civilization is a vital and pervasive force in contemporary Mexican life. Batalla suggests
that *México profundo* contains an enormous reservoir of accumulated knowledge
that can assist Mexican society face the future successfully.
me regañó: he scolded me
migra: Short for immigration, or U.S. immigration authorities, today better known
by its acronym, ICE (Immigration and Customs Enforcement). Long used in the
Mexican and Latino community for ICE and its predecessor organizations.
mi jefito: literally, "my dear chief"; in this context, my dad, my father, said with endearment, informally
mi jilguerito: literally, "my little bird"; in this context, my little songbird.
mi'jita, mi'ja: literally, "my dear little daughter"; a contraction of *mi hija*. Masc. *mi'jo*.
mi mamá: my mother
milpas: cornfields
morrito: a younger or smaller dude or guy; also *morro*, used without the dimunitive
música mexicana: Mexican music
negros: blacks
negros peor, los: the blacks worse still
norte, el: literally, "the north"; most often used to refer to going north to the United
States.
no te hallas: you can't keep up; overwhelmed
pachanga: a formally or informally organized gathering or party to celebrate something
partera: midwife
pero: but
¡Pues qué la chingada!: Well, what the fuck! Well, goddammit!
¡Pues sí!: Of course!
quinceañera: a Latin American tradition involving a fifteen-year-old's coming-of-age
ceremony and celebration hosted by families for their daughters, usually accompanied by elaborate religious and festive preparations.
ranchera music: a genre of Mexican music that is quite common and came into its own
in the twentieth century
respeto de: respect of
río: river
sonorense: of or being from Sonora, Mexico
también: also

taquería: a restaurant that serves tacos and other Mexican food
teatros: theaters; theatrical groups.
tienditas: little neighborhood stores, usually mom-and-pop operated.
todo [el] tiempo: all the while
todos [los] mexicanos: all the Mexicans
trocas: trucks
troquero: truck driver
tucsonenses: Mexicans from Tucson, Arizona
up the chingao: idiomatic phrase; as used here, similar to "up the kazoo"
un poco tiempo: a short time
vatos: dudes, guys; in some parts of the U.S., especially Texas, also spelled *batos*
veteranos: veterans
vida loca, la: the crazy life
yo soy mexicano: I am Mexican

The idea to include this glossary was proposed by the historian Roberto Calderón, a reviewer of the manuscript. He deserves much of the credit for its basic structure and content. I have made some modifications but wish to acknowledge his labor and foresight in making the text more accessible to non-Spanish-speaking readers.

BIBLIOGRAPHY

"Basic Information about the DREAM Act Legislation."Retrieved January 10, 2011, from http://dreamact.info/students.
Canellos, Peter S. "Obama Victory Took Root in Kennedy-Inspired Immigration Act" [electronic version]. *Boston Globe*, November 11, 2008. Retrieved January 5, 2011, from www.boston.com/news/politics/2008/articles/2008/11/11 /obama_victory_took_root_in_kennedy_inspired_immigration_act/.
Executive Office of the President. "Immigration's Economic Impact." Washington, DC: Council of Economic Advisers, June 2007. Retrieved January 5, 2011, from http:// isites.harvard.edu/fs/docs/icb.topic803549.files/Week%205-October%206 /council_immigration.pdf.
Hajela, D., and F. Eltman. "Advocates Say Rhetoric Fuels Anti-Hispanic Crime" [Electronic version]. *USA Today*, November 12, 2008. Retrieved January 5, 2011, from www.usatoday.com/news/nation/2008–11–12–2775952356_x.htm.
Jordan, Judith V. "The Meaning of Mutuality." Paper presented at the Stone Center Colloquium, December 4, 1985. Retrieved March 15, 2011, from www.womensre viewofbooks.com/pdf/previews/preview_23sc.pdf.
Mendoza, L. "Voices and Images from a *Journey Across our America.*" *Progressive Planning* 178 (Winter 2009): 27–30.
Owens, G., J. Meyerson, and C. Otteson. *A New Age of Immigrants: Making Immigration Work for Minnesota.* Report prepared for Wilder Foundation, St. Paul, MN, August 2010.
Saenz, Rogelio. "The Demography of Latino Immigration: Trends and Implications for the Future." PowerPoint presentation, ASA Congressional Briefing on Immigration, April 19, 2004. Retrieved January 5, 2011, from www2.asanet.org/public /saenz_brief.ppt.
Scherer, Michael. "The GOP's Big Hispanic Problem." *Time Magazine*, November 10, 2008. Retrieved January 5, 2011, from Swampland: A blog about politics and policy, from http://swampland.blogs.time.com/2008/11/10 /the-gops-big-hispanic-problem/.
Zúñiga, Víctor, and Rubén Hernández-León, eds. *New Destinations: Mexican Immigration in the United States.* New York: Russell Sage, 2005.